THE EFTA COURT: TEN YEARS ON

The EFTA Court

Ten Years On

Edited by Carl Baudenbacher,
Per Tresselt,
Thorgeir Orlygsson

The EFTA Court

•HART•
PUBLISHING

OXFORD AND PORTLAND, OREGON
2005

Hart Publishing
Oxford and Portland, Oregon

Published in North America (US and Canada) by
Hart Publishing c/o
International Specialized Book Services
5804 NE Hassalo Street
Portland, Oregon
97213-3644
USA

Hart Publishing, Salter's Boatyard, Folly Bridge,
Abingdon Road, Oxford OX1 4LB
Telephone: +44 (0)1865 245533 or Fax: +44 (0)1865 794882
e-mail: mail@hartpub.co.uk
WEBSITE: http//www.hartpub.co.uk

British Library Cataloguing in Publication Data
Data Available
ISBN-13: 978–1–84113–569–4 (hardback)
ISBN-10: 1–84113–569–0 (paperback)

Typeset by Hope Services (Abingdon) Ltd.
Printed and bound in Great Britain by
TJ International, Padstow, Cornwall

Foreword

This volume contains the contributions made at the symposium which the EFTA Court held to mark its tenth anniversary. The Court had the honour of receiving on 21 October 2004 at the Cercle Municipal in Luxembourg some 200 participants from all the branches of the legal profession: Presidents and Chief Justices, judges national and international, advocates general, government lawyers and those representing European institutions, lawyers in private practice and academics. In addition, high-ranking politicians, diplomats and representatives of the EFTA Surveillance Authority and of the European Commission were present.

The contributions cover seminal topics of substantive and procedural law, reflecting the EFTA Court's and the Community Courts' experience in applying and interpreting law in the EEA and beyond the EEA over the last ten years. Accordingly, this book deals in Part I with 'Selected Topics of EEA Law in Practice', in Part II with the topics presented under the rubric 'Homogeneity as a Fundamental Principle of Economic and Legal Spaces', whereas Part III contains 'Additional Speeches' given in the course of informal proceedings.

We are deeply indebted to the speakers and participants, whose contributions made the symposium a memorable event. The Court is also indebted to Dirk Buschle and the members of his organizing team: Bryndís Pálmarsdóttir, Kerstin Schwiesow, Sigrid Hauser-Martinsen, Hrafnhildur Mary Eyjolfsdóttir and Mary Cox, who all worked hard and with dedication to make the conference a success. Our special thanks go to Bryndís for preparing the publication of this book, as well as to our publisher, Richard Hart, who committed himself to this project with uncommon enthusiasm.

March 2005

Carl Baudenbacher Per Tresselt Thorgeir Örlygsson

Contents

List of Speakers and Moderators

CARL BAUDENBACHER is President of the EFTA Court.

MARCO BRONCKERS is Professor of WTO Law, EU Law and Competition Law, University of Leiden; partner, Wilmer Cutler Pickering Hale and Dorr LLP, Brussels.

HANS PETTER GRAVER is Professor of Competition, Administrative and EEA/EU Law, University of Oslo.

PETER-CHRISTIAN MÜLLER-GRAFF is Professor of Civil, Commercial, Corporate and Economic Law, European Law and Comparison of Laws, University of Heidelberg.

THORGEIR ÖRLYGSSON is Judge at the EFTA Court; Lecturer in Law, University of Iceland.

ALLAN ROSAS is Judge at the European Court of Justice; President of Third Chamber.

LEIF SEVÓN is President of the Supreme Court of Finland (Korkein oikeus).

VASSILIOS SKOURIS is President of the European Court of Justice.

STEFÁN MÁR STEFÁNSSON is Professor of Procedural, Company and European Law, University of Iceland; ad hoc Judge at the EFTA Court.

PER TRESSELT is Judge at the EFTA Court.

KARL ARNE UTGÅRD is Judge at the Supreme Court (Høyesterett) of Norway.

BO VESTERDORF is President of the Court of First Instance.

Table of Cases

EFTA Court

Court of Justice of the European Communities

Court of First Instance

Other Courts (alphabetical)

Ten Years of the EFTA Court: Symposium 21 October 2004

CARL BAUDENBACHER

Good morning ladies and gentlemen, I cordially welcome you to this symposium, which is intended to mark the EFTA Court's Tenth Anniversary.

A. GENERAL

The EFTA Court took up its functions on 1 January 1994, in Geneva with five judges from the then EEA/EFTA countries Austria, Finland, Iceland, Norway and Sweden. It had not been an easy birth. The brave men who embarked on the adventure were: (1) The Court's first President, *Leif Sevón*, who later became a judge of the Court of Justice of the European Communities and is now the Chief Justice of Finland. His personal and professional reputation has greatly benefited the Court. (2) The Court's second President, Norway's Former Attorney General *Björn Haug*, shouldered the difficult task of winding up the five members' court and securing the transition to the three members court. (3) The Court's third President, my predecessor *Thór Vilhjálmsson*, brought to the EFTA Court his experience as a Chief Justice of his native Iceland as well as a judge and Vice-President of the European Court of Human Rights. (4) Former Judge *Sven Norberg*, now a Director at the European Commission's Competition Directorate General, acted as a Judge Rapporteur in cases in which essential foundations for the development of the Court's case law were layed. (5) Former Judge *Kurt Herndl*, at the time the only judge from a monist country, brought to the Court his immense experience, in particular, in procedural matters. After Leif Sevóns appointment to the ECJ, he was replaced by Judge *Gustav Bygglin*, now a Justice of the Supreme Court of Finland. Gustav Bygglin was very actively involved in finishing the five members' court pending cases by 30 June 1995. We are happy that all our former judges as well as most of the Court's former Registrars are participating in this celebration.

The founding fathers have also been responsible for providing the Court with crucial *accessories*, if I may say so. They gave the EFTA Court a very elegant emblem with a balance on an upright sword, which in heraldic circles means highest judicial power. Moreover, they were responsible for the choice of what I may describe as the most stylish robes you can imagine.

The EFTA Court is an example of what in legal theory is referred to as judicialization of international law. One will remember that unlike in the Community, the bilateral free trade agreements concluded between the EEC and the EFTA States in 1972/73 did not produce any effect in the EFTA Countries. This situation has been characterized as judicial restraint of trade by the late *Olivier Jacot-Guillarmod*, the man who by the way would have become Switzerland's EFTA Court judge if Switzerland had been able to ratify the EEA Agreement.

Much of what was said at the Court's inaugural session on 4 January 1994 is still valid today. President Sevón emphasized that whatever the future will bring, 'the administration of justice will continue with the firmness and impartiality which must be expected from the EFTA Court' (1994–95 EFTA Ct Rep 176). The President of the EFTA Surveillance Authority *Knut Almestad* called the EFTA Court and the EFTA Surveillance Authority 'perhaps a bit daringly . . . the quintessence of the EEA Agreement' (1994–95 EFTA Ct Rep 177).

But, looking back to 1994, other parameters have changed. After only 18 months of existence, the Court was reduced from five judges to two due to the accession of Austria, Finland and Sweden to the EC. Since mid 1995, the Court has consisted of three judges from Iceland, Liechtenstein and Norway. Moreover, there is a list of six *ad hoc* judges. The EC Treaty, the model of reference for the EEA Agreement, has been amended three times since the conclusion of the latter. On 1 September 1996, the seat of the Court was moved from Geneva to Luxemburg, a step that proved to be the right one. On 1 May 2004, due to eastern enlargement of the EC, the EFTA Court's 'big sister courts', the Court of Justice of the European Communities and the Court of First Instance of the European Communities, have grown from 15 to 25 judges each.

B. THE EFTA COURT'S CASE LAW

The EFTA Court has dealt with legal problems that could have come up in any modern economy and society. There are, however, *cultural and geographic features* of the EEA/EFTA States, which may be at the origin of certain procedures. Mention must be made of the series of cases related to Nordic import and retail *alcohol monopolies*. In these cases, the Nordic Governments argued that their Alcohol policy is deeply rooted in modern history and in Nordic societies and that its aim is to fight the harms to society and the individual which may result from the consumption of alcoholic beverages. The Court found the

Finnish alcohol import monopoly to be incompatible with the EEA rules on free movement of goods, but essentially upheld the Norwegian retail monopoly.

Another cultural feature is the strong tradition of *workers' protection* in the north. A series of transfer of undertaking cases were referred to the EFTA Court, most of them focusing on legal problems related to the applicability of the relevant directive to the succession of contracts. In two cases, the EFTA Court had to deal with the concept of abuse within the meaning of the Insolvency Directive. Mention must also be made of the *Landorganisasjonen* case in which the Court held upon reference by the Norwegian Labour Court that provisions of a collective agreement, which pursue the objective of improving conditions of work and employment, fall outside the scope of the EEA competition rules. If, however, the national court were to find that the contested provisions do, in fact, not pursue their apparent objectives, they may, according to the Court, in light of the objectives actually pursued, fall within the scope of Articles 53/54 EEA.

In parallel trade cases it has become quite obvious that the EFTA countries in general and Norway in particular have a tradition of favouring *free trade* and thereby fostering the *interests of consumers* over market partitioning through the use of intellectual property rights. In *Maglite*, the Court ruled that EEA/EFTA countries had retained the right to opt for international exhaustion of trademark rights under the Trademark Directive. In *Astra Norge*, it held that enforcement of a national copyright in a summary of product characteristics (SPC) would constitute a disguised restriction on trade in pharmaceuticals and be disproportionate to the aim of protecting the copyright in the SPC. In *Merck v Paranova*, the Court found that the legality of a parallel importers' strategy of product presentation cannot mechanically be assessed on the basis of the necessity criterion along the lines developed in the case law of the Court of Justice of the European Communities in the context of the repackaging.

Consumer protection was also the key issue in the trans-frontier television broadcast cases the EFTA Court had to deal with. The Court emphasized the importance of the transmitting state principle, but made it clear at the same time that control measures of receiving states are not thereby excluded, if they can be based on a legal foundation inside or outside the TV Directive.

In other proceedings, the special Norwegian concern for the *protection of health* became apparent. In two cases, the Court essentially found that Norway had been given the power by the EEA Joint Committee to deviate from the EC requirements for polyacrylamide to be labelled as carcinogenic. In *Kellogg's* the EFTA Court rejected the Norwegian government's argument that in order to ban the marketing of a fortified product it was sufficient to demonstrate a lack of nutritional need in the Norwegian population, but held at the same time that if certain conditions were fulfilled, Norway was entitled to invoke the *precautionary principle*.

Norway is considering itself a champion of *gender equality* not only in terms of equal opportunity, but of equal results. That policy has lead to the enactment of legislation permitting the reservation of a number of academic posts for members of the underrepresented gender, ie women. The EFTA Court held this to be incompatible with the Equal Rights Directive, which is based on the recognition of the right to equal treatment as a fundamental right of the individual.

In a case involving state aid in the form of regionally differentiated social security taxation, the special *geographical situation* of Norway was at stake. In a free movement of flight services case, the same happened with regard to *Iceland* where the longest air-route within the domestic market is 379 km, while the shortest route in service between Iceland and the rest of the EEA is approximately 1350 km. One of *Liechtenstein's* main geographical features has led to cases being brought before the EFTA Court: the country's *scarcity of (building) land* and, as a consequence thereof, the fear to be overrun. The EFTA Court held in five cases that residence requirements for managers and members of the board of directors of a domiciliary company, as well as the so-called single practice rule for doctors and dentists were not compatible with the right of establishment.

C. RELEVANCE OF THE CASE LAW OF THE COMMUNITY COURTS

Based on the EEA homogeneity rules, which as law in the books essentially constitute a one way street, the EFTA Court has, as a matter of principle, always followed existing ECJ and CFI case law on the interpretation of Community law that is identical in substance to EEA law. The EFTA Court has, however, from the very beginning, also been called upon to answer legal questions that have not or not fully been decided by the Community Courts in the past. In such cases, the ECJ and the CFI have shown their readiness to enter a judicial dialogue with the EFTA Court.

When interpreting the main part of the Surveillance and Court Agreement which deals, *inter alia*, with the types of procedure, the EFTA Court will consider the case law of the Community courts relevant when the expressions used in Community law are identical in substance to those of the SCA.

As far as effect is concerned, the EFTA Court's case law consists of three elements: (1) Implemented EEA rules (the vast majority of all EEA rules) that are sufficiently precise and unconditional may be invoked in national courts and take precedence over conflicting rules of national law. (2) The principle of state liability is part of EEA law. (3) It follows from the general objective of the EEA Agreement of establishing a dynamic and homogeneous market, in the ensuing emphasis on the judicial defence and enforcement of the rights of individuals, as well as in the public international law principle of effectiveness, that national courts will consider any relevant element of EEA law whether implemented or not, when interpreting international law.

This jurisprudence differs from the constitutional principles the ECJ has erected. In the EEA/EFTA we do not have the giant gothic cathedral with three naves which is characteristic for EC law, our construction rather resembles a simple Nordic stave church. But worshipping is possible in both places with the same results. To my best knowledge no individual whether from EFTA nor from the Community, has ever been prevented from invoking a precise and unconditional provision of EEA law before a national court of an EEA/EFTA State in a vertical context.

Both Community courts have made important contributions to this outcome, the CFI in its 1997 *Opel Austria* judgment and the ECJ in its 1999 *Rechberger* ruling. After the EFTA Court's ruling in *Sveinbjörnsdóttir* and the ECJ's judgment in *Rechberger*, the Common Market Law Review has stated in Editorial comments that the assumption underlying the ECJ's famous Opinion 1/91 that the EEA Agreement only creates rights and obligations between governments has been too one-sided and that with its reference to EFTA Court *Sveinbjörnsdóttir* in *Rechberger*, the ECJ has admitted that. The respective issue of the Common Market Law Review does not name the author of those editorial comments, but I have reason to believe that he is sitting in this room today.

In view of the effect issue, the EEA Agreement has been described as an attempt to mix oil and vinegar. In cuisine, that is not an insurmountable task. Every chef will confirm that oil and vinegar can easily be mixed provided you take first class—*extra vergine*, olive—oil and excellent—probably *Modena balsamic*—vinegar and you are good in mixing or, rather, whipping. It was not that easy in EEA law, but it has happened anyway. Supranationalism—the oil—has been combined with dualism—the vinegar—with a result that at least for individuals and economic operators constitutes a tasty dressing. Let me add one remark concerning the ECJ's Opinion 1/91: Seen from today, it was the right thing to bury the idea of creating an EEA court (which would have been a mixed breed) and to establish a structurally fully independent EFTA Court. This has not hindered the Community Courts to enter a judicial dialogue with the EFTA Court.

D. COOPERATION WITH THE NATIONAL COURTS OF EEA/EFTA STATES

The EFTA Court is cooperating with the national courts of the EEA/EFTA States under the preliminary reference procedure. Generally speaking, the number of references from national courts is comparable to the ones from Swedish and Finnish courts to the ECJ. Unlike ECJ rulings under the Article 234 EC procedure, EFTA Court opinions lack legally binding effect. In practice, they are, however, not weaker than preliminary rulings of the ECJ. Of equal importance is the fact that although national supreme courts of the EEA/EFTA States are not obliged to refer European law questions to the EFTA Court, the latter has received requests by the Supreme Courts of Iceland (1), Norway (3), and Sweden

(1) as well as by the Supreme Administrative Court of Liechtenstein (5) in the fields of *public procurement*, *requirement for provision of security costs by a foreign plaintiff*, *motor vehicle insurance law*, *law of parallel trade and repackaging*, and *freedom of establishment of managers, trustees, doctors and dentists*. Overall, it is fair to say that the EFTA Court has developed a fruitful relationship with the national judiciaries of its Member States.

I would like to welcome the Chief Justice of Iceland, Markús Sigurbjörnsson, the Chairman of the Supreme Administrative Court of Liechtenstein, Andreas Batliner, and Justices Eilert Stang Lund and Karl Arne Utgård who are representing the Chief Justice of Norway as well as the many judges from our three Member States.

E. DIALOGUE WITH THE COMMUNITY COURTS

In a number of fields such as *Television without frontiers*, *labour law*, *equal rights*, the *law of parallel trade and of repackaging*, *state aid law* and—in particular—*food safety law*, the case law of the EFTA Court has prompted reactions on the side of the ECJ, the CFI, Advocates General or national courts of EC Member States in cases in which they interpreted EC law. To give an example: Recent case law of the ECJ and the CFI concerning fortification of foodstuffs, fortification of animal food with antibiotics, and release of genetically modified organisms is largely based in the EFTA Court *Kellogg's* 2001 judgment.

The cross-fertilization between the Community courts and the EFTA Court is particularly intense in those cases in which the Community courts have to give interpretation of EEA law. Cases concerning the *principle of homogeneity in the EEA*, *state liability in EFTA States*, *free movement of capital* and *food safety law* may be mentioned here. In the *Bellio Fratelli* case, the ECJ rejected the Advocate General's assertion that Community law always prevails over EEA law and examined acts of Community secondary law with regard to their compatibility with the EEA Agreement.

With this, the EFTA Court has in its relationship with the Community courts come rather close to the position that the planned EEA Court would have had.

The EFTA Court would like to thank the Community courts for their openness and friendship. We are particularly pleased that so many colleagues from those Courts are participating in this symposium and I welcome particularly the President of the Court of Justice of the European Communities, Vassilios Skouris, First Advocate-General Ad Geelhoed and the President of the Court of First Instance of the European Communities, Bo Vesterdorf.

F. FUNDAMENTAL RIGHTS

The EFTA Court held in the *Bacalhao* case that provisions of the EEA Agreement as well as procedural provisions of the SCA are to be interpreted in the light of fundamental rights and that the provisions of the European Convention of Human Rights and the judgments of the European Court of Human Rights are important sources for determining the scope of these rights. In detail, the Court has referred to the freedom of expression granted by Article 10 ECHR, and to the landmark ruling of the European Court of Human Rights in the *Handyside* case, to the principle of access to justice constituting an essential element of the EEA legal framework and to the right to a fair trial within reasonable time guaranteed in Article 6(1) ECHR.

The EFTA Court is honoured that the President of the European Court of Human Rights, Luzius Wildhaber, is attending this symposium.

G. CONCLUSIONS

The EFTA Court has manyfold relations with the EFTA governments. I welcome the Minister of Justice and Ecclesiastical Affairs of Iceland, Björn Bjarnason, the Former Prime Minister of Norway and Member of the Storting, Thorbjörn Jagland, the former Prime Ministers of Liechtenstein Hans Brunhart and Mario Frick, but also the Members of the ESA/Court Committee, Ambassadors Bjørn Grydeland, and His Serene Highness Prince Nikolaus of Liechtenstein.

The EFTA Surveillance Authority has been involved in all the cases dealt with by the EFTA Court, either as a party or as a presenter of observations. A warm welcome to the College Members of the EFTA Surveillance Authority, President Hannes Hafstein, Bernd Hammermann and Einar Bull.

The European Commission has submitted observations in every single case. We are honoured that the Deputy Director-General of its Legal Service, Giuliano Marenco, has accepted our invitation.

I also cordially welcome the President of the Supreme Court of Switzerland, Heinz Aemisegger, the Vice-President of the Supreme Court of Luxembourg, Marc Schlungs, and the Secretary General of the Ministry of Foreign Affairs of Luxembourg, Ambassador Georges Santer.

Today's event is called a symposium. Symposium is a Greek word. I am speaking here under the supervision of ECJ President Skouris. Symposium can mean a feast, a banquet with food and wine and entertainment. That is not exactly what we are aiming at, at least not at this time of the day. We understand symposium in its second meaning, namely as a scientific convention in which issues of European and International law are dealt with, in presentations and discussions in a rather informal way.

You all have received the papers in advance, and I would like to thank our speakers for having made this possible. Therefore, we want to limit the interventions and leave enough time for discussion. The papers and the discussions will be published in a special volume.

In substance, the symposium consists of two parts, which, however, hang together. The morning session will be chaired by my colleague Thorgeir Örlygsson. Speakers will deal with certain issues related to the case law of the EFTA Court, issues that, however, reach beyond that case law. Professor Peter-Christian Müller-Graff from the University of Heidelberg will speak on the impact of climate, geography, and other non-legal factors on EC and EEA law. Professor Hans Petter Graver from the University of Oslo will analyze the effects of EFTA Court jurisprudence on the legal orders of EEA/EFTA States. Marco Bronckers, Attorney at Law and Professor at the University of Leiden, will deal with the precautionary approach in foodstuff law and environmental law, a subject that has not only regional, but also global implications.

The afternoon session, which will be chaired by my colleague Per Tresselt, will be dedicated to the subject of homogeneity as a fundamental principle of economic and legal spaces. Whenever more than one court or administrative authority in a given legal or economic area, is competent to apply legal rules that are identical in substance, the question arises how a homogeneous or coherent application of that law can be ensured. Ensuring homogeneity in such a constellation seems to be a genuine European concern. Inhomogeneous or incoherent interpretations will in that view lead to unequal treatment, distortion of competition, a 'race to the bottom', and forum shopping. Such consequences are unwarranted and must be avoided. It is to be noted that U.S. law takes a much more relaxed stance with regard to inter-circuit conflicts, ie, conflicts between Federal Appellate Courts that have not (yet) been resolved by a ruling of the US Supreme Court, the reason being that unlike Europe, the U.S. has for a long time been a single market with a common language, a single currency, a common culture (also in the legal field), and a common history. The President of the Court of Justice of the European Communities, Vassilios Skouris, will give us the honour of opening the afternoon session with a speech on 'The ECJ and the EFTA Court under the EEA Agreement'. Justice Karl Utgård from the Supreme Court of Norway will then address the issue of procedural aspects of homogeneity. One will remember in that context that the homogeneity provisions of the EEA Agreement have been modelled on the template of the Lugano Convention. Professor Stefán Már Stefánsson from the University of Iceland, one of the Court's *Ad Hoc* Judges, will deal with the subject of 'State liability in the EC, the EEA and under the European Human Rights Convention'. Judge Allan Rosas from the Court of Justice of the European Communities will speak on 'The Luxembourg and Strasbourg Courts', before I will make some closing remarks.

Participants in our symposium are judges, advocates general, representatives of governments, of the EFTA Surveillance Authority and of the European

Commission, lawyers in private practice and academics. They all contribute to a noble cause: How to resolve conflicts, which are inherent in human nature in a peaceful and fair way under the rule of law. We all know that it is difficult if not impossible to define what a just solution of a legal problem is. But we may agree on the concept of justice through procedure as developed in particular by German lawyer and sociologist Niklas Luhmann.

I wish us all a fruitful day and I thank you for your attention.

I. Selected Topics of EEA Law in Practice

The EFTA Court Ten Years On

CARL BAUDENBACHER

A. THE ESTABLISHMENT OF THE THIRD EUROPEAN COURT

THE EFTA COURT, the third European court after the Court of Justice of the European Communities and the European Court of Human Rights, took up its functions on 4 January 1994 in Geneva with five judges from the EFTA States participating in the EEA Agreement: Austria, Finland, Iceland, Norway, and Sweden. Much of what was said at the inaugural session 10½ years ago is still valid today. The Court's first President, Leif Sevón, emphasized that whatever the future will bring, 'the administration of justice will continue with the firmness and impartiality which must be expected from the EFTA Court'.[1] He also pointed to the independence of both the Surveillance Authority and the Court from the EFTA States. And he mentioned that the establishment of the EFTA Court was greatly facilitated by the help of the Court of Justice of the European Communities and the Court of First Instance of the European Communities. The President of the EFTA Surveillance Authority, Knut Almestad, called the EFTA Court and the EFTA Surveillance Authority 'perhaps a bit daringly. . . the quintessence of the EEA Agreement'.[2] Seen from today, this contention was, however, quite appropriate.

In fact, the EFTA Court is an important example of what in legal theory is referred to as judicialization of international law or, by using a rather problematic term, the proliferation of international courts.[3] One will remember that the bilateral free trade agreements concluded between the EEC and the EFTA States in 1972/73 were characterized by an imbalance with regard to the role of courts.

[1] (1994) 95 EFTA Ct Rep 176.

[2] (1994) 95 EFTA Ct Rep 177.

[3] See for instance, C Romano, 'The Proliferation of International Judicial Bodies: The Pieces of the Puzzle' (1999) 31 *NYU J Intl L & Politics* 710 ff; JI Charney, 'The Impact on the International Legal System of the Growth of International Courts and Tribunals' (1999) 31 *NYU J Intl L & Politics* 697 ff; JE Alvarez, 'The New Dispute Settlers: (Half) Truths and Consequences' (2003) 38 *Texas Intl L J* 405 ff; with regard to the EFTA Court in particular, C Baudenbacher, 'The EFTA Court—An Example of the Judicialization of International Economic Law' (2003) 28 *European L Rev* 880 ff.

With the Court of Justice of the European Communities, there was a common court of the EC states, which was competent to apply the provisions of the FTAs and which ruled in the *Kupferberg* case that provisions of the FTAs were able to have direct effect.[4] On the EFTA side there was no equivalent. A common court was not all that was lacking. The Supreme Courts of Switzerland and of Austria, the two EFTA countries which were deemed to follow the monist tradition, ruled in cases *Stanley Adams*, *Omo*, and *Austro Mechana* that the provisions of the FTAs on free movement of goods and on competition were not able to produce direct effect.[5] In the dualistic Nordic countries, such effect was excluded *a priori*, due to the lack of implementation of these agreements into the respective domestic legal orders.[6] This asymmetric situation was characterized as 'judicial restraint of trade' by the late Olivier Jacot-Guillarmod, the man who, by the way, would have become Switzerland's EFTA Court judge had Switzerland been able to ratify the EEA Agreement.[7]

But looking back to 1994, other parameters have changed. After only 18 months of existence, the Court was reduced from five judges to three due to the accession of Austria, Finland, and Sweden to the EC. Since mid-1995, the Court has consisted of three judges from Iceland, Liechtenstein, and Norway. Moreover, there is a list of six *ad hoc* judges. The EC Treaty, the model of reference for the EEA Agreement, has been amended three times since the conclusion of the latter, at Maastricht, Amsterdam, and Nice. On 1 September 1996, the seat of the Court was moved from Geneva to Luxembourg, a step with far-reaching consequences, a step that proved to be the right thing to do. On 1 May 2004, due to eastern enlargement of the EC, the EFTA Court's 'big sister courts', the Court of Justice of the European Communities and the Court of First Instance of the European Communities, have grown from 15 to 25 judges each. At the inaugural session of 4 January 1994, President Sevón rightly emphasized that the homogeneity rules, which essentially oblige the EFTA Court to follow or take into account the relevant case law of the ECJ (cf Articles 6 EEA, 3 II SCA), are at the very heart of the EEA Agreement.[8] That is still true. But after ten years, we can state that as far as law in action is concerned, homogeneity in the EEA is not a one-way street. Both the ECJ and the CFI have made important contributions to the homogeneous development of the case law in the EEA as a whole in a way that could hardly have been foreseen ten years ago.

[4] Case C–104/81 *Kupferberg* [1982] ECR 3641.

[5] Swiss Supreme Court, BGE 104 IV 175(1978)—*Adams*; 105 II 49(1979)—*Omo*; Supreme Court of Austria of 10 July 1979, *Austro–Mechana/GRAMOLA* Winter & Co, *Revue Internationale du Droit d'Auteur* 1980, no 104, GRUR Int 1980, 185.

[6] See U Bernitz, 'The EEC-EFTA free Trade Agreements with special reference to the position of Sweden and the other Scandinavian EFTA Countries' (1986) *CML Rev* 567, 578; J Forman, 'The EEA Agreement Five Years On: Dynamic Homogeneity in Practice and its Implantation by the Two EEA Courts' (1999) *CML Rev* 751.

[7] (1982) *CML Rev* 427 ff.

[8] (1994) 95 EFTA Ct Rep 176.

B. THE EFTA COURT'S CASE LAW

1. Number of Cases

The classical question EFTA Court judges are asked is: How many cases does the Court have? The answer is: The number of cases that in view of the size of the three EEA/EFTA countries can be expected. The vast majority of cases are references from national courts of EEA/EFTA States under the preliminary reference procedure. The numbers of references from national courts of EEA/EFTA countries are comparable with those from Finnish and Swedish courts to the ECJ.[9] There is, however, no clear line. The numbers of cases tend to go up and down. The Court has taken steps to intensify its relations with the national judiciaries so that national judges become more aware of the possibilities offered to them under the Article 34 SCA procedure.

The EFTA Court does not get many cases brought directly by the EFTA Surveillance Authority. ESA appears to be less active in bringing EFTA Member States before the Court than the EC Commission is in the framework of the European Community. ESA takes the view that as long as EEA/EFTA countries comply with their obligations under the EEA Agreement, it sees no reason to go after them in an aggressive way. In fact, one will notice that according to the so-called scoreboard, a list of best performing states, the EEA/EFTA countries have been, at least in the last years, among the top achievers or in the midfield.[10] The scoreboard, however, only refers to the fact that Directives have been implemented in good time. ESA has won all of its direct action cases so far. It is a well-known fact that in court you never can be absolutely sure. There is the famous saying in the Hanseatic Court of Appeal in Bremen that in court as on the high seas we are all in the hands of God. Some have concluded from the fact that the Authority has won all its cases that it may have a tendency to bring 'waterproof' cases, whereas the Commission seems to be willing to seek a clarification of the law also in cases where the result may not be that obvious.

[9] Sweden has 8.8 million inhabitants. Since 1995, the ECJ has received 49 requests under the Art 234 EC procedure from Swedish courts; 3 references had originally been lodged with the EFTA Court and were withdrawn after Sweden's accession to the EU; 9 more references are actually pending (as of 4 July 2004). Finland has a population of 5.2 million. The ECJ has received 36 references from Finnish courts; 9 more references are pending (as of July 2004). Norway's actual population is 4.5 million. The EFTA Court has since 1994 received 23 references from Norwegian courts, 4 more are actually pending (as of 4 July 2004). Iceland has a population of 280,000. The EFTA Court has received 9 references from Icelandic courts. Liechtenstein's population is 34,000. The EFTA Court has received 5 references so far, all from the Supreme Administrative Court.

[10] See EFTA Surveillance Authority, Internal Market Scoreboard EFTA States, July 2004.

2. Types of Cases

One may ask the question why the EFTA Court has received cases in certain areas of the law and not in others. One answer is that there have been some *leftovers from the EEA negotiations*. The negotiators were not able to resolve certain issues, but they knew that those issues could be brought before the Court. We are familiar with that pattern of conduct from our national legislatures. For instance, it was quite clear to the negotiators that the Nordic alcohol monopolies which at the time were covering the import, wholesale, and retail business would lead to problems, but they preferred to shift the responsibility for the details to the future EFTA Court. Moreover, it had not been made totally clear whether certain products, for instance beer, were covered by the rules of the EEA Agreement. In the Court's second alcohol monopoly case, *Wilhelmsen*,[11] that came up as an issue. The Norwegian government pleaded that beer did not fall within the scope of the EEA Agreement and asked the Court to throw out the case on that basis. The Court did not follow that suggestion.

Moreover, there are *cultural and geographical features* of the EFTA States, which may be at the origin of certain procedures:

(1) In the case of the Nordic countries, the *alcohol monopolies* are again an important example. Nordic governments have repeatedly argued that their alcohol policy is deeply rooted in modern history and in Nordic societies and that its aim is to 'curb to the greatest possible extent the harm to society and the individual that may result from the consumption of alcoholic beverages'.[12] The Court has demonstrated a certain understanding of this policy.[13] It declared the Finnish import monopoly incompatible with the EEA rules on free movement of goods in *Restamark*,[14] but upheld the Norwegian retail monopoly in *Wilhelmsen* provided that such an exclusive right does not give rise to discrimination between domestic products and products from other EEA States.[15] Alcohol policy considerations were also behind the provision of the Norwegian Automobile Liability Act, which stated that in principle a passenger injured in a traffic accident may not

[11] Case E–6/96 [1997] EFTA Ct Rep 53, paras 17 ff, 33.

[12] Case E–9/00 *EFTA Surveillance Authority v Norway ('Alcopops')* [2002] EFTA Ct Rep 72, para 32.

[13] See Case E–9/00 *EFTA Surveillance Authority v Norway ('Alcopops')* [2002] EFTA Ct Rep 72, paras 55 and 56.

[14] Case E–1/94 (1994) 95 EFTA Ct Rep 15. See, with regard to the Icelandic alcohol import monopoly, Case E–4/01 *Karlsson* [2002] EFTA Ct Rep 240.

[15] Case E–6/96 [1997] EFTA Ct Rep 53. The Court furthermore held that a provision of national law which automatically grants a wholesale licence—a pre-condition for supplying beer containing more than 4.75% alcohol by volume to a State alcohol retail monopoly in that State—to a domestically established producer of beer and does not do so for a foreign producer of beer constitutes a discrimination prohibited by Arts 11 and 16 EEA that cannot be justified under Art 13 EEA.

obtain compensation if he or she knew or must have known that the driver of the vehicle was under the influence of alcohol at the time of the accident. The EFTA Court held that legislation to be incompatible with the so-called Motor Vehicle Insurance Directives.[16] Admittedly, the case was decided on other grounds that did not include an evaluation of the legitimate fight against driving under the influence of alcohol.

(2) Another cultural feature is the strong tradition of *workers' protection* in the north. That tradition led to a series of transfer of undertaking cases being referred to the EFTA Court. At least the first ones were most probably thought to be test cases in order to find out how far the EFTA Court was willing to go with regard to the question of whether the succession of contracts constituted a transfer of undertaking within the meaning of the relevant Directive.[17] In two cases, the EFTA Court had to deal with the concept of abuse within the meaning of the Insolvency Directive. It held in *Samuelsson* that a provision of Swedish law which excluded employees from any further remuneration from a guarantee institution if they had received remuneration for claims arising from the same activity within the two years prior to the declaration of bankruptcy was incompatible with Article 10(a) of the Directive.[18] And it found in *Sveinbjörnsdóttir*[19] that Articles 1(2) and 10 of the Directive precluded Iceland from maintaining a provision of national law which excluded persons in a sibling relationship with the owner of a considerable part of the shares in the employer company from the scope of the national wage guarantee. Mention must also be made of the *Landorganisasjonen* case, in which the Court held upon reference by the Norwegian Labour Court that provisions of a collective agreement which pursue the objective of improving conditions of work and employment fall outside the scope of the EEA competition rules. If, however, the national court were to find that the contested provisions do not, in fact, pursue their apparent objectives, they may, according to the Court, fall within the scope of Articles 53/54 EEA. The Court held that, in any case, the good faith of the parties in concluding and implementing a collective agreement must also be taken into account.[20]

(3) In parallel trade cases it has become quite obvious that the EFTA countries in general and Norway in particular have a tradition of favouring *free trade* and thereby fostering the *interests of consumers* over market partitioning through the use of intellectual property rights. In *Maglite*, the EFTA Court

[16] Case E–1/99 *Finanger* [1999] EFTA Ct Rep 1.

[17] See Case E–2/95 *Eidesund* [1995/1996] EFTA Ct Rep 1; Case E–3/95 *Langeland* [1995/1996] EFTA Ct Rep 36; Case E–2/96 *Ulstein* [1995/1996] EFTA Ct Rep 65; Case E–3/96 *Ask v ABB and Aker* [1997] EFTA Ct Rep; moreover Case E–3/01 *Viggósdóttir* [2002] EFTA Ct Rep 202, and E–2/04 *Rasmussen* (not yet reported); below.

[18] Case E–1/95(1994) 95 EFTA Ct Rep 145.

[19] Case E–7/97 [1998] EFTA Ct Rep 95, paras 17 ff.

[20] Case E–8/00 *LO and NKF v KS* [2002] EFTA Ct Rep 114.

ruled that EEA/EFTA countries had retained the right to opt for international exhaustion of trademark rights under the Trade Mark Directive.[21] In *Astra Norge*,[22] the Court held that enforcement of a national copyright in a summary of product characteristics (SPC) would lead to an artificial partitioning of the market in the European Economic Area, constitute a disguised restriction on trade in pharmaceuticals, and be disproportionate to the aim of protecting the copyright in the SPC. The enforcement of the copyright would have prevented the competent national authority from giving out/approving/laying down the same SPC for a product imported by way of parallel import as for a directly imported medicinal product. In *Merck v Paranova*,[23] a repackaging case, the EFTA Court found that the legality of a parallel importer's strategy of product presentation cannot mechanically be assessed on the basis of the necessity criterion along the lines developed in the case law of the ECJ in the context of the repackaging itself. Instead, the EFTA Court found, a comprehensive balancing of the interests of the trademark proprietor and the parallel importer must be carried out.

(4) *Consumer protection* was also the key issue in the transfrontier television broadcast cases the EFTA Court had to deal with.[24] The Court emphasized the importance of the transmitting state principle, but made it clear at the same time that control measures of receiving states are not thereby excluded if they can be based on a legal foundation inside or outside the TV Directive.

(5) In other cases, the special Norwegian concern for the *protection of health* became apparent. In two cases, the Court had to deal with the question of whether Norway was entitled to require polyacrylamide to be labelled as carcinogenic when it contains residual acryl amide in a concentration of less than 0.1% by total volume although the relevant Directives did not allow that.[25] The Court essentially found that Norway had been given that power by a Joint Statement of the EEA Joint Committee and that the Committee was competent to adopt such a statement.[26] The *Kellogg's* case, one of the EFTA Court's landmark cases, was about strict Norwegian health policy with regard to the fortification of foodstuffs with vitamins and iron.[27] The EFTA Court rejected the Norwegian government's argument that in order to ban the marketing of a fortified product it was sufficient to demonstrate a lack of nutritional need in the Norwegian population, but held at the same

[21] Case E–2/97 [1997] EFTA Ct Rep 127.

[22] Case E–1/98 [1998] EFTA Ct Rep 140; see below.

[23] Case E–3/02 [2003] EFTA Ct Rep 101; see below.

[24] Joined Cases E–8/94 and E–9/94 *Mattel/Lego* [1994–95] EFTA Ct Rep 113, and E–8/97 *TV 1000* [1998] EFTA Ct Rep 68; see below.

[25] Council Directive 67/548/EEC of 27 June 1967 on classification, packaging and labelling of dangerous substances; Council Directive 88/379/EEC of 7 June 1988 on classification, packaging and labelling of dangerous preparations.

[26] Case E–6/01 *CIBA Speciality Chemicals Water Treatment Ltd v The Norwegian State* [2002] EFTA Ct Rep 281; E–2/00 *Allied Colloids v Norwegian State* [2000–01] EFTA Ct Rep 35.

[27] Case E–3/00 *EFTA Surveillance Authority v Norway* [2000–01] EFTA Ct Rep 73; see below.

time that if certain conditions were fulfilled, Norway was entitled to invoke the *precautionary principle*. The recognition of the precautionary principle must be regarded as a shift of paradigm in dealing with the justification ground of health protection.

(6) Norway considers itself a champion of *gender equality* in terms not only of equal opportunity, but of equal results. In connection with that policy, legislation has been enacted permitting the reservation of a number of academic posts for members of the underrepresented gender, ie, women, at the University of Oslo. The EFTA Court held this to be incompatible with the Equal Rights Directive 76/207/EEC of 9 February 1976, which is based on the recognition of the right to equal treatment as a fundamental right of the individual.[28] The Court found that derogations from that right can be permissible only when they show sufficient flexibility to allow a balance between the need for the promotion of the underrepresented gender and the opportunity for candidates of the opposite gender to have their situation objectively assessed. It rejected the defendant's submissions that Article 2(2) of the Directive applies since gender constitutes a determining factor for carrying out the activities in question and that the positions in question are new posts so that male applicants are not in a more difficult position with respect to career advancement than they would be without the earmarking scheme. However, the EFTA Court also pointed to the importance of the criteria for assessing the qualifications of candidates and found that in such an assessment there appears to be room for considering those factors that, on empirical experience, tend to place female candidates in a disadvantaged position in comparison with male candidates.

(7) In a state aid case, the *geographical situation of Norway* was at stake. The EFTA Court dismissed the application by Norway for annulment of a decision of the EFTA Surveillance Authority that found state aid in the form of regionally differentiated social security taxation incompatible with the functioning of the EEA Agreement.[29] But it noted that ESA had not fully considered the effect of harsh weather conditions or other circumstances which may justify an improvement of the employment situation by lowering the costs of labour in the affected areas. This alone was, however, found not to be sufficient for annulling ESA's decision. In a free movement of services case, the special *geographical situation of Iceland* was an issue. ESA had brought an action arguing that by maintaining in force legislation which subjected flights from Iceland to other EEA States to a higher tax rate than that charged for domestic flights, Iceland had failed to fulfil its obligations under EEA law. Iceland contended, *inter alia*, that the markets and services for international and domestic flights are not comparable, particularly in light of the geographical situation of Iceland, the longest air-route within

[28] Case E–1/02 *EFTA Surveillance Authority v Norway* [2003] EFTA Ct Rep 1.

[29] Case E–6/98 *Norway v EFTA Surveillance Authority* [1999] EFTA Ct Rep 74; see below.

the domestic market being 379 km, while the shortest route in service between Iceland and the rest of the EEA is approximately 1350 km. The EFTA Court held that geographic distance does not affect the nature of the service provided and rejected the defendant's argument that domestic flight services and intra-EEA flight services cannot be compared.[30] One of *Liechtenstein's main geographical features* has led to cases being brought before the EFTA Court: the country's *scarcity of (building) land* and, as a consequence, the fear of being overrun. Liechtenstein already has a very high percentage of foreign inhabitants. Everybody foresaw during the negotiations that this would lead to problems, and in fact, most of the cases originating from Liechtenstein have had to do with the freedom of establishment. The EFTA Court held in five cases that residence requirements for managers and members of the board of directors of a domiciliary company, as well as the so-called single practice rule for doctors and dentists, were not compatible with the right of establishment.[31]

The EFTA Court has finally dealt with problems that could have come up in any modern economy and society. Examples concern certain cases on *locus standi* of associations, on free movement of goods and of capital, but also on vertical restraints of competition and state aid in the form of state guarantees for a publicly owned mortgage bank.[32]

3. Relevance of the Case Law of the Community Courts

(a) General

EEA law is essentially identical in substance to Community law. The EFTA Court has, as a matter of principle, always followed ECJ case law on the interpretation of Community law that is identical in substance to EEA law. This holds true, in particular, for the concept of fundamental freedoms and for the elements of the rules prohibiting cartels and abuses of dominant positions as well as of the rules on public undertakings and on state aid. The Court has rejected attempts to construe the fundamental freedoms in a less integration-friendly way than the ECJ does in Community law.[33] The politically important distinction between old and new case law (cf Articles 6 EEA, 3 II SCA) has in practice, largely been qualified. The term 'Court of Justice of the European

[30] Case E–1/03 *EFTA Surveillance Authority v Iceland* [2003] EFTA Ct Rep 143.

[31] Cases E–3/98 *Herbert Rainford–Towning* [1998] EFTA Ct Rep 205; E–4/00 *Brändle* E–5/00 *Mangold*; and E–6/00 *Tschannet* [2000–01] EFTA Ct Rep 123, 163, 203; E–2/01 *Pucher* [2002] EFTA Ct Rep 44.

[32] See for instance, Cases E–5/98 *Fagtún* [1999] EFTA Ct Rep 51; E–1/00 *Íslandsbanki* [2000–01] EFTA Ct Rep 8; E–2/02 *Bellona* [2003] EFTA Ct Rep 52; E–4/97 *Norwegian Bankers' Association v EFTA Surveillance Authority II* [1999] EFTA Ct Rep 1.

[33] See below.

Communities' has been understood as comprising also the Court of First Instance.[34]

At the same time, it has always been plain that the homogeneity goal relates primarily to the outcome of a case and to a lesser extent to the reasons. It is to be borne in mind that arriving at a judicial decision is a psychological process running its course within a framework determined by the cornerstones of positive law and the hierarchical order of the judicial constitution.[35] What is more important is that the EFTA Court has from the very beginning, been called upon to answer legal questions that have not or not fully been decided by the ECJ in the past.[36] In such cases, the ECJ and the CFI have shown their readiness to enter into a judicial dialogue with the EFTA Court.[37]

(b) Access to Justice

As far as access of individuals and economic operators to the EFTA Court is concerned, two features need to be dealt with: Access to the preliminary reference procedure and *locus standi* to bring an action for nullity against a decision of the EFTA Surveillance Authority. The EFTA Court has made it clear that although it is not required by Article 3(1) SCA to follow the case law of the ECJ when interpreting the main part of the Surveillance and Court Agreement which deals, *inter alia*, with the types of procedure, that case law is relevant when the expressions used in Community law are identical in substance to those of the SCA.[38]

The Court in its very first case, *Restamark*,[39] was asked to give an interpretation of the notion of court or tribunal within the meaning of Article 34 SCA. Under the six-factor test usually applied by the ECJ when interpreting the parallel provision of Article 234 EC, to constitute a 'court or tribunal' within the meaning of that provision, the referring body must (1) be established by law, (2) be permanent, (3) have compulsory jurisdiction, (4) conduct inter-partes procedures, (5) apply rules of law and evidence, and (6) be independent.[40] The

[34] Cases E–2/94 *Scottish Salmon Growers* [1994–95] EFTA Ct Rep 59, para 13; E–2/02 *Bellona* [2003] EFTA Ct Rep, para 40.

[35] C Kohler, 'Integration und Auslegung—Zur Doppelfunktion des Europäischen Gerichtshofes' in E Jayme (ed), *Ein internationales Zivilverfahrensrecht für Gesamteuropa* (Heidelberg, CF Müller Juristischer Verlag, 1992) 11–28, III2.

[36] C Baudenbacher, 'Homogenität–Parallelität—Going First—Betrachtungen zur Rechtsstellung des EFTA—Gerichtshofs am Beispiel der Rechtsprechung zur Betriebsübergangsrichtlinie', *Festschrift für Bernhard Grossfeld zum 65. Geburtstag* (Heidelberg, Verlag Recht und Wirtschaft GmbH, 1999) 55 ff.

[37] See in detail below.

[38] Cases E–1/94 *Restamark* [1994–95] EFTA Ct Rep 15, para 24; E–2/94 *Scottish Salmon Growers* [1994–95] EFTA Ct Rep 59, para 11; E–1/95 *Samuelsson* [1994–95] EFTA Ct Rep 145, para 14; E–2/02 *Bellona* [2003] EFTA Ct Rep, paras 38 and 39.

[39] Case E–1/94 [1994–95] EFTA Ct Rep 15.

[40] See for instance, Case C–393/92 *Municipality of Almelo* [1994] ECR I–1477, para 21. The first five elements of the test for establishing whether a body constitutes a 'court or tribunal' were identified in the early case of *Vaassen–Gobbels* (Case C–61/65 [1969] ECR I–1277 *Vaassen (née Gobbels)*, while the sixth was added later in the *Pretore di Salò* case; Case C–14/86 [1987] ECR 2545).

EFTA Court took that as a starting point, but followed a rather liberal approach. It held that the Tullilautakunta, a Finnish customs appeal body that appeared to be closely linked to the central customs administration, constituted a 'court or tribunal' within the meaning of Article 34 SCA, based on the following criteria: It was a permanent body entrusted by law to exercise its functions, it had compulsory jurisdiction, its composition was defined by law, it had to apply the law, the procedure before it was similar to that before the administrative courts, and its decisions were binding and enforceable. The independence granted and assumed to be practiced, and the elements characteristic of judicial procedures prescribed for it, led the EFTA Court to the conclusion that, on balance, the Tullilautakunta was, in fact and law, independent and impartial. The Court observed that in the proceedings at issue only one party appeared before the Tullilautakunta. However, that frequently occurs in Finland as well as in Sweden in proceedings before administrative courts, including the Supreme Administrative Court. The Court noted that if the right to request an Advisory Opinion were subject to the procedure before the national court being adversarial, this would result in the administrative courts in Finland (and also in Sweden) being largely unable to refer a question to the EFTA Court. The request was therefore considered admissible. The Court confirmed its approach in cases *Mattel/Lego*[41] and recognized the right of the Norwegian Market Council to request an Advisory Opinion. That court recently referred another case to the EFTA Court.[42] When the EFTA Court had to give judgment in the *Restamark* case in December 1994, the ECJ's case law on whether there is a requirement that the procedure be inter-partes was not entirely clear. In *Vaassen Gobbels*[43] the fact that the referring body was bound by rules of adversary procedure similar to those used by ordinary courts of law was one of the reasons which led the ECJ to conclude that it constituted a court or tribunal under Article 234 EC. In *Greis Unterweger*,[44] the ECJ pointed to the fact that the proceedings were not inter-partes in ruling the reference inadmissible. In other cases, however, the ECJ came to the conclusion that fulfillment of the inter-partes requirement is not essential in determining whether a body constitutes a court or tribunal. In the *Politi* case,[45] the ECJ accepted a reference from the President of the Tribunale di Torino in the context of summary proceedings for an injunction during which the defendant does not appear. In addition, in the *Simmenthal* case,[46] the absence of inter-partes proceedings did not prevent the ECJ from accepting the reference. In its judgments in *Dorsch Consult* of 1997[47] and

[41] Joined Cases E–8/94 and E–9/94 [1994–95] EFTA Ct Rep 113, para 15.

[42] Case E–4/04 *Pedicel AS* (not yet reported).

[43] Vaassen Gobbels, above.

[44] Case C–318/95 *Greis Unterweger* [1986] ECR 955.

[45] Case 43/71 *Politi* [1971] ECR 1039.

[46] Case 70/77 [1978] ECR 1453.

[47] Case C–54/96 [1997] ECR I–4961.

Gabalfrisa of 2000,[48] the ECJ emphasized that the inter-partes factor is not an absolute requirement.

With regard to the admissibility of a request for an Advisory Opinion and of the questions of the national court, the EFTA Court has followed ECJ case law on Article 234 EC.[49] In one of its first cases, *Samuelsson*,[50] it held that the national court, which alone has direct knowledge of the facts of the case, is in the best position to appreciate, with full knowledge of the matter before it, the necessity for an Advisory Opinion to enable it to give a judgment. The EFTA Court has no jurisdiction where the interpretation of a provision of EEA law has no connection whatsoever with the circumstances or purpose of the main proceedings. It is not for the Court to give Opinions on general or hypothetical questions. In *Nille*,[51] the EFTA Court stated that it is for the national court to determine, in light of the particular circumstances of the case, both the need for an Advisory Opinion in order to enable it to give judgment and the relevance of the questions it submits to the Court. Whereas in *Samuelsson* and in *Nille* the Court came to the conclusion that the questions were closely related to the proceedings before the national court and could not be considered hypothetical, it found in *Wilhelmsen*[52] that two out of four questions were general and hypothetical and therefore inadmissible. The EFTA Court found that the national court had not submitted any factual information concerning these questions, but only referred to a request by one of the parties that these questions also be referred to the EFTA Court.[53] In *Ásgeirsson*,[54] the EFTA Court confirmed its now well-established case law on the need for and necessity of Advisory Opinions.

With respect to the question of *locus standi* to bring an action for nullity of a decision of the EFTA Surveillance Authority, the EFTA Court found in *Scottish Salmon Growers*[55] that an association representing the overwhelming majority of, if not all, salmon growers in a given country and negotiating on their behalf with the authorities in that country and with the EC Commission or ESA is to be considered as directly and individually concerned under Article 36 SCA. It therefore had *locus standi* to challenge a decision of ESA not to investigate a complaint concerning alleged state aid granted to the Norwegian salmon industry. In these circumstances, the EFTA Court held, it was not necessary to examine whether or not the applicant was the addressee of the decision of ESA. In *Husbanken I*,[56] the Court held that if state aid proceedings are governed by

[48] Cases C–110/98 to C–147/98 *Gabalfrisa* [2000] ECR I–1577.
[49] See for instance, Case C–412/93 *Leclerc–Siplec* [1995] ECR I–1790.
[50] Case E–1/95 [1994–95] EFTA Ct Rep 145.
[51] Case E–5/96 [1997] EFTA Ct Rep 30, para 12.
[52] Case E–6/96 [1997] EFTA Ct Rep 53, para 40.
[53] *Ibid*, para 40.
[54] Case E–2/03 [2003] EFTA Ct Rep 185.
[55] Case E–2/94 [1994–95] EFTA Ct Rep 59.
[56] Case E–4/97 *Norwegian Bankers' Association v EFTA Surveillance Authority* [1999] EFTA Ct Rep 38.

Article 1(2) of Protocol 3 to the Surveillance and Court Agreement, the provision mirroring Article 88(2) EC, an association's involvement in the proceedings before ESA may, in certain circumstances, warrant standing for that association to bring an action for annulment before the Court. This is particularly so where (1) the association is, as a representative of its members, at the origin of a complaint to ESA, (2) the association's views were heard during the procedure and information was gathered from the State in question with regard to the complaint from the association, and (3) a decision effectively was a decision not to object to the state aid complained of.

In *Bellona*,[57] the Bellona Foundation, a Norwegian environmental foundation which had lodged the original complaint with ESA, and TBW, a German environmental consulting firm, jointly sought annulment of an ESA decision before the EFTA Court. In that decision, ESA found that it would not raise objections to new Norwegian tax legislation setting favourable depreciation rates for natural gas exploitation projects (in particular the so-called *Snøhvit*-field) as being incompatible with EEA law on state aid. The EFTA Court held that the action was inadmissible because the decision, which was addressed to Norway, was not of direct and individual concern to the applicants as required under Article 36(2) SCA, the provision mirroring Article 230(4) EC. The Court found that the applicants had not shown that the contested state aid decision could adversely affect their legitimate economic interests. An environmental foundation could not institute proceedings before the Court either in a representative capacity on behalf of members or on the grounds of its involvement in the administrative procedure before ESA. An environmental consulting firm was not affected by any competition arising from the adoption of the contested decision. The Applicants therefore lacked *locus standi*.

On balance, the EFTA Court has in all these matters, essentially followed the case law of the ECJ (without being obliged to do so). There appears, however, to be a tendency toward being liberal in cases of doubt, which may also be a consequence of the fact that the Court, unlike the ECJ, is not overburdened.

(c) The Effect Issue

(i) The Starting Point From early on, the question has been discussed of whether the so-called constitutional principles of community law—direct effect, primacy, and state liability—which the ECJ recognized in 1963, 1964, and 1991, respectively, on the basis of a free law approach, also form part of EEA law. It goes without saying, that by this case law the ECJ has established a monist system in EC law. Monism does thereby not follow from a decision of Member States' law, but from Community law itself. The EEA Agreement contains regulations that at first sight seem to speak in favour of a dualist approach. Article 7 EEA states that acts corresponding to an EEC regulation are not directly

[57] Case E–2/02 [2003] EFTA Ct Rep 52.

applicable, but shall be made part of the internal legal order of the EFTA States. Furthermore, Protocol 35 stipulates that the aim of achieving a homogeneous European Economic Area, based on common rules, does not require the Contracting Parties to transfer legislative powers to any institution of the EEA. On the other hand, the EEA Agreement emphasizes on a number of occasions that the protection of individual rights is of paramount importance, that the overriding goal of the EEA Agreement is to create a dynamic and homogeneous European Economic Area and that the EEA Agreement as well as the Surveillance and Court Agreement contain specific homogeneity rules addressing the EFTA Court in particular, and that the Contracting Parties are under a duty to loyally cooperate within the framework of the EEA Agreement (Article 3 EEA).[58]

The governments of the Nordic states, focusing on Article 7 EEA and on Protocol 35 to the EEA Agreement, took the view that the EEA Agreement had recognized traditional Nordic dualism, which meant that direct effect and state liability were unthinkable in EEA law.[59] They seemed to find comfort in the ECJ's Opinion 1/91, in which that Court declared the establishment of an EEA judiciary consisting of ECJ and EFTA judges incompatible with Community law, and assumed that the EEA Agreement was a simple public international law treaty conferring rights only on the participating EFTA States on the one hand and the Community on the other. The principles of direct effect and primacy were found to be 'irreconcilable with the characteristics of the agreement'.[60] But influential authors, including two former judges of the EFTA Court and an Advocate-General of the ECJ, took the view that the constitutional principles of EC law in question were at least on balance part of EEA law.[61]

(ii) The EFTA Court's Answers The legal point of departure may be characterized as a *dilatorischer Formelkompromiss*, a compromise which aimed at handing over the power to shape the final decision either to the Court or to the Contracting Parties. The EFTA Court picked up the hot potato and went for

[58] See insofar, P Tresselt and K Mahieu, 'Hugtakid skadabótaábyrgd ríkisins innan EES–réttar' (2004) *Tímarit lögfræðinga*, part 4.

[59] See the written submissions of the Norwegian government in cases *Restamark* (Case E–1/04 Report for the Hearing (1994) 95 EFTA Ct Rep 15, points 89 ff); *Sveinbjörnsdóttir* (Case E–7/97 Report for the Hearing [1998] EFTA Ct Rep 127, points 66 ff); and *Karlsson* (Case E–4/01 Report for the Hearing [2002] EFTA Ct Rep 240, points 51 ff) and of the Icelandic and the Swedish government in *Sveinbjörnsdóttir* (Case E–7/97 Report for the Hearing [1998] EFTA Ct Rep 127, points 52 ff, 76 ff) as well as the oral submissions of the Swedish government in *Restamark*.

[60] Opinion 1/91 [1992] ECR I–6097 ff, para 28.

[61] See L Sevón, 'Primacy and Direct Effect in the EEA—Some Reflections' in *Festskrift til Ole Due, Liber Amicorum* (Copenhagen, Forlaget Thomson, 1994) 34; W van W van Gerven, 'The Genesis of EEA Law and the Principles of Primacy and Direct Effect' [1992/93] 16 *Fordham Intl L J* 955, 989; T Bruha, 'Is the EEA an Internal Market?' in Müller-Graff and Selvig (eds), *EEA–EU Relations* (Berlin, Berlin Verlag Arno Spitz GmbH, 1999) 97, 122 ff.; L Sevón and M Johansson, 'The Protection of the Rights of Individuals under the EEA Agreement' (1999) *European L Rev* 373, 385; S Norberg, 'Perspectives on the Future Development of the EEA Agreement' (Reykjavik, Bokautgafa Orators, 2000) *Afmælisrit Thór Vilhjálmsson* 367 ff.

what may be called *quasi-direct effect, quasi-primacy,* and *full state liability.* It held in its very first case, *Restamark,* on 14 December 1994, that it follows from Protocol 35 that individuals and economic operators must be entitled to invoke and to claim at the national level any rights that could be derived from the provisions of the EEA Agreement, as being or having been made part of the respective national legal order, if they are unconditional and sufficiently precise.[62] In its 2002 *Einarsson* judgment, the Court found that, according to Protocol 35, such provisions take precedence over conflicting provisions of national law.[63] National courts must be entitled to ask the EFTA Court for an Opinion on these matters under Article 34 SCA. In its 1998 *Sveinbjörnsdóttir* ruling, the EFTA Court found, that the principle of state liability for breaches of EEA law must be assumed to be part of that law.[64] The Court rejected the argument of the Icelandic government that if, in the absence of state liability, homogeneity should be affected, the matter would have to 'be dealt with politically and through diplomatic channels as set out particularly in Articles 105 to 111 EEA and not by the EFTA Court'.[65] After having confirmed its state liability jurisprudence in the 2002 *Karlsson* case, the EFTA Court held, without having been asked by the national court, ie, in *dicta,* that EEA law does not require that individuals and economic operators be able to rely directly on non-implemented EEA rules before national courts. At the same time, it was considered inherent in the general objective of the EEA Agreement of establishing a dynamic and homogeneous market, in the ensuing emphasis on the judicial defence and enforcement of the rights of individuals, as well as in the public international law principle of effectiveness, that national courts will consider any relevant element of EEA law, whether implemented or not, when interpreting international law.[66]

(iii) Contributions of the Community Courts The CFI and the ECJ have made important contributions to the development of the EFTA Court's case law in the field in question. The CFI turned out to become the 'ice-breaker' in its *Opel Austria* judgment of 1997, where it found that the EEA Agreement involves a high degree of integration, with objectives which exceed those of a mere free-trade agreement, and that the significance in regard to the interpretation and application of the agreement and of the Contracting Parties' objective to establish a dynamic and homogeneous EEA had not been diminished by the ECJ's Opinion 1/91. The CFI further held that Article 10 of the EEA Agreement, the provision corresponding to Articles 12, 13, 16, and 17 of the EC Treaty, has direct effect in community law.[67]

[62] Case E–1/94 (1994) 95 EFTA Ct Rep 15.
[63] Case E–1/01 [2002] EFTA Ct Rep 1.
[64] Case E–7/97 [1998] EFTA Ct Rep 95.
[65] Case E–7/97 Report for the Hearing [1998] EFTA Ct Rep 127, point 62.
[66] Case E–4/01 [2002] EFTA Ct Rep 240, para 28.
[67] Case T–115/94 [1997] ECR II–39.

In *Rechberger*,[68] the ECJ was, *inter alia*, asked by the Landesgericht Linz whether the principle of state liability applied in Austria after 1 January 1994, in view of the fact that Austria had become part of the European Economic Area on that date. Austria had not implemented the Package Tour Directive in good time, and travellers had suffered damage. In view of the planned accession of four of them to the EU, the five EFTA/EEA States had entered into an Agreement on transitional arrangements for a period after the accession of certain EFTA States to the EU on 28 September 1994.[69] According to Article 5 of this Agreement, after accession, new preliminary reference proceedings could only be brought before the EFTA Court in cases in which the facts occurred before accession, and where the application was lodged with the Court within three months after accession. Under Article 7 of that Agreement, the EFTA Court of five judges was to conclude all pending cases within six months after accession.[70] On 1 January 1995, Austria, Finland, and Sweden joined the European Union. In its ruling of 15 June 1999, the ECJ held that Austria was, according to Article 7 EEA in conjunction with Section 11 of Protocol 1 to the EEA Agreement, required to transpose the directive in question on the day the EEA Agreement entered into force, ie, on 1 January 1994. The Court, however, declared itself not competent to rule on a question of interpretation related to the application by Austria of the EEA Agreement during the period preceding its accession to the Community. The Court went on, however, by stating:

> Moreover, in view of the objective of uniform interpretation and application which informs the EEA Agreement, it should be pointed out that the principles governing the liability of an EFTA State for infringement of a directive referred to in the EEA Agreement were the subject of the EFTA Court's judgment of 10 December 1998 in *Sveinbjörnsdóttir*.[71]

One will have to conclude from this that the Austrian judge was at least indirectly encouraged to grant compensation in this case if the conditions set out by the EFTA Court in *Sveinbjörnsdóttir* (which, by the way, correspond to those developed in Community law by the ECJ) are fulfilled.

It must finally be pointed out that in *Ospelt* the ECJ emphasized that 'one of the principal aims of the EEA Agreement is to provide for the fullest possible realisation of the four freedoms within the whole EEA, so that the internal market established within the European Union is extended to the EFTA States'.[72] One will notice that in this case the ECJ did not refer to its EEA-critical Opinion 1/91 anymore, but to its EEA-friendly Opinion 1/92.[73]

[68] Case C–140/97 [1999] ECR I–3499.

[69] Agreement on transitional arrangements for a period after the accession of certain EFTA States to the European Union.

[70] Case E–1/95 *Samuelsson* was referred to the EFTA Court by the Varbergs tingsrätt, Sweden, on 2 March 1995 and decided by the EFTA Court on 20 June 1995; (1994) 95 EFTA Ct Rep 145.

[71] Case C–140/97 [1999] ECR I–3499, para 39.

[72] Case C–452/01 *Margarethe Ospelt and Schlössle Weissenberg Familienstiftung* [2003] ECR I–9743, para 29.

[73] Opinion of the Court of 10 April 1992 [1992] ECR I–2821.

(iv) Consequences Many observers from the Community and from the EFTA side have for a long time been of the opinion that the constitutional principles of direct effect, primacy, and state liability are unique features of Community law, features that make Community law stand out against all international law. This is usually deduced from the ECJ's finding in its 1963 *Van Gend en Loos* judgment that 'the Community constitutes a new legal order of international law for the benefit of which the states have limited their sovereign rights.[74] The ECJ's Opinion 1/91, which was rendered 28 years later, still breathes that spirit, although, as Danish scholar Ole Spiermann has alleged, the Community legal order was not that new anymore in 1991.[75]

There are those who think that with the case law in question the EFTA Court has gone supranational. This is deemed to be sensitive in light of the declaration in Protocol 35 to the EEA Agreement that no Contracting Party is required to transfer legislative powers to any institution of the EEA.[76] Others focus on the fact that the EEA Agreement has created a market.[77] And as we all know, markets can work only if individuals and economic operators are able to carry out their functions, ie, to freely produce, distribute, and consume within the limits of the relevant legal framework, in order to create wealth. It has also been argued that it does not automatically follow from the fact that the EEA Contracting Parties have limited their sovereign rights that they have transferred legislative powers to the EEA institutions.[78] In this writer's view, one must bear in mind that the specific EC law concept of supranationalism has been developed against the background of traditional public international law. EEA law escapes such conceptualization. Accordingly, the EFTA Court has characterized the legal nature of the EEA Agreement as an international treaty *sui generis* that has created a distinct legal order of its own. Even if the integration is less far-reaching than under the EC Treaty, the scope and objective of the EEA Agreement go beyond what is usual for an agreement under public international law.[79] In any case, one may, with respect, say that the ECJ is, after the EFTA Court's rulings in *Restamark*, *Einarsson*, and *Sveinbjörnsdóttir*, no more the only saving church when it comes to protecting the rights of individuals and economic operators. The EFTA Court may with that jurisprudence, also have made a contribution to fostering the development of general international law towards an approach that would grant individuals and economic operators

[74] Case E–26/62 [1963] ECR 1.

[75] O Spiermann, 'The Other Side of the Story: An Unpopular Essay on the Making of the European Community Legal Order' (1999) 10 *Eur J Intl L* 763, 767.

[76] See F Sejersted, in F Sejersted, *et al*, *EØS-rett*, 2nd edn (Oslo, Universitetsforlaget, 2004) 108–9.

[77] See K Almestad, 'The Duties of Co-Operation of National Authorities and the Community Instutitions under Article 10 (ex Article 5) of the Treaty of Rome: The EEA Variant' (2000) *FIDE XIX Congress*, vol I, 427 ff.

[78] L Sevón and M Johansson, 'The Protection of the Rights of Individuals under the EEA Agreement' (1999) 24 *European L Rev* 373, 382.

[79] Case E–7/97 *Sveinbjörnsdóttir* [1998] EFTA Ct Rep 127, para 59.

subjectivity. As for the rest, it would hardly have been possible to maintain homogeneity with regard to the protection of individual rights had the EFTA Court not taken the steps it took in the cases in question. Such pragmatic considerations, which indeed focus on the fact that the EEA has created an internal market, must always be part of a European court's equation. It has rightly been said that the homogeneity goal includes an *obligation de résultat* on the part of the EEA/EFTA side with regard to the level of protection of individual rights.[80] One may assume that this obligation has been fulfilled. The development described above shows that similarly to the European Convention on Human Rights (as held by the European Court of Human Rights on many occasions),[81] the EEA Agreement is a living instrument, which in particular due to the homogeneity link with the Community may need interpretation in light of present-day circumstances. For the sake of completeness, it must be added that from a homogeneity perspective dynamic interpretation of EEA law may in particular be required in cases in which the relevant provisions of Community law have been amended since the conclusion of the EEA Agreement in 1992.[82]

Opinion 1/91 led to a certain disappointment in EFTA circles at the time it was rendered. Seen from today, it was the right thing to do to bury the idea of creating an EEA Court (which would have become a mixed breed) and to establish a structurally fully independent EFTA Court. As subsequent development has shown, this has not hindered the Community courts from entering into a judicial dialogue with the EFTA Court. Other parts of Opinion 1/91, such as the prognosis that direct effect and primacy will not be possible in EEA law, have to a large extent been falsified through the jurisprudence of the EFTA Court.[83] It appears that the ECJ itself has had second thoughts in that respect. After the EFTA Court's ruling in *Sveinbjörnsdóttir* and the ECJ's judgment in *Rechberger*, the Common Market Law Review has stated in editorial comments that the thesis, according to which the EEA Agreement only creates rights and obligations between governments, has been too one-sided and that with its reference to EFTA Court *Sveinbjörnsdóttir* in *Rechberger*, the ECJ has given 'more than a "coup de chapeau", a salute to the EFTA Court. With this statement, it is important to note, the EC Court appears to endorse the EFTA Court's judgment'.[84]

In concluding, one may say that even if EC-style direct effect and primacy are as such lacking in EEA law, homogeneity has not been impaired in this field.

[80] See T Bruha, 'Is the EEA an Internal Market?' in Müller-Graff and Selvig (eds), *EEA–EU Relations* (Berlin, Berlin Verlag Arno Spitz GmbH, 1999) 97, 123.

[81] See for instance, *Tyrer v UK* 2 EHRR 1 (25 April 1978).

[82] See C Baudenbacher, 'Der EFTA–Gerichtshof, das EWR–Abkommen und die Fortentwicklungen des EG–Vertrages', *Festschrift zum 75. Geburtstag von Prof Dr Dr Herbert Batliner* (Vaduz, ex jure Verlagsanstalt, 2004) 59 ff.

[83] While this writer is speaking of falsification, he is referring to the philosophy of science approach of Sir K Popper, *Logik der Forschung*, 6th edn (Berlin, Akademie-Verlag, 1976).

[84] Editorial Comments: 'European Economic Area and European Community: Homogeneity of Legal Orders?' (1999) *CML Rev*, 697, 700.

First of all, the EEA Main Agreement has been implemented in the domestic legal orders of the EFTA States.[85] EEA secondary law is being implemented in an ongoing process. The same holds true for the rulings of the EFTA Court.[86] There has, to this writer's knowledge, never been a case in which a national court refused to set aside a conflicting rule of domestic law, at least not in a *vertical context*.[87] That is also important from a reciprocity perspective. '[S]ince EFTA operators benefit from the characteristics of direct effect and supremacy of the EC legal order to enforce their EEA rights within the EC national Courts, their EC counterparts should be in a similar position to obtain a comparable level of legal redress in the EFTA national Courts'.[88]

4. Fundamental Rights

The Court of Justice of the European Communities has a long-standing tradition of referring to the European Convention on Human Rights and to judgments of the European Court of Human Rights in cases involving fundamental rights.[89] Fundamental rights are part of the general principles of EC law. The EFTA Court has followed suit on the first occasion. In *TV 1000,*[90] the Court interpreted the transmitting state principle underlying the Television without Frontiers Directive 89/552/EEC and referred to the freedom of expression granted by Article 10 ECHR as well as, with regard to the limitations of that freedom, to the landmark ruling of the European Court of Human Rights in *Handyside*.[91] In *Bellona*[92] the EFTA Court dealt with an action for nullity against a decision of the EFTA Surveillance Authority approving state aid. It held that access to justice constitutes an essential element of the EEA legal

[85] One will notice that Advocate–General Geelhoed, has in his Opionion in *Ospelt,* stated that the principle of free movement of capital has, according to the case law of the EFTA Court, direct effect; below.

[86] See with regard to Iceland, T Örlygsson, 'Hvernig hefur Ísland brugdist vid ákvördunum EFTA-dómstólsins?' (2004) 54 *Tímarit lögfrædinga* 375.

[87] In its *Finanger* judgment, the Norwegian Supreme Court declared itself unable to set aside a clear provision of Norwegian law that conflicted with the EEA Motor Vehicle Insurance Directives. The Court emphasized that the judgment was given in a horizontal context. See Judgment of 16 November 2000, Rt 2000, p 1811.

[88] Editorial comments: 'European Economic Area and European Community: Homogeneity of Legal Orders?' (1999) *CML Rev,* 697, 698; see in this respect also Sevón and Johansson, above, 384:

> If individuals and economic operators would not be ensured the same possibility of invoking the Agreement there would be an imbalance in the Agreement. While individuals and economic operators from the EFTA States would be in the position to invoke the Agreement before courts and administrative authorities in the EC Member States, this would not be the case for individuals and economic operators from the EC Member States in the EFTA States.

[89] See for instance Case C–44/79 *Hauer v Rheinland–Pfalz* [1979] ECR 3727; C–63/83 *Regina v Kent Kirk* [1984] ECR 2689; C–222/84 *Johnston v Chief Constable of the RUC* [1986] ECR 1651.

[90] Case E–8/97 [1998] EFTA Ct Rep 68.

[91] Judgment of 7 December 1976, A, vol 24.

[92] Case E–2/02 [2003] EFTA Ct Rep 52, paras 36 f.

framework. The EFTA Court stated that it was aware of the ongoing debate with regard to the issue of the standing of natural and legal persons in actions against Community institutions and referred, *inter alia*, to the Opinion of Advocate General *Jacobs* in *ECJ Pequeños Agricultores*.[93] It added that this discussion was important at a time when the significance of the judicial function which is inspired by the idea of human rights appeared to be on the increase, both on the national and international level. The EFTA Court's case law culminated in *Ásgeirsson*,[94] also referred to as the *Bacalhao* case. In these proceedings, one of the defendants in the national proceedings had alleged that the reference of the case to the EFTA Court prolonged the duration of the proceedings and thereby infringed Article 6 of the European Convention on Human Rights. The EFTA Court held in a general way that provisions of the EEA Agreement as well as procedural provisions of the SCA are to be interpreted in light of fundamental rights and that the provisions of the European Convention on Human Rights and the judgments of the European Court of Human Rights are important sources for determining the scope of these rights. With regard to the right to a fair and public hearing within a reasonable time granted by Article 6(1) ECHR, the EFTA Court observed that the European Court of Human Rights held in a case concerning a delay of two years and seven months due to a reference by a national court to the ECJ for a preliminary ruling that to take this period into consideration would adversely affect the system instituted by Article 177 of the EEC Treaty (now Article 234 EC) and work against the aim pursued in substance in that Article.[95] The EFTA Court held that the same must apply with regard to the procedure established under Article 34 of the SCA, which, as a means of inter-court cooperation, contributes to the proper functioning of the EEA Agreement to the benefit of individuals and economic operators. The EFTA Court added that in the present case the period from the registration of the request to the delivery of judgment amounted to a little more than five months.

5. The Role of Governments and Institutions

The governments of the EEA/EFTA States and the EFTA Surveillance Authority may be parties in the proceedings before the EFTA Court. In cases in which they are not parties, they have, according to Article 20 of the EFTA Court's Statute, the right to participate by way of submitting statements of case or written observations. The same right is given to the Community (read: the EC Member States) and to the European Commission. Under Article 36(1) of the Statute, the EEA/EFTA States, the EFTA Surveillance Authority, the Community (read: the

[93] Case C–50/00 *Unión de Pequeños Agricultores v Council* [2002] ECR I–6677.
[94] Case E–2/03 [2003] EFTA Ct Rep 185, para 28.
[95] Case *Pafitis v Greece* (26 February 1998) Reports 1998–I, para 95.

EC Member States), and the European Commission may intervene in cases before the EFTA Court. For the sake of order, it must be mentioned that in cases before the Court of Justice of the European Communities, EEA/EFTA States and the EFTA Surveillance Authority have corresponding rights if one of the fields of application of the EEA Agreement is concerned (Article 40 of the Statute, Article 93 of the Court's Rules of Procedure, and Articles 155, 116 of the Rules of Procedure of the Court of First Instance, Article 23 of the Statute). The participation rights in question are important means intended to contribute to the homogeneous development of the case law in the EEA.

That *governments* tend to take a tough stance in cases in which they are involved as parties or in which their interest is at stake seems normal. Proceedings concerning access to (European) justice, fundamental freedoms, state monopolies, discriminatory taxation, state aid, effect, and state liability are cases in point. In such constellations, governments tend to show an attitude that is not exactly pro-integration, for instance by arguing that provisions of EEA law need to be interpreted differently from parallel provisions of EC law[96] or that discriminations and restrictions following from the legislation of EEA/EFTA States are justified on grounds whose acceptance would be doubtful in comparable cases in Community law.[97] A classical pattern of government behaviour consists in preferring to be taken to Court rather than to ask the national legislatures to comply with EEA law on their own initiative. This motive sometimes becomes apparent in actions for violation of the EEA Agreement brought by the EFTA Surveillance Authority. But it may also be present in preliminary reference cases, for instance if in the national proceedings an individual or an economic operator is seeking a ruling by an administrative court against a government.[98] In preliminary reference cases involving private litigants, however, governments often take a pro-integration stand. The EFTA Court was faced with this kind of situation in particular in a series of cases concerning the relationship between the principle of free movement of goods and national intellectual property rights.[99]

The *EFTA Surveillance Authority* has been a party in all direct action cases dealt with by the EFTA Court, either by bringing actions against EEA/EFTA States in its capacity as the guardian of the EEA Agreement or as a defendant in action for nullity cases brought by private operators or by governments. In all the preliminary reference cases decided by the EFTA Court, ESA has submitted observations. In these cases, ESA has made extremely valuable contributions to

[96] See for instance, Cases E–3/98 *Herbert Rainford–Towning* [1998] EFTA Ct Rep 205; Case E–1/03 *EFTA Surveillance Authority v Iceland* [2003] EFTA Ct Rep 143; Case E–1/04 *Fokus Bank ASA v Norwegian State*, (23 November 2004).

[97] See for instance, Case E–1/01 *Einarsson* [2002] EFTA Ct Rep 1, in particular para 42.

[98] In the three cases involving the compatibility of the Liechtenstein single practice rule for doctors and dentists Cases E–4/00, E–5/00 and E–6/00 [2000–01] EFTA Ct Rep 123, 163, 203, *Dr Braendle*, *Dr Mangold* and *Dr Tschannet*. ESA had dealt with the same issue before in proceedings that could have led to an action for infringement of the EEA Agreement.

[99] See below.

the Court's jurisprudence. Mention must be made, in particular, of its submissions in the cases on effect and on state liability, on fundamental freedoms, but also in the parallel trade and competition law cases.

The *European Commission* has submitted observations in every single case, be it a reference by a national court or a direct action. Its interventions are of great importance in particular from the perspective of homogeneity, and the Court is very grateful for them. Experience shows that the Commission's view is of considerable weight, in particular in cases fundamental freedom cases. In a majority of cases, the Court has followed the path proposed by the Commission (often together with ESA). But in a couple of high-profile cases (concerning state liability, international exhaustion of trademark rights, and the relationship between collective agreements and EEA competition law),[100] the Court has not done that.

When it comes to the substance of cases, one sometimes gets the impression that the Commission is (not surprisingly) wearing more than one hat. First of all, the Commission seems to feel that it bears a special responsibility for the maintenance of homogeneity, particularly in light of the fact that the EFTA Court is operating without an Advocate-General. One must also bear in mind that the Commission is representing the Community in the EEA Joint Committee, the body which would be competent to settle a dispute arising from a judicial conflict between the ECJ and the EFTA Court. Moreover, the Commission may have a special interest in the outcome of an EFTA Court case because one or several cases involving the same or similar issues are pending before the Community courts or because such cases are in the pipeline. It may then try to use the proceedings before the EFTA Court as a testing ground, so to speak. If things go well for the Commission, it will take the EFTA Court's ruling as persuasive authority and ask the Community courts to go for the same solution in EC law. This has happened a couple of times, the most important example being the EFTA Court's *Kellogg's* case.[101] In *Commission v Denmark*, the Commission largely referred to the EFTA Court's *Kellogg's* judgment which, in its view, had to be seen 'as an element in the development of the law'[102] and successfully urged the ECJ to reject the Danish government's argument that the mere finding by a national authority of the absence of a nutritional need is sufficient to justify a general prohibition on foodstuffs enriched with vitamins or minerals.[103]

Governments of EC States have presented their arguments in a number of EFTA Court proceedings, in particular in cases in which the EFTA Court had

[100] See Cases E–7/97 *Sveinbjörnsdóttir* [1998] EFTA Ct Rep 127; E–2/97 *Maglite* [1997] EFTA Ct Rep 127; E–8/00 *LO* [2002] EFTA Ct Rep 114.

[101] Case E–3/00 *EFTA Surveillance Authority v Norway* [2000–01] EFTA Ct Rep 73.

[102] Cited in pt 79 of the Opinion of Advocate-General Mischo in Case C–192/01 *Commission v Denmark* [2003] ECR I–9693.

[103] Case C–192/01 [2003] ECR I–9693, in particular para 25.

to deal with a legal problem as the first court in the European Economic Area[104] or in cases involving issues of particular significance, for instance if a case may affect the interest of EC States or of businesses operating in such States.[105] EC State governments will have a special interest in making their views known if they are facing a parallel problem in proceedings before the Community courts or if such proceedings are looming. An example would be the participation of Denmark, France, and the Netherlands in the EFTA Court's *Kellogg's* case.[106]

C. DIALOGUE WITH NATIONAL COURTS OF EEA/EFTA STATES, IN PARTICULAR SUPREME COURTS

The EFTA Court is cooperating with the national courts of the EEA/EFTA States in the framework of the Article 34 SCA procedure, which has been modeled on the template of Article 234 EC. In order to avoid constitutional problems in certain EEA/EFTA States, the drafters of the Surveillance and Court Agreement have deviated from Community law in particular in two respects: (1) Unlike national courts of last resort in the EC with respect to the ECJ, national supreme courts of the EEA/EFTA States are not obliged to refer European Law questions to the EFTA Court. (2) Unlike preliminary rulings of the ECJ under the Article 234 EC procedure, decisions rendered by the EFTA Court in response to a question by a national court are, strictly speaking, not legally binding on the referring national court. In the SCA they are therefore referred to as 'Advisory Opinions'. In practice, the differences between EEA Law and Community law are, however, not visible. The EFTA Court has received requests under the Article 34 SCA procedure by the Supreme Courts of Iceland, Norway, and Sweden as well as by the Supreme Administrative Court of Liechtenstein in the fields of *public procurement*,[107] the *obligation of a foreign plaintiff to provide security for costs of court proceedings*,[108] *motor vehicle insurance law*,[109] the *law of parallel trade and repackaging*,[110] and

[104] See the 'Television Without Frontier' cases, E–8/94 and E–9/94 *Mattel and Lego* [1994–95] EFTA Ct Rep 113; and E–8/97 *TV 1000* [1998] EFTA Ct Rep 68; or the 'Transfer of Undertakings' cases, E–2/95 *Eidesund* [1995/1996] EFTA Ct Rep 1; E–3/95 *Langeland* [1995/1996] EFTA Ct Rep 36; E–2/96 *Ulstein* and *Røiseng* [1995/1996] EFTA Ct Rep 65; E–3/96 *Ask v ABB and Aker* [1997] EFTA Ct Rep 1.

[105] See for instance, the submissions of France, Germany, and the United Kingdom in Case E–2/97 *Maglite* [1997] EFTA Ct Rep 127, or of the United Kingdom in Case E–1/04 *Fokus Bank ASA v Norwegian State*, (23 November 2004).

[106] Case E–3/00 *EFTA Surveillance Authority v Norway* [2000–01] EFTA Ct Rep 73. See Cases C–192/01 *Commission v Denmark* [2003] ECR I–9693; C–24/00 *Commission v France*, (5 February 2004); C–41/02 *Commission v Netherlands*, (2 December 2004).

[107] Case E–5/98 *Fagtún* [1999] EFTA Ct Rep 51 (Supreme Court of Iceland).

[108] Cases E–5/97 *European Navigation* [1998] EFTA Ct Rep 59 (Supreme Court of Norway); E–7/94 *Data Delecta* (1994) 95 EFTA Ct Rep 109 (Supreme Court of Sweden). After Sweden's accession to the European Community, the latter case was withdrawn and subsequently referred to and decided by the Court of Justice of the European Communities (Case C–43/95 [1996] ECR I–4461).

[109] Case E–1/99 *Finanger* [1999] EFTA Ct Rep 119 (Supreme Court of Norway).

[110] Case E–3/02 *Merck v Paranova* [2003] EFTA Ct Rep 101 (Supreme Court of Norway).

freedom of establishment of managers, trustees, doctors, and dentists.[111] Moreover, Opinions of the EFTA Court have always been followed by the referring national courts. If a national court were to refuse to comply with such an Opinion, it would bring its country into a status of breach of the EEA Agreement.[112] Justice Hans Flock, writing for the unanimous Norwegian Supreme Court, stated in the first *Finanger* case that although the Opinion of the EFTA Court is advisory, it must be accorded preeminent weight due to the task of the EFTA Court to guarantee homogeneous interpretation, the specialized knowledge of the EFTA Court, and the fact that Member States and institutions of EFTA and EC have the right to submit observations.[113] It may be added that the EFTA Court, in a case involving a second request for an Advisory Opinion by the same national court, referred to the ECJ's judgment in the *Wünsche* case[114] and held that a further reference may only be justified when the national court encounters difficulties in understanding or applying the first judgment, when it refers a fresh question of law, or when it submits new considerations that might lead to a different answer to a question submitted earlier. However, it was not held permissible to use the right to refer questions as a means of contesting the validity of the earlier Opinion.[115] Validity translates into German as *Rechtskraft*. Opinions of the EFTA Court are—from a sociological standpoint—not weaker than preliminary rulings of its 'big sister court', the ECJ.[116] It is fair to say that the legal nature is not the only *sui generis* feature in EEA law. The rulings rendered under the preliminary reference procedure, too, are of *sui generis* nature. That is why the EFTA Court calls them 'judgments'.

D. DIALOGUE WITH THE COMMUNITY COURTS

1. Community Courts Interpreting EC Law

The foregoing considerations show that EC State governments tend to base their decision to participate in EFTA Court cases on the assumption that the outcome of those proceedings may have an influence on the course of action in the Community Courts interpreting Community law. In fact, the EFTA Court has, with its limited means and its limited caseload, acted as a giver of ideas in

[111] Cases E–3/98 *Herbert Rainford–Towning* [1998] EFTA Ct Rep 205; E–4/00 *Brändle*, E–5/00 *Mangold*, and E–6/00 *Tschannet* [2000–01] EFTA Ct Rep 123, 163, 203; E–2/01 *Pucher* [2002] EFTA Ct Rep 44 (Supreme Administrative Court of Liechtenstein).

[112] See H Bull, 'The EEA Agreement and Norwegian Law' (1994) 5 *EBL Rev* 291, 296.

[113] Case 55/1999, (16 November 2000), Rt 2000, p 1859, *translation by European Courts Procedure* (London, 2002) 3.042.

[114] Case C–69/85 [1986] ECR 947, para 15.

[115] See Cases E–2/00 *Allied Colloids* [2000–01] EFTA Ct Rep 35; and E–6/01 *CIBA* [2002] EFTA Ct Rep 281, in particular paras 11–13.

[116] See also HP Graver, 'Die Ausdehnung des Europäischen Gemeinschaftsrechts auf Nichtmitglieder der Union—das Beispiel Norwegens', *ARENA Working Papers 01/21*.

fields such as *Television without frontiers*, *labor law*, the *law of parallel trade and of repackaging*, *state aid law*, and—in particular—*food safety law*. It must be emphasized in this context, that the ECJ is under no obligation to take into account the EFTA Court's jurisprudence. That means that the only way by which the EFTA Court can make itself heard is through argument. Advocates-General of the ECJ have played an important role in this dialogue.[117] In recent times, the EFTA Court has, for its part, referred to Opinions of Advocates-General.[118]

(a) Control of Transfrontier TV Broadcasts by the Receiving State Based on a Foundation Outside the TV Directive

In joined cases *Mattel* and *Lego*, the EFTA Court, upon a question referred to it by the Norwegian Market Council, held in a judgment of 16 June 1995 that Articles 2(2) and 16 of the Television Directive must be interpreted as preventing an EEA State from applying a national general ban on television advertising specifically aimed at children if the advertisements are part of a television programme which is received from another EEA State. The Court referred in *dicta* to the 17th recital of the Television Directive's preamble, according to which the Directive 'is without prejudice to existing or future Community acts of harmonization', particularly if they serve to protect consumers and safeguard fair trade and competition. This was held to be, *inter alia*, a reference to Directive 84/450/EEC concerning misleading advertising. The Court noted that the Television Directive was not meant to preclude Members States from taking measures under Directive 84/450/EEC with regard to advertisements deemed misleading within the meaning of that Directive.[119] The legal questions the EFTA Court dealt with in *Mattel/Lego* were faced by the ECJ in joined cases *De Agostini* and *TV-Shop i Sverige*, which had originally been referred to the EFTA Court. After Sweden's accession to the EU, the market court withdrew the request for a preliminary ruling and, on 7 March 1995, referred it to the ECJ.[120] In its ruling of 9 July 1997, the ECJ fully endorsed the line previously taken by

[117] See below.

[118] See Cases E–2/02 *Bellona* [2003] EFTA Ct Rep 52, para 37 (reference to A-G Jacobs in C–50/00 *Pequeños Agricultores* [2002] ECR I–6677); E–8/00 *LO* [2002] EFTA Ct Rep 114, para 35 (reference to A-G Jacobs in Cases C–67/96 *Albany*, Joined Cases C–115/97 to C–117/97 *Brentjens'* and C–219/97 *Drijvende Bokken*); E–1/02 *EFTA Surveillance Authority v Norway* [2003] EFTA Ct Rep 1, paras 37 and 40 (reference to A-G Tesauro in Case C–450/93 *Kalanke* [1995] ECR I–3051, and Saggio in Case 158/97 *Badeck* [2000] ECR I–5539); E–1/04 *Fokus Bank ASA v Norwegian State*, (23 November 2004) para 23 (reference to A-G Geelhoed in Case C–452/01 *Ospelt and Schlössle Weissenberg* [2003] ECR I–9743).

[119] Cases E–8/94 and E–9/94 (1994) 95 EFTA Ct Rep 113.

[120] Cases E–4/94 *Konsumentenombudsmannen v De Agostini (Svenska) Förlag AB* [1994–95] EFTA Ct Rep 89; and E–5/94 *Konsumentenombudsmannen v TV–shop i Sverige AB* [1994–95] EFTA Ct Rep 93, and later dealt with by the Court of Justice of the European Communities (Joined Cases C–34/95 *Konsumentenombudsmannen v De Agostini (Svenska) Förlag AB* and C–35/95 and C–36/95 *Konsumentenombudsmannen v TV–shop i Sverige AB* [1997] ECR I–3843.

the EFTA Court. It reasoned that 'the Directive is to be interpreted as precluding the application to television broadcasts from other Member States of a provision of a domestic broadcasting law which provides that advertisements broadcast in commercial breaks on television must not be designed to attract the attention of children under 12 years of age'.[121] The ECJ noted, however, that Directive 84/450/EEC concerning misleading advertising 'could be robbed of its substance in the field of television advertising if the receiving Member State were deprived of all possibility of adopting measures against an advertiser and that this would be in contradiction with the express intention of the Community legislature' and referred to the EFTA Court's *Mattel/Lego* judgment.[122] On the strength of this, the ECJ came to the conclusion that the Television Directive

> does not preclude a Member State from taking, pursuant to general legislation on protection of consumers against misleading advertising, measures against an advertiser in relation to television advertising broadcast from another Member State, provided that those measures do not prevent the retransmission, as such, in its territory of television broadcasts coming from that other Member State.[123]

One will notice that Advocate-General Jacobs had proposed that the ECJ follow the holding of the EFTA Court in *Mattel/Lego*, but not the dicta.[124]

(b) Control of Transfrontier TV Broadcasts by the Receiving State Based on a Foundation in the TV Directive

In *TV 1000*,[125] a Swedish broadcasting company operated a film channel. Transmissions were sent via satellite. The programmes could be received only via pay TV. In Norway, the broadcasts were retransmitted in the cable net and by satellite. The films in question consisted of explicit hard-core pornography. The Norwegian authorities prohibited their transmission. The EFTA Court found that an exceptional procedure of temporary suspension of retransmission was allowed pursuant to Article 2(2) of the Directive. The reference in Article 2(2)(a) of the Directive to a television broadcast infringing Article 22 was to be understood as being a reference to the criterion that it 'might seriously impair the physical, mental or moral development of minors.' The Court denied the question of whether there exists a common standard of pornography in the whole of the EEA and held that broadcasts of programmes which might seriously impair the physical, mental, or moral development of minors are not lawful because they are sent at night or because there is a technical device. In *R v Secretary of State for Culture, Media and Sport*, the Queens Bench Division had to decide a case involving the broadcasting of pornographic movies by Danish

121 Cases C–34/95, 35/95, 36/95 [1997] ECR I–3843, para 62 and operative part.
122 Para 37.
123 Para 38.
124 Opinion, para 85.
125 Case E–8/97 [1998] EFTA Ct Rep 68.

Satellite TV (DSTV) from Denmark to the United Kingdom. After having informed the Commission (and DSTV) that in its view the broadcasts had manifestly, seriously, and gravely infringed Article 22 of Directive 89/552, the UK government prohibited the broadcast and informed the Commission, which by a decision addressed to the U.K. stated that the measure was not discriminatory and appropriate for the purpose of protecting minors. That Act was notified to DSTV. The High Court, referring to EFTA Court *TV 1000*, dismissed an application by DSTV against the order of the U.K. government. The judge also rejected DSTV's alternative request for a question to be referred to the ECJ under the Article 234 EC procedure stating that the judgment was unequivocal.[126] Moreover, the High Court refused DSTV leave to appeal to the Court of Appeal. DSTV's application for leave to appeal was dismissed. An action for annulment against the Commission by DSTV was dismissed as inadmissible by the Court of First Instance of the European Communities. The CFI found that DSTV was not directly concerned for the purposes of what is now Article 230(4) EC.[127]

(c) Succession of Contracts and the Transfer of Undertakings Directive

The preliminary reference series of *Eidesund*, *Langeland*, *Ulstein and Røiseng*, and *Ask v ABB and Aker* was primarily concerned with the question of whether the Directive on Transfers of Undertakings was applicable to the replacement of independent service providers, ie, the termination of a contract with one service provider followed by the conclusion of a contract with a new, more competitive company. In the wake of the ECJ's affirmation in the *Christel Schmidt* case of the Directive's applicability in cases of mere outsourcing of an activity,[128] this question had become a bone of contention, particularly in Germany and the United Kingdom. In *Eidesund*,[129] the operator of an oil-drilling platform in the North Sea terminated a contract relating to the provision of catering and cleaning services by an independent company, invited tenders, and, based on those tenders, awarded the contract to another company. After obtaining the contract, the second employer offered 14 of the first contractor's employees continued work on the platform. There were no contractual relations between the first service provider and the second, and tangible assets were taken over to a very limited extent. With regard to the question of whether the succession of two independent service providers constituted a transfer, the EFTA Court ruled that, first, the business or part of business in question was to be the business activity carried out by the service provider; second, for a service provider's business activity to be considered a separate economic entity it needed to be

[126] *R v Secretary of State for Culture, Media and Sport ex parte Danish Satellite TV and another*, 12 February 1999 (CO/3153/98).

[127] Case T–69/99 [2000] ECR II–4039.

[128] Case C–392/92 [1994] ECR I–1311.

[129] Case E–2/95(1995) 96 EFTA Ct Rep 1.

distinguishable from his other service activities, and normally have employees mostly assigned to that unit; and third, for a supply of services, or goods, to be considered a separate business, a certain minimum of activity and continuity was required. The taking over of assets could constitute an important element in the overall assessment of the transaction. The EFTA Court furthermore found that the supply of services and goods alone did not constitute part of a service provider's business within the meaning of the Directive. Accordingly, the loss of one customer to a competing company would normally not qualify as a transfer of a business within the meaning of the Directive. Nonetheless, the EFTA Court concluded that the replacement of an independent service provider with another might constitute a transfer of business within the meaning of the Directive, depending on the circumstances of the individual case. The EFTA Court changed its approach in *Ulstein and Røiseng*. In that case, an outside company that had carried out ambulance services for a hospital was no longer considered after public tenders had been invited, but replaced by a second company. No tangible assets were taken over. The second company reemployed four of the original 19 employees. In its ruling, the EFTA Court held that 'a mere succession of two contracts for the provision of the same or similar services will not, as a rule, be sufficient for there to be a transfer of an undertaking, business or part of a business' within the meaning of the Directive.[130] The EFTA Court confirmed its jurisprudence in the *Ask v Aker and ABB* case.[131] In its *Süzen* judgment of 11 March 1997,[132] the ECJ did not qualify the replacement of a service provider as falling within the scope of the Transfer of Undertakings Directive, making reference to the EFTA Court's ruling in *Ulstein* and *Røiseng*. In *ADI v Willer & Ors*, a case on succession of contracts, the Court of Appeal based itself on the ECJ's *Süzen* judgment and indirectly referred to EFTA Court *Ulstein* by way of quoting the paragraph in which the ECJ cites that EFTA Court ruling verbatim.[133] The Austrian Supreme Court interpreted the notion of transfer by reference to EFTA Court *Ulstein*.[134] The question was whether the transfer rules would also apply if the worker is an apprentice. The Supreme Court answered in the affirmative.

In the *Eidesund*, *Ulstein and Røiseng*, and *Ask v ABB and Aker* cases,[135] the EFTA Court found furthermore that the Transfer of Undertakings Directive was applicable where in the event of succession of contracts the new contract was awarded after a public tender had taken place. However, the Court expressed the reservation that in most cases of public tendering, regardless of whether it was stipulated by EEA law or not, the replacement of a service provider would not constitute a transfer of an undertaking, business, or part of

[130] Case E–2/96(1995) 96 EFTA Ct Rep 67, para 27.
[131] Case E–3/96 [1997] EFTA Ct Rep 1.
[132] Case C–13/95 [1997] ECR I–1259.
[133] EWCA Civ 971, [2001] IRLR 542.
[134] 9 ObA 193/98t, (7 October 1998), DRdA 1998, 269 ff.
[135] See above.

a business within the meaning of the Transfer of Undertakings Directive. The ECJ followed EFTA Court *Eidesund* and *Ask v ABB and Aker* in *Oy Liikenne*, holding that a public tender does not exclude the applicability of the Directive.[136]

In the cases *Eidesund* and *Langeland*,[137] the national courts asked whether an obligation of the transferor of a business or of part of a business to pay premiums into a supplementary pension scheme would be transferred to the purchaser. The Court found that the Directive exempted all the rights and obligations regarding old age, invalidity, and survivors' benefits. It noted that the accrual of pension benefits and the payment of pension premiums were inseparable and that it would make no economic sense to transfer the obligation to pay premiums once it was clear that any obligation to pay pensions was ruled out. The England and Wales Court of Appeal held in the *Adams* case[138] that Article 3(3) of the Transfer of Undertakings Directive exempts all the rights concerning supplementary pension schemes in case of old-age, invalidity, and survivors' benefits from the transfer. It referred, *inter alia*, to EFTA Court *Eidesund* holding that the ruling was not binding, but 'persuasive authority'. Appellation to the House of Lords was denied. The Employment Appeal Tribunal came to the same conclusion in *Frankling* and referred to the EFTA Court's *Eidesund* ruling.[139]

(d) Equal Rights

In the *Briheche* case, Advocate-General Poiares Maduro proposed the ECJ to hold that the Equal Rights Directive 76/207/EEC and Article 141(4) EC preclude national legislation that discriminates between widowers and widows who have not remarried as regards the age limit imposed on them for access to posts in the administration, without being aimed either at removing existing inequalities or at compensating them.[140] The Advocate-General emphasized that positive measures, ie, measures that favour women in order to reduce their underrepresentation in professional life, must be reconciled as far as possible with the equal treatment principle and referred, *inter alia*, to the EFTA Court's judgment in the *University of Oslo* case.[141] In that case, the EFTA Court held that 'earmarking' of academic posts for women was contrary to the principle of equal treatment.[142] No judgment has been delivered by the ECJ so far.

[136] [2001] ECR I–745.

[137] See above.

[138] *Adams v Lancashire County Council and BET Catering Services Ltd* [1997] ICR 834, [1997] IRLR 436.

[139] *Frankling v BSP Public Sector Ltd* [1999] IRLR 212.

[140] Case 319/03 *Serge Briheche v Ministère* de l'intérieur, *de la sécurité intérieure et des libertés locales*, Opinion of 29 June 2004.

[141] *Ibid*, point 36, as well as nn 16 and 26.

[142] See above.

(e) Parallel Trade

In *Maglite*,[143] a Norwegian business had directly imported trademarked Maglite flashlights from California to Norway without the trademark owner's consent. According to Article 7(1) of the Trade Mark Directive, the trademark shall not entitle the proprietor to prohibit its use in relation to goods which have been put on the market in a Member State under that trademark by the proprietor or with his consent. The EFTA Court held on 3 December 1997 that this provision is to be interpreted as leaving it up to the EFTA States parties to the EEA Agreement to decide whether they wish to introduce or maintain the principle of international exhaustion of rights conferred by a trademark with regard to goods originating from outside the EEA. The Court found that the principle of international exhaustion is in the interest of free trade and competition and thus in the interest of consumers, that it is in line with the main function of a trademark, to allow consumers to identify with certainty the origin of the goods, and that this interpretation of Article 7(1) of the Trade Mark Directive was also consistent with the TRIPs Agreement, which left the issue open for the Member States to regulate. The EFTA Court mentioned that there is a difference in scope between the EEA Agreement and the EC Treaty. The EEA Agreement does not establish a customs union, but a free trade area, and it does not entail a common commercial policy towards third countries. The EFTA States therefore remain free to conclude treaties and agreements with third countries relating to foreign trade. It is for them to decide whether they want to stick to the principle of international exhaustion of trademark rights. In its *Silhouette* judgment of 16 July 1998, the ECJ came to the opposite conclusion, holding that national rules of EC Member States providing for international exhaustion of trademark rights were incompatible with Article 7(1) of the Trade Mark Directive.[144] The ruling was essentially based on the consideration that the result found is the only one that is in line with the goal of securing the functioning of the internal market. The ECJ did not make reference to the EFTA Court's *Maglite* judgment. But Advocate-General Jacobs did. He distinguished the two cases on the facts (in *Maglite*, unlike in *Silhouette*, the parallel imports stemmed from the US, ie from outside the EEA) and on the law (unlike the EC Treaty, the EEA Agreement has not established a customs union, but a free trade area in which sovereignty in foreign trade matters lies with the Contracting Parties). Mr Jacobs moreover found the argument put forward in *Silhouette* by the Swedish government that the function of trademarks is not to enable the trademark owner to divide up the market and to exploit price differentials and that the adoption of international exhaustion would bring substantial advantages to consumers, and would promote price competition, 'extremely attractive'.[145] One will notice that this

[143] Case E–2/97 [1997] EFTA Ct Rep 127.
[144] Case C–355/96 [1998] ECR I–4799.
[145] *Ibid*, pts 48 f.

approach is also underlying the EFTA Court's *Maglite* ruling. However, the Advocate General concluded that the ECJ's case law on the function of trademarks was developed in the context of the Community, not the world market, and to allow Member States to opt for international exhaustion would itself result in barriers between Member States. It is not for the President of the EFTA Court to comment on the ECJ's *Silhouette* judgment. But it may be doubted that the actual situation constitutes a contribution to making Europe 'the most competitive and dynamic economy in the world' in this decade.[146] For the sake of order, it may be added that in the *Zino Davidoff* case, which in the meantime has led to a judgment by the ECJ,[147] the Chancery Division referred in its decision to ask the ECJ for a preliminary ruling, *inter alia*, to EFTA Court *Maglite*.[148]

In *Merck v Paranova*,[149] the American pharmaceutical manufacturer *Merck* brought a lawsuit against the Danish parallel importer *Paranova*. *Paranova* repackaged the original products and reaffixed onto the new packaging *Merck's* original trademark as well as information on the identity of the repackager. Moreover, along the edges of the repackaging, it affixed vertical or horizontal stripes, whose colours would vary in accordance with those employed by the original producer. The action brought by *Merck* against *Paranova* before the Norwegian courts aimed at prohibiting the use of those coloured stripes. The Norwegian Supreme Court essentially asked the EFTA Court whether, in a case where it has been established that repackaging of a pharmaceutical product was necessary to allow a parallel importer effective access to the market, 'legitimate reasons' within the meaning of Article 7(2) of the Directive existed on the grounds that the parallel importer has equipped the new packaging with coloured stripes, and whether the use of such packaging design should be measured against a 'necessity test', along the lines developed in the case law of the Court of Justice of the European Communities. The EFTA Court emphasized the importance of free trade in markets partitioned along national boundaries, such as the pharmaceutical market. In recognition of their contribution to overcoming this partition, certain privileges are conferred on parallel importers. Once the right to repackage and to reaffix the original trademark is established and market access is thereby ensured, the parallel importer is to be considered as an operator on basically equal footing with the manufacturer and trademark proprietor within the framework of the Trade Mark Directive. Consequently,

[146] As formulated at the EU Feira Summit in March 2001.

[147] Joined Cases C–414/99 to C–416/99 [2001] ECR I–8691; see C Baudenbacher, 'Internationale Erschöpfung des Markenrechts und der Begriff der Zustimmung' (2001) *Eur L Reporter* 382 ff.

[148] EWCA Civ 971, [2001] IRLR 542, (22 June 2001). For the sake of completeness, the judgment of the Zurich Commercial Court in the *Kodak* case may be mentioned. In this case, the Commercial Court found by 4:1 votes that patent rights were subject to international exhaustion. The Court referred, *inter alia*, to EFTA Court *Maglite* (*Kodak SA/Jumbo–Markt AG*, ZR 1998 Nr 112). Upon appeal by the patent owner, the judgment was overruled by the Swiss Federal Supreme Court in a 3:2 decision (BGE 126 III 129).

[149] Case E–3/02 [2003] EFTA Ct Rep 101.

its strategy of product presentation and the new design cannot mechanically be assessed on the basis of the necessity criterion. Instead, the EFTA Court found, a comprehensive balancing of the interests of the trademark proprietor and the parallel importer must be undertaken. In doing so, the national court must take into account whether the packaging design used by *Paranova* is liable to damage the reputation of *Merck's* trademark, whether the trademark is used in a way that may give rise to the impression that there is a commercial connection between Paranova and Merck, and whether the marketing of *Merck's* products under the same trademark by various parallel importers with various package designs would evoke the risk of degeneration of the mark. If this were the case, the EFTA Court concluded, the trademark owner would have 'legitimate reasons' within the meaning of Article 7(2) of the Trade Mark Directive to oppose Paranova's use of coloured stripes. The EFTA Court's ruling in *Merck v Paranova* prompted the England and Wales Court of Appeal in *Boehringer* to refer to the ECJ the question of whether the use of its own design elements (referred to as 'co-branding') by a parallel importer and repackager of pharmaceuticals is in line with the Directive provisions on the exhaustion principle and the ECJ's case law related thereto, in particular the 'necessity test'.[150] The Court of Appeal emphasized that with regard to this question, there appear to be two schools of thought in European justice: Whereas the EFTA Court's jurisprudence shows a positive approach towards the parallel importer creating a package design of its own, the Supreme Courts of Austria, Denmark, and Germany, as well as the Court of Appeal of Sweden, apply a strict necessity test and tend to prohibit conduct such as Paranova's in the EFTA Court's judgment. As a result, once again the ECJ will have to deal with a question which has already been answered in the EFTA pillar of the EEA–this time, however, without any differences in scope in the respective legal bases. Nobody knows how the ECJ will answer this question. But that is not the point. Taking into account other courts' rulings and openly stating possible value judgments underlying a decision will in any case improve the quality of a judgment. In other words: Judicial dialogue will enhance the rationality of a judgment no matter what the outcome of that process will be. In this respect, one may refer to the theory of judicial dialogue or of judicial globalization[151] as well as to Jürgen Habermas'

[150] [2004] EWCA Civ 129.

[151] C L'Heureux–Dubé, 'The Importance of Dialogue: Globalization and the International Impact of the Rehnquist Court' (1998) 34 *Tulsa L J* 15; A-M Slaughter, 'Judicial Globalization' (2000) 40 *Virginia J Intl L* 1003; A-M Slaughter, 'A Global Community of Courts' (2003) 44 *Harvard Intl L J* 201; C Baudenbacher, 'Judicial Globalization: New Development or Old Wine in New Bottles?' (2003) 39 *Texas Intl L J: Special Symposium: Globalization and the Judiciary* 505 ff; F Jacobs, 'Judicial Dialogue and the Cross-Fertilization of Legal Systems: The European Court of Justice' (2003) 39 *Texas Intl L J: Special Symposium: Globalization and the Judiciary* 547, 552; J Bornkamm, 'The German Supreme Court: An Actor in the Global Conversation of High Courts', *TILJ* vol 39, *Special Symposium: Globalization and the Judiciary: Key Issues of Economic Law, Business Law, and Human Rights Law*, 415 ff; Sir C Bellamy, 'Focusing on the European Perspective of Judicial Dialogue: Issues in the Area of Competition Law', *TILJ* vol 39, *Special Symposium: Globalization and the Judiciary: Key Issues of Economic Law, Business Law, and Human Rights Law*, 461 ff.

'Theorie des herrschaftsfreien Diskurses'[152] and to the doctrine of justice through procedure as developed in particular by German lawyer and sociologist Niklas Luhmann.[153]

(f) State Aid

In *Husbanken II,*[154] the EFTA Surveillance Authority, upon a complaint by the Norwegian Bankers' Association, found that the state guarantee for Husbanken, the Norwegian State Housing Bank, amounted to state aid within the meaning of Article 61(1) EEA, but that it was essentially justified under Article 59(2) EEA, as constituting an operation of services of general economic interest. The Norwegian Bankers' Association brought an action for annulment of that decision under Article 36 SCA. The EFTA Court held that an institution performing the tasks of Husbanken may be considered as an undertaking entrusted with the operation of a service of general economic interest within the meaning of that provision and that the aid in question was necessary for Husbanken to perform the tasks entrusted to it. However, the Court annulled the decision of ESA on the grounds that the latter had not considered the following points to the extent necessary: the definition of the relevant market, the question of whether there were alternative means less distortive of competition, the issue of a cost-benefit analysis, and the application of a proportionality test. ESA had thereby, wrongly interpreted Article 59(2) EEA. The Court confirmed in *Íslandsbanki*[155] that a state guarantee system for a publicly owned bank may constitute state aid within the meaning of Article 61 EEA. At the same time, it found that a national court does not have the competence to declare that state aid granted by an EFTA State is contrary to the EEA Agreement.

In *GEMO*, Advocate-General Jacobs mentioned the EFTA Court's *Husbanken II* judgment as a reference for the so-called 'state aid approach' with regard to the issue of whether financial compensation granted by a Member State to an undertaking providing a public service should be regarded as State aid.[156] The question was and partly still is one of the most controversial in EC State aid law and has recently been answered by the ECJ in cases *Ferring* and *Altmark* conversely, ie, in favour of the so-called 'compensation approach'.[157]

In *Norway v EFTA Surveillance Authority,*[158] the EFTA Court dismissed an application brought by Norway for the annulment of a decision of ESA regard-

[152] J Habermas, *Theory of Communicative Action* (Frankfurt, Suhrkamp, 1981) vol 2.

[153] N Luhmann, *Legitimation durch Verfahren* (Frankfurt, Suhrkamp, 1983).

[154] Case E–4/97 *Norwegian Bankers' Association v EFTA Surveillance Authority II* [1999] EFTA Ct Rep 1.

[155] Case E–1/00 [2000–01] EFTA Ct Rep 8.

[156] Opinion of 30 April 2002, Case C–126/01 *GEMO*, n 64, 77.

[157] Cases C–53/00 *Ferring* [2001] ECR I–9067; C–280/00 *Altmark Trans* [2003] ECR I–7747; as a matter of interest see also Case E–3/03 *Transportbedriftenes Landsforening and Nor-Way Bussekspress AS*, [2004] EFTA Ct Rep 1 (withdrawn).

[158] Case E–6/98 [1999] EFTA Ct Rep 74.

ing state aid in the form of regionally differentiated social security taxation in Norway. The National Insurance Act of 28 February 1997 provided for an insurance scheme under which employees and employers pay social security contributions. The contribution rates for employers, ranging from 0 to 14.1%, were calculated on the basis of the individual employee's gross salary income, with the contribution rate depending on in which of five designated zones the employee had his or her registered permanent residence. The highest rate was payable in central municipalities in southern Norway and a zero rate applied in certain areas in northern Norway. Following an investigation, ESA adopted the contested decision, finding that the scheme involved state aid in breach of Article 61(1) EEA. ESA found that a general exemption was not warranted but that parts of the aid might, subject to certain conditions, be exempted under Article 61(3)(c) EEA. The EFTA Court held the contribution system to be selective, favouring certain undertakings, and thus constituting state aid within the meaning of Article 61(1) EEA. The argument that it constituted a general measure falling outside the scope of that provision was rejected. Whereas, as a general rule, a tax system of an EEA/EFTA State was not deemed to be covered by the EEA Agreement, such a system may have consequences that would bring it within the scope of application of Article 61(1) EEA. The EFTA Court considered the fact that a system applies to all undertakings within a given EFTA State a primary criterion for its generality. Although in the case at hand the advantageous contribution rates were formally open to all undertakings, the EFTA Court held that the system in fact conferred direct competitive advantages on undertakings in the favoured regions due to the high correlation between the zone of location of an undertaking and the place of residence of its workforce. Legitimate policy considerations, such as employment and settlement considerations, were found not to be decisive for the assessment under Article 61(1) EEA. The Court further ruled that ESA was correct in basing its assessment on the characteristics of the aid scheme as such. The fact that the lower rates also applied to economic activities not exposed to international competition was not considered capable of eliminating an otherwise established effect on trade.

In *Salzgitter AG v Commission*,[159] the Court of First Instance of the European Communities had, *inter alia*, to answer the question of whether the Commission had wrongly classified the tax provisions of Paragraph 3 of the German law on the development of the border zone between the former German Democratic Republic and the former Czechoslovak Socialist Republic (*Zonenrandförderungsgesetz, ZRFG*). That provision provided for tax incentives in the form of special depreciation allowances and tax-free reserves for investments made in any establishment of an undertaking situated along the border area between the former German Democratic Republic and the former Czechoslovak Socialist Republic. The Commission found that these privileges constituted state aid within the meaning

[159] Case T–308/00, (1 July 2004).

of the ECSC Treaty. The CFI rejected Salzgitter's plea that the tax provisions in question constitute general tax provisions. It noted that Paragraph 3 of the ZRFG applied without distinction to all sectors of activity, all types of investments, and all undertakings regardless of size, sector of activity, or seat. The advantage conferred by the measures was, however, subject to the condition that the investments were made in the zone in question, ie, in a geographically limited area within a Member State. That was, in the CFI's view, sufficient for the measures to be viewed as relating to a specific category of undertakings. The CFI concluded that it does not matter that the selective nature of the measure flows from a sectoral criterion or, as on the case at hand,

> from a criterion relating to geographic location in a defined part of the territory of a Member State. What matters, however, for a measure to be found to be State aid, is that the recipient undertakings belong to a specific category determined by the application, in law or in fact, of the criterion established by the measure in question (see, to that effect, Case E–6/98 *Norway v EFTA Surveillance Authority* [1999] EFTA Court Report 74, paragraph 37).[160]

(g) Food Safety Law

In its 1983 *Sandoz* judgment, the ECJ held that the Member States have to give marketing permission for fortified foodstuffs if the addition of vitamins will satisfy a real need, in particular of technological or nutritional nature. At the same time, the ECJ found that a national regulation according to which the marketing approval for foodstuffs fortified with vitamins which have been lawfully put on the market in other Member States depends on whether the importer shows that there is a need on the market is incompatible with Community law.[161] In *EFTA Surveillance Authority v Norway*,[162] Norway had banned the import and marketing of Kellogg's cornflakes fortified with vitamins and iron which had been lawfully manufactured and marketed in other EEA States. The EFTA Court rejected the argument of the Norwegian government that in order to justify a marketing ban on cornflakes produced in Denmark it was sufficient to show the absence of a nutritional need for the fortification with vitamins and iron in the Norwegian population. The question of need with regard to additives to foodstuffs may have a proper place in the context of the proportionality test. At the same time, the EFTA Court found that in examining whether the marketing of fortified cornflakes may be banned on grounds of the protection of human health, a national government may, in the absence of harmonization, invoke the precautionary principle. According to that principle, it is sufficient to show that there is relevant scientific uncertainty with regard to the risk in question. The Court stressed that measures taken must be based on scientific

[160] See para 38.
[161] Case C–174/82 [1983] ECR 2445.
[162] Case E–3/00 [2001–02] EFTA Ct Rep 73.

evidence; they must be proportionate, non-discriminatory, transparent, and consistent with similar measures already taken. The conditions to be fulfilled by a proper application of the precautionary principle were, in the view of the Court, firstly, an identification of potentially negative health consequences, and secondly, a comprehensive evaluation of the risk to health, which must be based on the most recent scientific information. The EFTA Court added that the precautionary principle can never justify the adoption of arbitrary decisions and can justify the pursuit of the objective of 'zero risk' only in the most exceptional circumstances. The Norwegian fortification policy did not fulfil these requirements. It was in particular inconsistent due to the long-standing fortification of certain products initiated by the government and was therefore held to be contrary to Article 11 EEA.

The EFTA Court's *Kellogg's* judgment had a considerable influence on the case law of the Court of Justice of the European Communities and has also influenced the practice of the Court of First Instance of the European Communities. In September 2002, the CFI in two cases involving the fortification of animal food with antibiotics acknowledged the precautionary principle as being part of Community law and referred to EFTA Court *Kellogg's*.[163] In September 2003, the ECJ in *Monsanto* had to decide on a case concerning the release of genetically modified maize. It too relied on EFTA Court *Kellogg's* when stating that 'protective measures . . . may not properly be based on a purely hypothetical approach to risk, founded on mere suppositions which are not yet scientifically verified'.[164] The most important judgment in the field is undoubtedly the ECJ's ruling in *Commission v Denmark*. The facts of the case were similar to the ones in EFTA Court *Kellogg's*. Advocate General Mischo proposed that the Court acknowledge the precautionary principle along the lines developed by the EFTA Court in *Kellogg's*, but he wanted to save the nutritional need argument and took the view that the ECJ should dismiss the Commission's application. The ECJ followed the EFTA Court's ruling in its entirety. It held that it was not sufficient for a government to make the argument that a marketing ban on fortified foodstuffs may be justified by the sheer lack of a nutritional need in the respective country. At the same time, the ECJ recognized the precautionary principle and formulated essentially the same conditions for its application as the EFTA Court had done in *Kellogg's*. In a preliminary ruling case, the ECJ confirmed its stand with regard to the significance of the precautionary principle in foodstuff law. In this case, the link to the EFTA Court was established by Advocate-General Mischo.[165] Finally, the ECJ relied on the EFTA Court; Kellogg's judgment in *Commission v Netherlands* when it held that after having authorised the marketing of a foodstuff fortified with a given nutrient, the national authorities 'remain free to refuse a subsequent

[163] Cases T–13/99 *Pfizer Animal Health* [2002] ECR II–3305; T–70/99 *Alpharma* [2002] ECR II–3495.
[164] Case C–236/01 *Monsanto Agricoltura Italia* [2003] ECR I–8105, para 106.
[165] Opinion of 16 May 2002, C–95/01 *Greenham and Abel*, paras 44, 53 ff.

application for marketing authorisation on the basis of the situation brought about by the first authorization'.[166] AG Poiares Maduro had, as the ECJ in *Monsanto* and in *Commission v Denmark*, referred to the EFTA Court's statement that it is not sufficient for a government to invoke hypothetical considerations when establishing the relevant scientific uncertainty.[167]

2. Community Courts Interpreting EEA Law

It goes without saying, that the cross-fertilization between the EFTA Court and the Community courts is particularly intense in those cases in which the Community courts have to give an *interpretation of EEA law*. Cases concerning *the principle of homogeneity* in general, *EEA/EFTA States' liability*, *free movement of capital*, and *food safety law* are to be mentioned here.

(a) EEA Homogeneity

In CFI *Opel Austria*,[168] a case on the compatibility with the EEA Agreement of a Council Regulation withdrawing tariff concessions by imposing a 4.9 percent duty on certain F–15 car gearboxes produced by General Motors Austria and originating in Austria, the CFI dealt with the homogeneity goal informing the EEA Agreement and referred, with regard to the interpretation of Article 3(2) SCA, to the judgments of the EFTA Court in *Restamark* and in *Scottish Salmon Growers*.[169]

The ECJ's *Bellio Fratelli* case concerned, *inter alia*, the compatibility of two decisions of the Council and the EC Commission on certain BSE protection measures with Article 13 EEA.[170] Except for referring in a comprehensive way to the EFTA Court's *Kellogg's* judgment,[171] the ECJ stated that 'both the Court and the EFTA Court have recognised the need to ensure that the rules of the EEA Agreement which are identical in substance to those of the Treaty are interpreted uniformly'. Insofar the ECJ referred to its *Ospelt* judgment[172] and to the EFTA Court's judgment in *EFTA Surveillance Authority v Iceland*, which in the relevant paragraph itself contains a reference to ECJ *Ospelt*.[173] One will notice that ECJ *Ospelt*, a case on free movement of capital in the EEA, is, for its part, linked to the EFTA Court's ruling in *Íslandsbanki* by way of a reference in Advocate General Geelhoed's opinion.[174]

[166] Case C–41/02, (2 December 2004) para 62.
[167] Case C–41/02, Opinion of 14 September 2004, pt 28.
[168] Case T–115/97 [1997] ECR II–39. See with regard to that judgment also above.
[169] Cases E–1/94(1994) 95 EFTA Ct Rep 15; E–2/94 [1994] 95 EFTA Ct Rep 59.
[170] Case C–286/02 (1 April 2004).
[171] See below.
[172] Case C–452/01 *Ospelt and Schlössle Weissenberg Familienstiftung* [2003] ECR I–9743, para 29.
[173] Case E–1/03 *EFTA Surveillance Authority v Iceland* [2003] EFTA Ct Rep 143, para 27.
[174] See below.

(b) State Liability in EEA/EFTA States

As mentioned, the ECJ denied jurisdiction to rule on whether the principle of state liability applied in Austria after that country's accession to the EEA on 1 January 1994 in the *Rechberger* case.[175] At the same time, the ECJ explicitly referred to the EFTA Court's *Sveinbjörnsdóttir* judgment of 10 December 1998, which found that state liability is part of EEA law.[176] It appears that compensation was in fact paid in the framework of a settlement before the referring Austrian court. For the sake of completeness, it must be added that the Norwegian government sought a replay[177] over whether state liability was part of EEA law in the *Karlsson* case. In rejecting the government's position, the EFTA Court in turn referred to ECJ *Rechberger*. One commentator has noted that with this, the EFTA Court has in a skilful way, taken the ECJ on board as an ally.[178] Finally, on the day when the ECJ gave judgment in *Rechberger*, it delivered a second preliminary ruling in the case *Andersson*. In that case, the ECJ had to deal with similar questions concerning Sweden's membership in the EEA/EFTA in 1994. Again, the ECJ denied its jurisdiction without, however, referring to the EFTA Court *Sveinbjörnsdóttir* judgment. The ECJ did not sit in the same composition as in *Rechberger*. The first instance court in Sweden subsequently acknowledged state liability, but the court of appeals reversed. On 26 November 2004, the Swedish Supreme Court, relying on the EFTA Court's judgments in *Sveinbjörnsdóttir* and *Karlsson* as well as on the judgment of the Icelandic Supreme Court in *Sveinbjörnsdóttir*, held that state liability was part of EEA law and decided in favour of the plaintiffs.[179]

(c) Free Movement of Capital

In the *Ospelt* case, a Liechtenstein citizen owning agricultural land in Vorarlberg (Austria) had been refused authorisation to transfer that land to a foundation established in Liechtenstein. The ECJ held that a rule such as that of the Vorarlberger Land Transfer Law, making transactions between nationals of States party to the EEA Agreement relating to agricultural land subject to administrative controls, must be assessed in light of Article 40 and Annex XII of that Agreement, 'which are provisions possessing the same legal scope as that of Article 73b of the EC Treaty (now Article 56 EC), which is identical in substance'.[180] The ECJ stressed that 'one of the principal aims of the EEA Agreement is to provide for the fullest possible realisation of the free movement

[175] Case C–140/97 [1999] ECR I–3499.
[176] Case E–7/97 [1998] EFTA Ct Rep 95, para 17 ff.
[177] So the apt characterization by P Tresselt and K Mahieu, see above.
[178] G Gorton, 'Bestätigung der Staatshaftungsrechtsprechung des EFTA–Gerichtshofs' (2002) 7–8 *Eur L Reporter* 260, 263.
[179] Cases T 2593/01 and 2595/01.
[180] Case C–452/01 (23 September 2003), operative part [2003] ECR I–9743.

of goods, persons, services and capital within the whole European Economic Area, so that the internal market established within the European Union is extended to the EFTA States'.[181] It is to be noted that the ECJ referred in that respect to its EEA-friendly Opinion 1/92.[182] Based on these contentions, the ECJ found that the provisions of the EC Treaty on the free movement of capital (which are identical to the respective provisions of the EEA Agreement) do not preclude the requirement of a prior authorisation, but 'do preclude such authorisation being refused in every case in which the acquirer does not himself farm the land concerned as part of a holding and on which he is not resident'.[183] Advocate General Geelhoed had in his Opinion referred to EFTA Court *Íslandsbanki*, in which the EFTA Court had assumed that the provisions of the EEA Agreement and of the EC Treaty on free movement of capital are identical in substance in spite of the fact that the latter have been amended in Maastricht.[184]

(d) Food Safety Law

In the above-mentioned ECJ *Bellio Fratelli* case, Bellio had imported from Norway a consignment of fish flour for the production of feed for animals other than ruminants. After samples taken by the competent Italian authority showed that the fish meal contained fragments of unidentified animal bones, the consignment in question was seized. Bellio brought proceedings in the Treviso Court, which referred to the ECJ, *inter alia*, a question concerning the application of the precautionary principle. The seizure was based on two decisions of the Council and the EC Commission on certain BSE protection measures with Article 13 EEA, the provision mirroring Article 30 EC.[185] The ECJ found that the provisions on which the seizure had been based were compatible with Article 13 EEA. With regard to the precautionary principle and the conditions of its application, it referred to EFTA Court *Kellogg's* and to those judgments of the ECJ which are based on that ruling.[186]

E. CONCLUSIONS

The EFTA Court has, in its first ten years of existence, developed a fruitful relationship with the national courts of the EEA/EFTA States, in particular the Supreme Courts. The Advisory Opinion procedure has proven to be an essential means of (vertical) cooperation. Opinions of the EFTA Court are, on balance, not weaker than preliminary rulings of the ECJ. As far as the relationship with

[181] Case C–452/01 (23 September 2003), operative part [2003] ECR I–9743, para 29.
[182] *Ibid.*
[183] Operative part.
[184] Case C–452/01, Opinion of 23 September 2003 [2003] ECR I–9743, n 32.
[185] Case C–286/02 (1 April 2004).
[186] *Ibid*, paras 57, 58, 59, 60.

the Community courts is concerned, one will remember that in its Opinion 1/91 on the first version of the EEA Agreement, the ECJ struck down a provision according to which the Community courts would have been under an obligation to take into account the case law of the EEA courts.[187] In practice, the Community courts have however, shown such openness, at least in cases in which they agree with the outcome as well as with the reasons of an EFTA Court case. The EFTA Court is the only court besides the European Court of Human Rights, which is regularly referred to in the judgments of the ECJ and of the CFI. The Community courts' policy is less clear in cases in which they do not agree with the reasons of an EFTA Court case. In particular, the ECJ seems to be reluctant to enter a debate in such cases.[188] For the sake of order, it must be pointed out that there has not been a judicial conflict between the ECJ and the EFTA Court in the first ten years of EEA existence, not even in cases in which the EFTA Court had to decide on a legal question as the first EEA court.[189]

[187] See above.

[188] A case in point could have been the ECJ's judgment in *Franzén*, Case C–189/95 [1997] ECR I–5909 which dealt with essentially the same questions as the EFTA Court's *Wilhelmsen* ruling. See with regard to *Wilhelmsen* above.

[189] See with regard to the *Maglite* and *Silhouette* rulings above.

Thorgeir Örlygsson

Ladies and gentlemen, welcome to the symposium. I have the honour of introducing to you today our second speaker, Professor Dr Peter-Christian Müller-Graff, who will talk to us about 'The impact of climate, geography and other non-legal factors on EC law and EEA law'. Dr Müller-Graff is a member of the law faculty of the University of Heidelberg, and the Director of the Institute for Economic law and European law at the University of Heidelberg. He served as Dean from 1999 to 2004. He studied law at the Universities of Göttingen, Berlin, Tübingen, and at Cornell University Law School. He received his doctorate and habilitation at Tübingen University, where he worked as a research fellow. He was a Professor of Law at the law faculties at Cologne and Trier before being appointed in Heidelberg in 1994. Professor Müller-Graff has also been appointed a judge at the Court of Appeals. Dr Müller-Graff, the floor is yours.

The Impact of Climate, Geography and Other Non-Legal Factors on EC Law and EEA Law[1]

PETER-CHRISTIAN MÜLLER-GRAFF

THE IMPACT OF climate, geography and other non-legal factors on EC law and EEA law addresses the overarching legal issue of whether specific geographical locations, different climates and other distinguishing factors of this kind may have or even call for an impact, either on shaping legal rules (eg, in the economic and social cohesion policy), or on resolving legal issues (such as the taking into account of special climatic conditions by the jurisprudence of the ECJ on the free movement of goods),[2] or on the respect of law in general (as, eg, described by the writer *Hans Magnus Enzensberger* in his collection of essays on different countries under the title 'Ach, Europa!'), and may hence contradict the prime objective of the EEA Agreement, namely promoting trade with equal conditions of competition, and the respect of the common rules with a view to creating a homogeneous European Economic Area.[3] *Montesquieu,* in his great work 'L'Esprit des Lois', held the view that '*les lois politiques*' and '*les lois civiles*'

> 'doivent être relatives au physique du pays, au climat glacé, brûlant ou tempéré: à la qualité du terrain, à sa situation, à sa grandeur: au genre de vie des peuples,

[1] Extended text of the lecture given on the occasion of the celebration of the 10th anniversary of the EFTA Court in Luxembourg on 21 October 2004.

[2] Case 94/83 *Heijn* [1984] ECR 3263; Case 304/84 *Muller* [1986] ECR 1511.

[3] See Art 1 EEA Agreement; see, eg, HP Graver, 'Die Ausdehnung des Europäischen Gemeinschaftsrechts auf Nichtmitglieder der Union–Das Beispiel Norwegens' in PC Müller-Graff (ed), *Europäisches Integrationsrecht im Querschnitt* (Baden-Baden, Nomos Verlagsgesellschaft, 2003) 45, 49f; PC Müller-Graff, 'EEA Agreement and EC Law: A Comparison in Scope and Content' in PC Müller-Graff and E Selbig (eds), *The European Economic Area—Norway's Basic Status in the Legal Construction of Europe* (Berlin, Berlin Verlag Arno Spitz GmbH, 1997) 17; F Sejersted, 'Between Sovereignty and Supranationalism in the EEA Context—On the Legal Dynamics of the EEA Agreement', *ibid*, p 43.

labroureurs, chasseurs ou pasteurs . . ., à la religion des habitants, à leur inclinations, à leurs richesses, à leur nombre, à leur commerce, à leur moeurs, à leur manières.'[4]

In order to give this topic a systematic focus, it will be structured into three parts: First, a more precise definition of the subject, in particular of the 'non-legal factors' and the inherent overarching legal issue (A), second, the systematic position and handling of this issue in EC law will be considered (B), and third, the ramifications of these factors in the jurisprudence of the EFTA Court will be scrutinized (C).

A. DEFINITION OF THE SUBJECT

Defining the subject more precisely is necessary in view of the very general meaning of 'impact' and 'non-legal factors'.

While the mention of climate and geography may find rather clear pre-understandings, their generic description as 'non-legal factors' and the inclusion of several factors in the topic may cause confusion. It is evident that a 'non-legal factor' cannot be understood to include every factual aspect of a case as different from legal provisions. Otherwise, the problem to be tackled would be as blurred as the general philosophical distinction between facts and norms. Moreover, the terms 'climate' and 'geography' can be understood to point only to those 'non-legal' factors which are specific for one region or Member State or, at most, a few regions or Member States, but which are not necessarily common to all Member States. This perspective permits the inclusion—besides climate and geography—of factual aspects such as specific diets and nutritional habits, languages, religious beliefs, cultures, consumer awareness, animal populations, specific environment, size of economy or origin of products and so on. These will be referred to as 'specific factors'.

By defining the topic in this way, the overarching legal issue emerges of how European market law (EC law and EEA law) resolves conflicts between the objective of homogeneous legal standards and specific national or regional conditions; or, in other words, whether European market law is bound to uniformly solve conflicts between the objective of establishing equal conditions for the EEA[5] on one hand and regional conditions on the other hand or, on the contrary, grants discretion to consider such specific features and, hence, accepts special rules. Of course, there is no explicit simple answer laid down in the market law of the EEA Agreement, nor in the internal market law of the EC Treaty. However, conflicting elements and starting points for solution are seen both in EC law (B) and EEA law (C).

[4] Quotation taken from the publication in *Tome 2 des Oeuvres Complètes de la Pléiade*, by Roger Caillois (Editions Gallimard, 1951) and reproduced in P Pescatore, *La séparation des pouvoirs et l'office du juge, de Montesquieu à Portalis—Cahier Documentaire* (Luxemburg, 2004), p 4.

[5] See n 4.

B. THE IMPACT OF 'NON-LEGAL FACTORS' ON EC LAW

Turning first to EC law, being the older set of rules, the mentioned conflict can be found in both categories of EC primary law: on the level of legislative policy empowerments (1) and on the level of directly applicable rules (2).

1. Conflict and Rules in Policy Empowerments

On the level of policy empowerments of the Community the impact of specific factors is particularly well known in the provisions of internal market orientated approximation policy towards national rules (a), but is also visible in other policy areas (b).

(a) Internal Market Orientated Approximation Empowerments

Internal market orientated approximation policy aims at harmonising relevant national law (i), but to some extent contains options for Member States protecting public interests rooted in national and regional 'non-legal factors' (ii).

(i) Approximation The idea of approximation is inspired by the idea of establishing equal level market fields by way of positive legislative action of the Community and its implementation by the Member States.[6] The concrete intensity of the desired approximation on the basis of, eg, Article 95 EC-Treaty, may vary between full approximation in the defined area of rules and minimum harmonisation,[7] but, as far as it is deemed to be necessary, the objective to create substantially equal rules for the internal market is the overarching feature of alignment policies. However, already the method of minimum harmonisation gives leeway to Member States to serve specific public interests which are rooted in national or regional 'non-legal factors' as long as the adopted national measures do not contradict other Community law, in particular the basic freedoms.

(ii) Self-Protection of National or Regional 'Non-Legal Factors' In view of the strong standardising potential of these empowerments on one side and on the other side, the diverse realities of the Community, which range from the Atlantic shores of Portugal to the Eastern borders of Poland, and from Northern Finland to Mediterranean Cyprus, the potentially far reaching Article 95, paragraph 1 TEC, is reasonably accompanied by the general principle of necessity (Articles 3 paragraph 1 lit h, 5 paragraph 1 ans 3 TEC). However, this principle

[6] See eg, PC Müller-Graff, 'Die Rechtsangleichung zur Verwirklichung des Binnenmarktes' [1989] *Europarecht* 107 ff.

[7] See eg, HH Herrnfeld, in J Schwarze (ed), *EU-Kommentar* (Baden-Baden, Nomos Verlagsgesellschaft, 2000), Art 95, Rdz 39.

approaches the question of harmonisation from the viewpoint of the requirements of the internal market, but not from the viewpoint of the individual characteristics of a single Member State. The same approach is taken by the principle of subsidiarity (Article 5 paragraph 2 TEC), which, in addition, is disputed in its applicability to the use of the power of Article 95 paragraph 1 TEC.[8]

However, national or regional 'non-legal factors' can unfold within the opting-out clauses that accompany Article 95 paragraph 1 TEC, for every single Member State. They *distinguish* between maintaining national provisions and introducing new national provisions after the adoption of a harmonisation measure. It is well known that *maintaining* national provisions is governed by Article 95 paragraph 4 TEC which enables every Member State to maintain provisions on grounds of major needs referred to in Article 30 TEC, or relating to the protection of the environment or the working environment, notwithstanding the control procedure laid down in paragraph 6. While the array of mandatory public interests is smaller than under the directly applicable market freedoms, the assessment of their compatibility with Community law should follow similar lines, although it is partly differently worded in paragraph 6 (no means of arbitrary discrimination; no disguised restriction on trade between Member States; no obstacle to the functioning of the internal market). The option of introducing *new* national provisions after the adoption of a harmonisation measure is governed by additional rules, and is significantly narrower (Article 95 paragraph 3 TEC).

They have, first, to be based on new scientific evidence, which, second, relates to the protection of the environment or the working environment on, third, grounds of a problem specific to that Member State which, fourth, arises after the adoption of the harmonisation measure. Remarkably, the protection of public health is not included in this option. In this respect, Article 95 paragraph 8 TEC suggests that a Member State, raising a specific problem on public health in a field that has been the subject of prior harmonisation measures, shall bring it to the attention of the Commission, which shall immediately examine whether to propose appropriate measures to the Council.

(b) Empowerments in Other Policy Areas

Special rules, which enable or even require differentiations between regions, apply to other policy empowerments. In the realm of *state aid control,* certain regional situations can justify an exception to the general prohibition of state aid, which distorts or threatens to distort competition by favouring certain

[8] Against its applicability, eg, Case C–376/98 *Federal Republic of Germany v European Parliament and Council of the European Union* [2000] ECR I–8419 /8423, Opinion of Advocate General Fennelly, para 142, and parts of the scholarly literature, for its applicability, Case C–377/98 *Kingdom of the Netherlands v European Parliament and the Council of the European Union* [2001] ECR I–7079 para 30, and parts of the scholarly literature.

undertakings or the production of certain goods.[9] The *economic and social cohesion* policy is explicitly bound to aim at reducing disparities between the levels of development of the various regions and the backwardness of the least favoured regions and islands.[10] In the context of the *Trans-European networks* policy, one must take into account the need to link islands, landlocked areas and peripheral regions with the central regions of the Community[11] and in the context of the policy towards *certain overseas regions,* the structural social and economic situation which is compounded by their remoteness, insularity, small size, difficult topography, climate and economic dependence on a few products.[12] It is also evident that *education* policy, as well as *environmental* policy, has to take into account the peculiarities of different regions and cultures.[13] In *cultural policy* the Community shall, on one side, contribute to bringing the common cultural heritage to the fore, but shall, on the other side, contribute to the flowering of the cultures of the Member States and shall in other actions respect and promote the diversity of its cultures.[14]

2. Conflict and Rules in Directly Applicable EC Primary Law

Differentiation in response to specific factors is also present in directly applicable primary law, which is in its interpretation and application in the hands of the courts. On this level, the basic conflict of the issue is found in the transnational freedoms (a), which also form the dogmatic basis of rules for coping with a conflict (b).

(a) Basic Location

On the level of directly applicable EC primary law, it is well known that the direct applicability and supremacy of the basic transnational freedoms contain an asymmetrically uniforming potential. Certain types of national restrictions are barred by them, but they do not establish a set of common positive rules. Consequently, a considerable number of national rules have been found to be incompatible with the market opening requirements of the provisions on the free movement of goods, persons, services and capital.[15] On the other hand, it is also well known that the rules on the free movement of goods contain an explicit exemption for restrictions justified on the grounds of the protection of national

[9] Art 87 para 2 lit b and c, para 3 lit a, b, c and d, TEC.
[10] Art 158 para 2 TEC.
[11] Art 154 para 2 TEC.
[12] See Art 299 para 2 TEC and Art IV–424 Constitutional Treaty for Europe (CTE).
[13] See Arts 149 TEC and 174 TEC.
[14] See Art 151 TEC.
[15] See for an overview, commentaries on Arts 28 *et seq*, 39 *et seq*, 43 *et seq*, 49 *et seq*, 56 *et seq* TEC.

treasures possessing artistic, historic or archaeological value.[16] This raises the general question of whether present national or regional special features can also be protected in conformity with internal market law. And indeed, beyond the mentioned explicit respect for a 'non-legal factor', other exceptions (such as public morality, public policy or public security) and the broad range of implied restrictions in view of mandatory requirements may potentially cover and protect specific non-economic regional and national factors.

(b) Dogmatic Location and Rules for Resolving the Conflict

On this basis, explicit textual dogmatic rules to resolve the potential conflicts are rather scarce. Hence, the task has become the realm of jurisprudence and jurisdiction. The question of whether a national measure constitutes a transnational market access restriction at the very outset (in the sense of the *Dassonville*-formula[17] or the parallel formula for the other freedoms[18]), is reasonably assessed without taking into consideration any of the 'non-legal factors', except in the special form of the basic requirement for the applicability of the transnational freedoms that the movement of persons, capital, goods and services geographically originates in another Member State.[19] This may be understood as a uniforming tendency since only the hindering effect on the inner communitarian transnational market access is evaluated and, if this is established, any justification of such a restriction on the grounds of a specific non-economic regional or national factor is legally the burden of the Member State that is responsible for the measure.[20] Hence, the very decisive procedure in resolving those conflicts is left by primary law to the definition and the application of the justification criteria by the courts in view of the remaining discretion of the respective Member State to fix the intended level of protection of a public good or mandatory requirement in its territory.[21] While the well known abstract criteria of justification (mandatory public interest, nature of measure, suitability, necessity, proportionality) are not changed in cases in which a Member State claims justification by 'non-legal factors' their impact unfolds within the application of these criteria. In this respect, in particular three issues have surfaced in the relevant jurisprudence of the ECJ: the recognition of

[16] See Art 30 TEC.

[17] Case 8/74 *Dassonville* [1974] ECR 837.

[18] For the free movement of services, Case 33/74 *van Binsbergen* [1974] ECR 1299; for the right of establishment, Case 107/83 *Klopp* [1984] ECR 2971; for the free movement of workers, Case C–415/93 *Bosman* [1995] ECR I–4921; for the free movement of capital, Case C–367/98 *Commission of the European Communities v Portuguese Republic* [2002] ECR I–4731.

[19] See for this requirement, eg, in the free movement of services, Case 52/79 *Debauve* [1980] ECR 833.

[20] See in general for this burden, eg, in the question of health protection in the free movement of goods, Case C–205/89 *Commission v Griechenland* [1991] ECR I–1361.

[21] For this discretion in the area of health protection, see eg, Cases C–1/90 *Aragonesa* and C–176/90 [1991] ECR I–4151, 4184, para 16.

'non-legal factors' as mandatory public interests (i), their impact on the qualification of the nature of the measure (ii) and their assessment within the three classical criteria of justification (iii).

(i) Recognition of 'Non-Legal Factors' as Mandatory Public Interest First: 'Non-legal factors' may pose the question of whether they can be recognized as a mandatory public interest either within an explicit exception clause or within the implied restrictions of the *Cassis*[22]—*Gebhard*[23]—jurisprudence.

Within the latter the Court recognized, eg, in the rules on free movement of *goods*, eg, cultural policy (*Cinétheque*[24]), the protection of national or regional social and cultural specialities (in particular the observance of the English Sunday as a day of rest in *Torfaen*[25]), consumer protection in a certain country (eg, *Gut Springenheide*[26]), environmental protection (eg, case *Kramer*[27] on the protection of the richness of the sea) and the conditions of supply in remote areas (*TK-Heimdienst Sass*).[28] The protection of languages as a pre-eminent expression of national and regional culture should be included. In the rules on free movement of *services*, the Court recognized as mandatory requirements, eg, the preservation of the national historical and artistic heritage (*tourist guides in Italy*[29]), the increase in value of the cultural richness and the dissemination of knowledge of the artistic and cultural heritage of a country (cases on *tourist guides in France*[30] *and Greece*[31]) and the protection of the environment (*Cura/ASL*[32]). Within the rules on free establishment the Court recognized, eg, the protection of the public against misleading academic titles (eg, *Kraus*[33]) and the guarantee of a certain level of education (*Gebhard*[34]) or qualification (*architects in Italy*[35]).

Within the explicit exception clauses, apart from the explicit protection of *national treasures*, the Court valued 'non-legal factors' in particular in the area of *public morality* where it reasonably held that it is the matter of every Member State to put this idea into concrete forms and terms in accordance with its own values (*Henn and Darby*[36]). The impact of national or regional 'non-legal factors' also surfaces in particular in the jurisprudence of the Court concerning

[22] Case 120/78 *Rewe-Zentral-AG/Bundesmonopolverwaltung für Branntwein* [1979] ECR 649, 662.

[23] Case C–55/94 *Gebhard* [1995] ECR I–4165, para 37.

[24] Cases 60/84 and 61/84 *Cinétheque* [1985] ECR 2605.

[25] Case C–145/88 *Torfaen* [1989] ECR I–3851.

[26] Case 210/96 *Gut Springenheide* [1998] ECR I–4657.

[27] Cases 3, 4 and 6/76 *Kramer* [1976] ECR 1279.

[28] Case C–254/98 *TK-Heimdienst Sass* [2000] ECR I–151, 172, para 34.

[29] Case C–180/89 *Commission v Italy* [1991] ECR I–709, para 20.

[30] Case C–54/89 *Commission v France* [1991] ECR I–659, para 17.

[31] Case C–198/89 *Commission v Greece* [1991] ECR I–727, para 21.

[32] Case C–451/99 *Cura v ASL* [2002] ECR I–3193, paras 66, 68.

[33] Case C–19/92 *Kraus* [1993] ECR I–1663, para 32.

[34] Case C–55/94 *Gebhard* [1995] ECR I–4165, para 37.

[35] Case C–298/99 *Commission v Italy* [2002] ECR I–3129, para 38.

[36] Case 34/79 *Henn and Darby* [1979] ECR 3795, 3813.

health protection in respecting, in principle, the national definition of the pursued level of protection (eg, *Aragonesa*[37]) and thereby including national particularities such as habits of nutrition, the general health status and climate (eg, *Eyssen,*[38] *Heijn,*[39] *Mirepoix,*[40] *Muller*[41]). Concerning the health of animals, the survival of endangered regional species has been recognized in the cases of German freshwater crayfish[42] and the brown Laesö-bee (*Bluhme*[43]).

(ii) Impact of 'Non-Legal Factors' on the Qualification of the Nature of a Measure Second: 'Non-legal factors' can also influence the solution of the question whether a restrictive measure is indistinctly applicable or not and, by that, qualify the nature of the measure which determines, in principle, whether the measure is justifiable on grounds of mandatory requirements or not.[44] Here the 'non-legal factors' can have a decisive impact on resolving the issue whether a differentiating measure distinguishes between equal or unequal situations. In the famous Wallonian waste-disposal-site case,[45] in which the disposal of waste originating from other Member States was prohibited by regional law, the Court held that the geographically different origin constituted a difference of waste in the light of the primary law principle that environmental damage should as a priority be rectified at its source.[46] Hence, it was held that the different treatment concerned different goods. Consequently, the Court found that the different treatment of Wallonian waste and foreign waste could not be assessed as a distinctly applicable measure. While this abstract reasoning of inequality and indistinct applicability may pass, the rough drawing of the inequality line along national borders is hardly convincing.

(iii) Assessment of 'Non-Legal Factors' within the Classical Three Criteria of Justification The third gateway for the impact of 'non-legal factors' in the justification of transnational market access restrictions is opened by the three classical criteria of justification: suitability, necessity and proportionality of a measure to serve the pursued mandatory public interest. Without diving into the details of single cases, some general dogmatic lines have to be taken into account in this respect.

[37] Cases C–1/90 and 176/90 *Aragonesa* [1991] ECR I–4151, 4184, para 16.
[38] Case 53/80 *Eyssen* [1981] ECR 409.
[39] Case 94/83 *Heijn* [1984] ECR 3263.
[40] Case 54/85 *Mirepoix* [1986] ECR 1067.
[41] Case 304/84 *Muller* [1986] ECR 1511.
[42] Case C–131/93 *Kommission v Deutschland* [1994] ECR I–3303, 3320, paras 13, 17.
[43] Case C–67/97 *Bluhme* [1998] ECR I–8033, 8065, para 33.
[44] See for this feature of the Cassis-jurisprudence, PC Müller-Graff, in H von der Groeben (ed), *Vertrag über die Europäische Union und Vertrag zur Gründung der Europäischen Gemeinschaft* (Baden-Baden, Nomos Verlagsgesellschaft, 2004) Art 28 paras 194 *et seq.*
[45] Case C–2/90 *Commission v Belgium* [1992] ECR I–4431, 4480 paras 34, 36.
[46] See for this principle in primary law, Art 174 para 2 TEC.

(*α*) **Suitability** It is common knowledge, that the suitability test assesses whether a measure is capable of protecting the specific interest or not:[47] eg, whether an import restriction on beverages with alcoholic content beyond a certain tolerated degree in order to protect the general health of the population is capable of generating this effect in a situation in which other alcoholic beverages with the same alcohol content are freely marketed in this country. It is fair to state as a general rule in this respect that a standard of national protection is not capable of serving its objective if alternatives with lower protection are permitted on the national market (eg, in the *Cassis* case of a minimum alcohol requirement for fruit liquors[48] as different, eg, from the *Schindler* case[49] where the protection of the public against the dangers of lotteries was also applied against internal initiatives).

(*β*) **Necessity** In particular, the criterion of necessity reasonably serves the judiciary for the fine-tuning in resolving the conflict between transnational market access requirements and specific regional or national 'non-legal factors'. Hence, the authorisation of different quantities of pesticide residues in different types of food can reasonably respond to different necessities in view of the nutrition habits, the general health status of a population or particularities of the climate (*Heijn*).[50] Concerning climate, one can imagine cases in which the requirement for certain conservation additives in quickly perishable foodstuff may be necessary in hot and humid regions, but not in the freezing airs of the North. Moreover, in view of nutrition habits, certain additives in cheese may be necessary to protect a population with specific high cheese consumption, but may not meet a demand of a population without this diet.

(*γ*) **Proportionality** Eventually the weight of a measure aimed at protecting mandatory public interests, which root in 'non-legal factors', has to be assessed in its proportionality to the market access restrictions.[51] This question boils down to an assessment of the merits of the single case, in which the value of the protected public good (eg, the fostering of the regional language) can have decisive weight.

C. IMPACT OF 'NON-LEGAL FACTORS' ON EEA LAW AND THE JURISPRUDENCE OF THE EFTA COURT

Turning to the question of impact of 'non-legal factors' on EEA law the difference between the rather defined objective of the EEA Agreement to create a

[47] See PC Müller-Graff (n 45) Art 28, para 231, and Art 30, paras 129 *et seq*.
[48] See n 23.
[49] Case C–275/92 *Schindler* [1994] ECR I–1039, para 22.
[50] See n 40.
[51] See PC Müller-Graff (n 45) Art 30, paras 157 *et seq*.

homogeneous economic area and the wide array of objectives of the EC-Treaty does not require a fundamental deviation in the interpretation of identically worded basic freedoms in the EEA Agreement. On the contrary, it is fair to expect, in principle, parallels to EC law on the substantial level of the four freedoms[52] and the competition rules[53] in the light of the homogeneity objective of Article 1 of the EEA Agreement[54] and, in particular, since the EFTA Court has consistently based its jurisdiction, as a matter of principle, on the jurisprudence of the ECJ concerning provisions of Community law that are identical in substance to the provisions of EEA law, which the EFTA Court has to apply.[55] It is well known that this parallelism does not extend to the questions of direct applicability[56] and primacy.[57] The difference, because of the non-supranational nature of the EEA Agreement,[58] may factually allow for some leeway in the conduct of EFTA Member States, with a dualistic approach to international law in order to give credit to national or regional 'non-legal factors'. It is well established by Article 34 of the Surveillance and Court Agreement (SCA) that courts of last resort are not obliged to refer questions of EEA law to the EFTA Court, although all supreme courts of the present EFTA Members of the EEA have already done so.[59] Also in accordance with Article 34 SCA the EFTA Court 'advisory' opinions on the interpretation of the EEA Agreement in preliminary reference procedures lack legally binding effect.[60] In addition, the approximation of national law is governed by the special procedure of the EEA Joint Committee of transforming secondary EC law into EEA law.[61] Within this specific framework, the impact of national and regional 'non-legal factors' on EEA law can be looked at on the level of principles (1) and on the level of their handling in practice (2).

[52] Art 8 *et seq*, Art 28 *et seq* EEA Agreement.

[53] Art 53 *et seq* EEA Agreement.

[54] See n 4.

[55] See, The EFTA Court, Legal framework, case law, and composition 1994–2003 (Luxembourg 2004) p 27; eg, Case E–1/94 *Ravintoloitsijain Liiton Kustannus Oy Restamark* [1994–95] EFTA Ct Rep 15, para 32ff; Case E–3/98 *Rainford–Towning* [1998] EFTA Ct Rep 205, para 17ff; Case E–9/97 *Erla María Sveinbjörnsdóttir v The Government of Iceland* [1998] EFTA Ct Rep 95, para 47ff; Case E–1/03 *EFTA Surveillance Authority v Iceland* [2003] EFTA Ct Rep 145, para 27.

[56] See HP Graver, 'The EFTA Court and the Court of Justice of the EC: Legal Homogeneity at Stake?' in Müller-Graff and Selvig (eds), *EEA-EU Relations* (Berlin, Berlin Verlag Arno Spitz GmbH, 1999) 31, 53 *et seq*.

[57] *Ibid*.

[58] See PC Müller-Graff, 'Supranationality and National Legal Autonomy: Community Law and EEA Compared' in HP Graver (ed), *National Judicial Reaction to Supranationality in the EC and the EEA* (Oslo, Universitetsforlaget, 2004) 35.

[59] See for Norway, eg, Case E–5/97 *European Navigation Inc v Star Forsikring AS* under offentlig administrasjon [1998] EFTA Ct Rep 59; Case 1/99 *Storebrand Skadeforsikring AS v Veronika Finanger* [1999] EFTA Ct Rep 119; for Liechtenstein, Case E–3/98 *Herbert Rainford–Towning* [1998] EFTA Ct Rep 205; Cases E–4/00 *Brändle*, E–5/00 *Mangold*, and E–6/00 *Taschannet* [2000–01] EFTA Ct Rep 123, 163, 203; Case E–2/01 *Pucher* [2002] EFTA Ct Rep 44; for Iceland, Case E–5/98 *Fagtún ehf v Byggingarnefnd Borgarholtsskóla, the Government of Iceland, the City of Reykjavik and the Municipality of Mosfellsbaer* [1999] EFTA Ct Rep 51.

[60] See HP Graver, n 4 above, p 21.

[61] See also, Case E–3/97 *Jan and Kristian Jaeger AS v Opel Norge AS* [1996] EFTA Ct Rep 1.

1. The 'Non-Legal Factors' in Principle

Concerning the level of principles, it was already mentioned that the EEA Agreement with its aim to create a homogeneous European Economic Area contains a rather specific objective when compared with the wide array of objectives of Article 2 TEC. However, this difference in objectives does not require from the very outset, to deviate from the impact of 'non-legal factors' on the interpretation of identically worded basic market freedoms in the EEA Agreement.

2. The Handling of 'Non-Legal Factors' in Practice

Turning to the handling of 'non-legal factors' in the practice of the EFTA Court, the question at hand is whether the Court met its own standards to base its judgments on the jurisprudence of the ECJ in its first ten years of existence. In general, it can be submitted that the Court has indeed, closely followed the general patterns of interpretation of the basic freedoms as developed by the ECJ. This is in particular true, first, for the definition of *restrictions* of free movement (eg, cases *Restamark*[62] and *EFTA Surveillance Authority v Norway*, which dealt with the two-tier retail sale of alcoholic beverages,[63] and in which the EFTA Court interpreted the wording 'measures having equivalent effect' in Article 11 EEA along the lines of the *Dassonville*-formula); second for the *Keck*-restriction of the *Dassonville*-formula concerning certain selling arrangements (eg, in cases *Ullensaker kommune*[64] and *Tore Wilhelmsen*[65]); third, for the idea of implied restrictions of the prohibition (eg, *Restamark,* where the mandatory requirements formula of the *Cassis*-jurisprudence was taken up);[66] fourth, for the shape of the proportionality principle (eg, in the *Kellogg's*-case[67] and the cases of the professional trustee *Pucher*[68] and the medical professionals *Brändle,*[69] *Mangold*[70] and *Tschannet*[71]); fifth, for the principle of strict construction of an exception clause (eg, *Restamark* in view of Article 13 EEA Agreement which parallels Article 30 TEC);[72] and sixth, for the idea of burden of proof for justification (eg, *Restamark).*[73] The *specific* national or regional 'non-legal

[62] Case E–1/94 *Ravintoloitsijain Liiton Kustannus Oy Restamark* [1994–95] EFTA Ct Rep 15.
[63] Case E–9/00 *EFTA Surveillance Authority v Norway* [2002] EFTA Ct Rep 72.
[64] Case E–5/96 *Ullensaker kommune and Others v Nille AS* [1997] EFTA Ct Rep 30.
[65] Case E–6/96 *Tore Wilhelmsen AS v Oslo kommune* [1997] EFTA Ct Rep 53.
[66] See n 63.
[67] Case E–3/00 *EFTA Surveillance Authority v Norway* [2000–01] EFTA Ct Rep 73, paras 27 *et seq*.
[68] Case E–2/01 *Pucher* [2002] EFTA Ct Rep 4.
[69] See n 60.
[70] *Ibid.*
[71] *Ibid.*
[72] See n 63.
[73] *Ibid.*

factors' have surfaced in several cases at the dogmatic crossroads of the question of restriction (a), the recognition of a public interest as a mandatory requirement (b), the qualification of the nature of a national measure (c), and the application of the three classical criteria of justification (d).

(a) The Determination of a Restriction by a 'Non-Legal Factor'

Within the question whether a state measure constitutes a restriction of the free movement of goods, geography, in the sense of the origin of goods, plays a specific role for the applicability of the respective EEA provisions. Different from the customs union of the EC, the provisions of the EEA free trade area apply, in principle, only to goods originating in the EEA Member States (*Maglite*[74]), notwithstanding the possibility that products imported from outside the EEA can obtain EEA originating status under special rules (denied in the case of *Ásgeirsson*[75] for fish caught off the coast of Alaska and Russia, where defrosting, heading, filleting, boning, trimming, salting and packing of fish frozen whole, was not considered as constituting sufficient working and processing within the relevant Protocol 4 to the EEA Agreement). The inclusion of products originating outside the EEA has been affirmed by the Court for the specific rules of Article 16 EEA on State monopolies of a commercial character (*Restamark*).[76]

Apart from this specific impact of geography by way of the rules on the origin of goods, the general requirement of an internal border crossing movement for the applicability of the basic freedoms in EC law[77] can also be applied in the parallel provisions of the EEA Agreement (eg, for services, the case of *EFTA Surveillance Authority v Iceland* concerning flights).[78] Beyond these questions of general applicability, no special impact has to be given to national or regional 'non-legal factors' on the application of the general restriction formula of the basic freedoms.

In the different question of whether the qualification of geographically differentiated social security rates as a distortion of competition by a State aid within the meaning of Article 61 paragraph 1 of the EEA Agreement might be excluded by the geographical aspect of settlement deliberations, the EFTA Court dismissed this argument in the case at issue.[79] However, the *Altmark Trans*-jurisprudence of the ECJ[80] might open the door for enriching the assessment

[74] Case E–2/97 *Mag Instrument Inc v California Trading Company Norway, Ulsteen* [1997] EFTA Ct Rep 127.

[75] Case E–2/03 *Ákæruvaldid (The Public Prosecutor) v Ásgeir Logi Ásgeirsson, Axel Pétur Ásgeirsson and Helgi Már Reynisson* [2003] EFTA Ct Rep 187.

[76] See n 63.

[77] See n 20.

[78] Case E–1/03 *EFTA Surveillance Authority v Iceland* [2003] EFTA Ct Rep 145.

[79] Case E–6/98 *The Government of Norway v EFTA Surveillance Authority* [1999] EFTA Ct Rep 74.

[80] Case 280/00 *Altmark Trans* [2003] ECR I–7747.

under Article 61 paragraph 1 of the EEA Agreement by the idea of legitimate compensation for special area services of general interest.

(b) Recognition of 'Non-Legal Factors' as Mandatory Public Interests

In the question of whether national or regional 'non-legal factors' constitute a mandatory public interest the relevant cases before the EFTA Court dealt with particularities of geography, population and culture. It seems that the EFTA Court, in general, follows the tendency, which is long since visible in the jurisprudence of the ECJ, to be open, in principle, for the recognition of a potentially broad scope of reasonable non-economic public interests as mandatory requirements. This is an unavoidable balancing consequence of the extension of the definition of a restriction of a basic freedom. The broader their scope is drawn, the more pressing is the necessity of accepting mandatory requirements. In terms of *geographical* particularities, the EFTA Court convincingly recognised: securing access to medical, cultural and commercial infrastructure for the inhabitants of outer regions of Iceland (*Flight taxation* case),[81] the prevention of emigration from rural areas (same case)[82] and, in very general terms, the public policy concerning the special situation of Liechtenstein as a very small country (in the case of the managing director *Rainford-Towning).*[83]

In view of specific features of the relevant *population* the EFTA Court recognised as mandatory public interests: the nutritional need in the Norwegian population (in the *Kellogg's*-case which dealt with a marketing ban on Danish cornflakes which were fortified with vitamins and iron);[84] and combating alcohol abuse in Norway as a public health concern under Article 13 EEA Agreement (in cases *Wilhelmsen*[85] and *EFTA Surveillance Authority v Norway*[86]).

In view of *cultural* features, the EFTA Court recognised, in a case pertaining to the interpretation of Council Directive 89/552/EEC on the coordination of certain provisions concerning the pursuit of television broadcasting activities, the protection of the mental and moral development of minors as forming an important part of the protection of public morality (*TV 1000 Sverige),*[87] and convincingly added, in a parallel to the ECJ's jurisprudence,[88] that in this area no uniform European conception could be determined. Concerning the recognition of national or regional cultural policy as a mandatory public interest, the last word might not yet be spoken by the EFTA Court. In the *Ullensaker kommune* case[89] the explicit exception clause of Article 13 EEA was strictly

[81] See n 79.
[82] *Ibid.*
[83] Case E–3/98 *Herbert Rainford–Towning* [1998] EFTA Ct Rep 205.
[84] Case E–3/00 *EFTA Surveillance Authority v Norway* [2000–01] EFTA Ct Rep 73, para 27 *et seq.*
[85] Case E–6/96 *Tore Wilhelmsen AS v Oslo kommune* [1997] EFTA Ct Rep 53.
[86] Case E–9/00 *Surveillance Authority v Norway* [2002] EFTA Ct Rep 72.
[87] Case E–8/97 *TV 1000 Sverige AB v The Norwegian Government* [1998] EFTA Ct Rep 68.
[88] See n 37.
[89] See n 65.

interpreted in line with the general principles of interpretation pursued by the ECJ and hence was held to form no basis for the justification of national cultural policy. In the *Hördur Einarsson* case,[90] which emerged from a differentiated taxation scheme on books in Iceland, and focused on the interpretation of the special prohibition of discriminatory taxation under Article 14 EEA (the assessment of the taxation as 'discriminatory' by the Court being doubtful; see below), no justification was available in general and hence even cultural policy convincingly could not serve as a mandatory requirement in this specific context. The *Cassis*-jurisprudence neither addresses this special prohibition nor covers, in principle, discriminatory treatment. The Court's rejection of an analogous application of the obligation of the Community, laid down in Article 151 paragraph 4 TEC, to take cultural aspects into account in its action, in particular in order to respect and to promote the diversity of its cultures was unavoidable, since this provision, which does not even find a parallel provision in the EEA Agreement, addresses the political conduct, but not the interpretation of a legal provision. However, this observation does not exclude the recognition of national culture as a mandatory requirement justifying restrictions of the basic freedoms as shown by the jurisprudence of the ECJ.[91] In particular, the protection of national languages should be among the prime mandatory cultural requirements to be recognized in view of worrying tendencies of economic actors to impose a single language in the European market communication.

(c) Impact of 'Non-Legal Factors' on the Qualification of the Nature of a Measure

The impact of 'non-legal factors' on the qualification of a measure as being indifferently or differently applicable was rare and hidden in the question of whether differentiating measures were applicable to the same situations of fact or to different situations.

In the Icelandic flight taxation case[92] the non-comparability of international and domestic air transport services, in particular in light of the geographical location of Iceland was considered, but eventually rejected. However, it is noteworthy that the Court considered a potential justification of the differentiated air passenger tax for achieving public interest goals. The question of a specific situation dependent upon the taste of the consumers and raised in the *Tore Wilhelmsen* case,[93] whether local Norwegian taste for strong beer was a distinguishing element which justified the method of selection of products by a retail monopoly (ten domestic and seven foreign brands), or was a result of discriminatory application of this monopoly, was left to assessment of the national

[90] Case E–1/01 *Hördur Einarsson v The Icelandic State* [2002] EFTA Ct Rep 1.
[91] See n 25.
[92] See n 79.
[93] See n 86.

courts. In the Icelandic book taxation case[94] the question of whether books in the Icelandic language could be considered as being similar products to books in foreign languages was resolved by the somewhat very crude economic assumption that they are at least in partial competition, but was not sufficiently scrutinized under the viewpoint of whether books in different languages represent different cultures and hence can not be assessed as being similar goods.

(d) Classical Criteria of Justification

Within the classical criteria of justification (suitability, necessity, proportionality and burden of proof) national or regional 'non-legal factors' have played, in general, a parallel role in the EFTA Court to that in the jurisprudence of the ECJ with a record of a strict approach to their application.

(i) Suitability Suitability was a relevant question and denied in several cases: eg, in assessing the different treatment of beer and other alcoholic beverages in Norwegian retail sale, in relation to the health objectives pursued (beer mainly produced domestically and permitted to be sold outside the state retail alcohol monopoly, while other beverages with the same alcohol content, mostly imported from other EEA States, were required to be sold through the monopoly).[95] The suitability was also denied for the requirement of the residence and physical presence of a managing director in Liechtenstein in order to secure his compliance with national legislation or the control of that compliance by the public authorities.[96]

(ii) Necessity Necessity was denied in several cases: eg, for the marketing ban on cornflakes with certain fortifiers in pursuit of the Norwegian health policy based on the absence of a nutritional need for such fortification,[97] although, in general, the EFTA Court permitted a national government to invoke, for the protection of human health, the precautionary principle according to which it is sufficient to show that there is relevant scientific uncertainty with regard to the risk in question.[98] Necessity was also denied for the differentiated treatment of beer and other alcoholic beverages in the Norwegian retail sale in relation to the health objectives pursued,[99] and for the differentiated Icelandic air passenger tax in order to achieve the mentioned public interest goals of securing access to the infrastructure for the inhabitants of outer regions and to prevent migration from rural areas.[100]

94 See n 91.
95 See n 87.
96 Case E–3/98, see n 84.
97 See n 85.
98 *Ibid.*
99 See n 87.
100 See n 79.

(iii) Proportionality In the application of the criterion of proportionality national or regional 'non-legal factors' played a role for the EFTA Court in the context of the justification of measures taken on the basis of the precautionary principle in view of assessing a nutritional need of the Norwegian population.[101]

(iv) Burden of Proof Eventually the burden of proof (or explanation) was ascertained by the EFTA Court as a guiding principle,[102] and considered as not having been met in cases of 'non-legal factors': eg, for the differentiated Norwegian sale scheme for alcoholic beverages either because of lack of comprehensive explanation of this scheme (*Gundersen*[103]) or because of a failure to meet the burden of proof (*EFTA Surveillance Authority v Norway*).[104] These burdens were found as not having been met either for the necessity of the Icelandic differentiated air passenger tax.[105]

D. SUMMARY

The decisions of the EFTA Court do not allow for the statement of a significant tendency towards respecting or not respecting national or regional 'non-legal factors'. In comparison to the jurisprudence of the ECJ, the balance of the cases, when looking only at the results, might seem to be more critical towards accepting specific national or regional conditions. However, such a conclusion would be built on shaky ground. First, the number of relevant cases is rather limited until now. Second, cases have to be judged, as a matter of course, on the basis of their individual merits. Hence, it has still to be seen which balance the EFTA Court will strike in the conflict between the objective of homogeneity on the one hand and the respect for the specific national or regional 'non-legal factors' on the other hand. In any case, although it may seem paradoxical, their recognition in principle and their precise legal assessment can contribute to the overall scheme of homogeneous features in EC law and EEA law and this again can serve the good functioning of the EEA in the future. The EFTA Court on its side is on a good track and the ECJ has started to pay attention to that from its side. Congratulations.

[101] See n 87.
[102] Eg, in Case E–1/94, see n 63.
[103] Case E–1/97 *Fridtjof Frank Gundersen v Oslo kommune* [1997] EFTA Ct Rep 198.
[104] See n 87.
[105] See n 79.

E. DISCUSSIONS

THORGEIR ÖRLYGSSON

Thank you very much, Dr Müller-Graff, for your interesting and informative speech. Now we will open up for discussion. Those who want to put questions to our speaker can do it either from their seats, or by entering the podium, whichever they prefer. I see it on the face of my President that he is formulating a question in his mind.

CARL BAUDENBACHER

Thank you very much. Thank you for your most inspiring speech, Professor Müller-Graff. You said with regard to the case you referred to a couple of times, the Icelandic book case, which was on discriminatory taxation and the question of whether such discriminatory taxation may be justified, that in the long run you could see that language would have to play a more prominent role than it played in this case. Could you elaborate a little bit on that?

PETER-CHRISTIAN MÜLLER-GRAFF

The Icelandic book case had this special feature that it was assessed as discriminatory taxation of similar products by the EFTA Court and discriminatory taxation is prohibited by Article 14 EEA Agreement and by Article 90 EC Treaty. Once the conclusion is drawn that there is discriminatory taxation then there is no way to legitimacy. I don't see where you can find a justification for this type of discrimination because different from Article 30 EC Treaty, no parallel provision exists in the respective rules on taxation in EC law and in EEA law. Hence, what I was going to say is that one has to pay careful attention to this distinction between indifferently and differently applicable rules in view of the specific factors. Here the facts can come into play as seen in the Wallonian case on waste, where the ECJ had to deal with the question whether the Cassis justification was applicable to a restriction of the import of goods and came to the conclusion that waste originating from other countries of the Community was not equal to waste originating from Wallonia. Hence, the ECJ denied that the Wallonian prohibition of disposal of foreign waste was discriminatory. Thereby the Court referred to a special rule in the EC Treaty that waste should be taken care of at the source, at the origin. If one presumes that different rules do not constitute a discriminatory treatment as a consequence of different situations of fact, then the prohibition of Article 14 EEA Agreement or of Article 90 EC Treaty, does not apply and a restriction of the free movement of goods, if applicable at all, could be justified on the grounds of a mandatory requirement. Concerning now languages, in particular in the Icelandic book case, which implied a small language in size, we should understand languages as a prime expression of a culture. If we accept this, then a tax system which distinguishes between books in different languages is not discriminatory in the sense of Article 14 EEA Agreement, because the goods concerned are not similar products by their nature.

TORBJÖRN JAGLAND

My name is Torbjörn Jagland, I am the Chair of the Foreign Affairs Committee in the Norwegian Parliament. I have been a politician, but I don't know which category that belongs to, whether it is climate, geography or other non-legal factors. But as a matter of fact, politicians tend to put more attention on how we can avoid the laws and regulations than on how we can help securing the homogeneous market of the EEA. But that is normal, so it was very interesting that you put this topic on the agenda of the symposium. My question would be related to the relation between the EFTA Court and the EC Court—to what extent is the EFTA Court looking to decisions made by the EC Court in related cases, when it makes its decisions? To what extent is it easier for the EC Court to look to different necessities of nations, member nations, than the EFTA Court?

PETER-CHRISTIAN MÜLLER-GRAFF

Thank you for these two questions. To what extent is the EFTA Court working with a view to the jurisprudence of the ECJ? My impression is: very intensely. I even assume whenever a case comes up, whoever skims through the papers will look up leading commentaries, whether there is a comparable case in the jurisprudence of the ECJ. One can assume this when looking to the reasoning in the jurisprudence of the EFTA Court because of its references to the jurisprudence of the ECJ. This is in particular true for the general patterns, which have been outlined, concerning a couple of identically worded EEA provisions in the area of the basic freedoms, but also in competition rules. As a matter of course, when heading towards this prime objective of homogeneous rules, the Court will start to take this into consideration and there is even a kind of obligation to do that. Considering the reverse direction, President Baudenbacher is much more an expert than I am, for the question whether and how much the ECJ looks to the judgments of the EFTA Court.

There was a second question which you raised. I think this is a very interesting issue, whether there might be a structural tendency of the ECJ to accept more of the specific factors or give more weight to them than this is done by the

EFTA Court. I came to this point just at the end of my observations, and said that all cases have to be assessed on their individual merits. It is self-evident that a court cannot shape its own cases. A court gets the cases which are brought to it. Considering the limited number of relevant cases in this area, I am reluctant to draw a general conclusion. But it might be that the orientation to this prime objective of homogeneous rules in the EEA Agreement might shape a certain tendency to be very sceptical when looking to deviating regional conditions. It could well be that in the normative mind, which is orientated to the prime objective of Article 1 EEA Agreement, a certain tendency is generated. But I would not draw this conclusion from the mentioned decisions, because I don't think one could have decided them differently except the Icelandic book taxation case for the reasons which I named.

CHRISTA TOBLER

Good morning, I am Christa Tobler from the Universities of Basel, in Switzerland, and Leiden, in the Netherlands. If you allow me to briefly return to the previous question on the Icelandic book case. If I understood Professor Müller-Graff correctly, he was suggesting that one could see language as part of culture and culture in turn as a possible mandatory requirement that would allow justifications for restrictions in free movement in particular. In the particular context of taxation, and more specifically the internal taxation of goods, I wonder about the issue of comparability. Wouldn't it be much easier in this context to say that, in fact, books written in Icelandic and books written in other languages are simply not similar products for purposes of Article 90 EC and that, therefore, the issue is not one of mandatory requirements but rather of comparability? If there is no comparability of situations, the products are not similar, and accordingly there is no issue of discrimination in the first place. I am quite aware of the fact that this only works in the context of discrimination and not so much in the context of restrictions. Nevertheless, I would be interested in hearing your views on that. Thank you very much.

PETER-CHRISTIAN MÜLLER-GRAFF

Frau Tobler, this was exactly my point. You only worded it differently. It is the question of 'similar product' or 'non similar product' and it is well known that the ECJ has hammered out in its jurisprudence on Article 90 EC Treaty a competition orientated approach to the delineation of similar/non–similar products to find out whether at least a partial competition exists between the products concerned. When it comes to books in different languages, a different approach should be taken. Then, one would indeed come to the conclusion that a book in Icelandic language is not a similar product to a book in French language.

CHRISTA TOBLER

May I pursue: Are you then making your argument on two levels? Are you saying it could be either an issue of comparability, or an issue of mandatory requirements? Or are you saying that in the end this is the same?

PETER-CHRISTIAN MÜLLER-GRAFF

I put it in the area of comparability. This was not the point of a mandatory requirement but of the nature of the measure, whether it is differently or indifferently applicable. This is the proper systematic context in my view. So we are just in line with different words.

DIRK BUSCHLE

I would like to ask a question as to the role of cultural factors in harmonized law or, to be more precise, in the area of media law. You touched on the so-called transmitting state principle as established under the 'Television without Frontiers' Directive. Despite the unambiguous allocation of responsibilities following from this principle judgments were given by both the ECJ and by the EFTA Court—namely the *De Agostini* case of the former and the corresponding *Mattel/Lego* judgment of the latter—that came to the conclusion that the level of protection of consumers when it comes to misleading advertising may differ in the Member States. The result of this interpretation is that transborder television broadcasting can be blocked. You also mentioned the EFTA Court's case *TV 1000* where it held that there is no common standard of pornography under the Television Directive even though the rules governing the protection of minors are extensively harmonized in the Directive. My question would now be if taking into account cultural differences, the way it was done in these cases, actually undermines the clear objective of 'hard' harmonized law, as opposed to the area of fundamental freedoms where there is more space for an overall appreciation including cultural differences.

PETER-CHRISTIAN MÜLLER-GRAFF

Herr Buschle, this is basically a political question. It is a question which one has to pose to the legislator. If the legislator thinks that there should be a harmonized standard and implements this in a very strict way, then it will be very difficult for any court, be it the ECJ, be it the EFTA Court, to deviate from it. So the advice would go to the origin of such a directive, to the drafter of such a directive, to be always aware of the fact that there exist these specific factors. As a consequence, the directives have to be open to give leeway to Member States to adapt eg, in view of a specific public morality or a specific consumer awareness. The latter is indeed an issue that deserves perhaps a higher degree of sensibility than in the last 10 or 15 years. Eg, the awareness of consumers of misleading advertisement might vary between Member States. Some years ago Schricker compared the different national standards of protection against unfair competition and came to the conclusion that somehow Italian consumers did not seem to need as much protection as, eg, those in Germany because the former when dealing with a business man seemed to him to be presumed to be very much aware of the old Roman wisdom 'omnes mercator mendax'. I don't have to translate this since a bit of Latin might be permitted in the presence of the members of Curiae in Luxemburg. On the other side the jurisprudence of German courts on unfair competition shows cases in which one wonders about the presumed low degree of expected awareness of those consumers. My experience, as a former judge in competition law cases, taught me that the qualification of a concrete advertisement as being misleading or not for the addressees can become indeed, a very disputed issue.

LEIF SEVÓN

I hope that President Skouris listened to your intervention, and subsequently ask you to come across the street to the Court of Justice. The problem you have dealt with will presumably grow in importance, but more so in the European Union than in the EFTA States. The philosophy behind this is the following: The more the Union is enlarged, the more disparate it becomes, in cultural, geographical and other terms that you mentioned. The question is then, whether that would affect the Union's legislation. I don't think that the cultural diversities will be taken very seriously when the EU legislator faces a specific legislative problem. The problem will be resolved in a uniform manner for the whole Union. I think the future composition of the Commission will contribute to this. If the Commission does not have knowledge of all differences and needs, there is a risk that the legislation will not work properly in all Member States. The next question is then the following: Is it acceptable under such circumstances the courts adjust the rule by a more subtle case law, a case law distinguishing between the rules applicable in different Member States, in order to take into account the different needs?

PETER-CHRISTIAN MÜLLER-GRAFF

Of course, I agree. But there are the limits of clear language or a directive. Hence, I come again to the question of Herr Buschle. In the first place, it is the task of the Community legislator to take into account that in a European Union of 25 Member States, more differences might exist or arise in these specific factors as recognised in the last twenty or thirty years. This is a question, a task, a challenge for the legislator. But then it is also a task for the courts when it comes to the interpretation of this secondary law. Those factors have to be taken into account. It might sound paradox, but the respect for diversity in these areas is an element of homogeneous rules when they are recognized both in ECJ jurisprudence and in the jurisprudence of the EFTA Court. Your very first question was, whether somebody should listen carefully to what I have said. Well, I always like the recommendation that the audience pays attention to what is said. Thank you very much.

PIERRE PESCATORE

I was happy when I saw that my good old friend Professor Müller-Graff has been marching in the footsteps of Montesquieu. Montesquieu indicates climate and geography as main factors which influence the legislation of States, but he related them to the law of the savages. He says it is the law of the savages which is mostly oriented after climate and geography. When you come to civilized countries, he says, like China or Japan, for what it was at his time, there are more sophisticated criteria to be taken into consideration. Now, I think Professor Müller-Graff, you have been right in raising this matter from the angle of climate and geography and I was asking myself, how could I observe the influence of those factors in my actions as a community judge, especially in the light of the well-known *Cassis de Dijon* jurisprudence. I found two or three quite specific instances, the first one is about denominations of origin; we have a whole legislation on the protection of such denominations. The second area is mountain agriculture. We have happily special protective measures that take into account conditions under which agriculture has been developed in higher altitudes. I came across the problem also in cases concerning competition between beer and wine and competition between different brands of cheeses. I found out that there really is a difference of approach and mentality within the Community which varies from north to south, between beer producing and wine growing nations. This was resolved in one of our cases, where we said that the criteria here was the competitivity between final products. Just look at the trays as they are carried around in receptions, where you have open competition between beer and wine, between alcoholic and non-alcoholic beverages, and everybody chooses what they wish. So this is the basic criterion: whenever goods are in competition and are, as we say, 'substitutable' for each other, no matter what their nature and their origin are. The same applies to cheeses. I once was rapporteur in a cheese case about Roquefort. I was quite struck when I saw the statistics about the outlets for Roquefort. Do you know that the main outlet for Roquefort is American ketchup? By far the largest part of the Roquefort production goes into American ketchup. So, when the Americans take reprisals against the Community, those reprisals *comme par hazard* fall easily on Roquefort. So you see that there are certain incidences of geography and climate. But for the remainder I think that it is competition, comparability and substitutability which rules the place. Thank you very much.

PETER-CHRISTIAN MÜLLER-GRAFF

Thank you very much for this extremely rich and experienced contribution. I don't think I should spoil your very good comments, since in relation to you I have always found to have the privilege to learn from you, Mr Pescatore. And I am particularly aware of your hand in the *Cassis*-judgment which opened the door for honouring more specific mandatory requirements of the Member States.

THORGEIR ÖRLYGSSON

Ladies and Gentlemen, we will now continue. I have the honour of introducing to you, our third speaker, Professor Dr Hans Petter Graver, who is going to talk to us about 'The Effects of EFTA Court Jurisprudence on the Legal Orders of the EEA/EFTA States'. Dr Hans Petter Graver is cand iur and Dr iur from the University of Oslo. He has been involved in various research projects and legal work at the Faculty of Law of the University of Oslo, the Ministry of Public Administration and the Attorney General's Office. His main academic work is within the fields of administrative law, European law, legal sociology and legal theory. Mr Graver has published several books and numerous articles, mainly in the fields of administrative law and market law. He has been a professor at the University of Oslo since 1993. Professor Graver, the floor is yours.

The Effects of EFTA Court Jurisprudence on the Legal Orders of the EFTA States

HANS PETTER GRAVER

A. ABSTRACT

ESTABLISHMENT OF THE EEA with a court for the EFTA countries ten years ago gives an opportunity to examine more facets of interrelations between courts and legal orders of different jurisdictions. The EEA differs from the Community legal order in that it is constructed as an agreement under public international law without the referrals of power included in the EC Treaty. On the other hand, the object of the agreement is to mirror the law of the Single Market into the relations between the EFTA States and the EC.

Formally, the EFTA Court has a position more of an international tribunal than that of a supranational Court. Figures from the first ten years do not reflect this difference between the EFTA Court and the Court of Justice of the European Communities (ECJ). Differences between the two courts regarding matters like legal basis, history, recruitment, workload and duration of proceedings, at least taken together, do not seem to influence the supply of referrals from national courts. Other factors such as similarities between the Nordic countries and construction of the national legal order have greater explanatory potential than differences between the EEA and the EC and the institutional arrangements of the two courts.

In the reception of the jurisprudence of the EFTA Court and the ECJ, the Norwegian Supreme Court does not distinguish according to legal obligations, but seems to take an approach similar to national courts in Member States of the EU.

B. INTRODUCTION

In this paper, I discuss the effects of EFTA Court jurisprudence on the legal orders of the EFTA States. I do this by contrasting the EEA experience with the

EU experience. I therefore start by pointing out the ways in which the position of the EFTA Court formally differs from the position of the ECJ. Because this is well known, this section will be brief. I then look at the EFTA Court cases in numbers and compare these numbers to the statistics of the ECJ. Then focus is turned to the national courts, more specifically the Supreme Court of Norway. I here assess the impact of the EFTA Court and the ECJ both quantitatively and qualitatively. An important part of the argument here is comparing the approach of the Norwegian Supreme Court to the approach of national courts in the Member States, both as to how the courts relate to the Community Courts and how the Supreme Court has treated main features of Community law such as the loyalty obligation, supremacy and direct effect and the interpretation obligation. A main finding is that on such issues there seems to be surprisingly few differences between being a court in a Member State and being an EFTA State court. The final part of the paper is therefore dedicated to a discussion of various factors that may explain how Community jurisprudence influences national legal orders. Although my focus is on the EEA and Norway, the contrast of two different systems may shed some more light on legal integration more generally.

The theme of the paper is effects of *EFTA Court* jurisprudence. As we shall see, when assessing the effects of the EEA Agreement on national law, it is in many ways difficult to distinguish between effects of the EFTA Court and effects of the jurisprudence of the ECJ. I therefore include effects of the jurisprudence of the ECJ and draw some comparisons between the two courts. When speaking of both, I use the term the 'EEA courts'. On the other hand, since the effects of the EEA Agreement on national legal orders is a question of national law, I will for practical reasons focus on the effects on the Norwegian legal order. I have not had the possibility to study sources of Icelandic and Liechtenstein law directly. This may limit the relevance of my contribution somewhat. On the other hand, the challenges posed by the Agreement toward the national legal orders are the same, and the approach taken by actors of the national legal orders thus replies to the same questions. On this basis, I hope an examination of the Norwegian experience may have a wider interest than the national audience itself.

C. THE LEGAL BASIS

In contrast to the European Community, the EEA was constructed as a regular agreement under international law. The EEA has no legal personality, and the contracting parties strived to maintain their formal sovereignty and at the same time mirror the legal effects of the single European market. This construction of the Agreement also had consequences for the court set-up. Following the opinion 1/91 of the ECJ, there is no EEA court. The EFTA States are according to the EEA Agreement Article 108(2) under an obligation to establish a court of justice.

The EFTA Court is set up pursuant to the SCA (Surveillance and Court Agreement) in compliance with this obligation. Article 108(2) states that the EFTA States shall establish a court of justice (EFTA Court). The Article further provides that the court in particular shall be competent for:

—actions concerning the surveillance procedure regarding the EFTA States;
—appeals concerning decisions in the field of competition taken by the EFTA Surveillance Authority;
—the settlement of disputes between two or more EFTA States.

We see here that the EEA Agreement does not go further than to demand the establishment of a court with the functions often attributed to an international tribunal, which is disputes between states, and disputes with regard to actions of institutions established in an international treaty.

The jurisdiction of the court is defined in the second paragraph of Article 31 SCA, which states that if a state concerned does not comply with a reasoned opinion of the EFTA Surveillance Authority, the latter may bring the matter before the EFTA Court, and in Article 32, that the EFTA Court shall have jurisdiction in actions concerning the settlement of disputes between two or more EFTA States regarding the interpretation or application of the EEA Agreement, the Agreement on a Standing Committee of the EFTA States or the Surveillance and Court Agreement itself. Article 35 states that the EFTA Court shall have unlimited jurisdiction in regard to penalties imposed by the EFTA Surveillance Authority and Articles 36 and 37, that the EFTA Court shall have jurisdiction in actions brought by an EFTA State or any natural or legal person against a decision of the EFTA Surveillance Authority or a failure on the part of the Authority to act in infringement of its obligations under the Agreement.

In such matters as described here, the Contracting States have given binding powers to the Court under international law. The EFTA States concerned by a ruling shall take the necessary measures to comply with the judgments of the EFTA Court and if an action against a decision the EFTA Surveillance Authority is well founded, the decision shall be declared void.

Reaching further than the obligation under the EEA Agreement, Article 34 of the SCA Agreement states that the EFTA Court shall have jurisdiction to give advisory opinions on the interpretation of the EEA Agreement. This type of procedure is modelled on Article 234 EC where the ECJ has jurisdiction to give preliminary rulings concerning the interpretation of Community law. The main differences between the two procedures are that the ECJ gives *rulings* and the fact that if any such question is raised in a case pending before a court or tribunal of a Member State, against whose decisions there is no judicial remedy under national law, that court or tribunal *shall* bring the matter before the ECJ.

There is no provision in the EEA Agreement or the SCA Agreement providing that the case-law of the EFTA Court should have status as precedents when deciding later cases of law. The doctrine of precedents in Community law is not explicitly stated in the EC Treaty, but is generally inferred from Article 220 which states that the ECJ shall ensure that in the interpretation and application of the Treaty the law is observed and Article 292 where the Member States undertake not to submit a dispute concerning the interpretation or application of the Treaty to any method of settlement other than those provided for therein. Read together these provisions state that the ECJ rules according to the law, and that it is for the Court alone to decide on the law.[1]

The status of the ECJ case-law as precedents and part of the *acquis communautaire* is reflected also in the EEA Agreement Article 6 which states that the provisions of the Agreement, in so far as they are identical in substance to corresponding rules of the EC Treaty shall, in their implementation and application, be interpreted in conformity with the relevant rulings of the Court of Justice of the European Communities given prior to the date of signature of the Agreement.

D. THE FIGURES

In its first ten years, 62 cases have been lodged before the EFTA Court; 18 direct actions, 42 requests for advisory opinions and 2 others (legal aid and suspension of measure). The composition of the cases differs substantially from the ECJ, where close to 60 per cent of the cases lodged are direct actions.[2] This difference should not, in my opinion, be attributed to characteristics of the two courts, but rather to differences between the Member States in how efficiently they implement their duties and how they relate to the Commission and the EFTA Surveillance Authority. The Nordic countries are all similar in this respect and have few infringement cases before the courts.[3] If we look at only the Nordic States, of a total of 238 preliminary rulings and actions for failure to fulfil an obligation, 25% of the cases are failure to act cases, a number corresponding very well with the composition of the cases before the EFTA Court.[4]

[1] See more explicitly ECJ Opinion 1/91 of the EEA Court [1991] ECR I–06079:

> Although, under the agreement, the Court of the European Economic Area is under a duty to interpret the provisions of the agreement in the light of the relevant rulings of the Court of Justice given prior to the date of signature of the agreement, the Court of the European Economic Area will no longer be subject to any such obligation in the case of decisions given by the Court of Justice after that date. Consequently, the agreement's objective of ensuring homogeneity of the law throughout the European Economic Area will determine not only the interpretation of the rules of the agreement itself but also the interpretation of the corresponding rules of Community law.

It follows that in so far as it conditions the future interpretation of the Community rules on the free movement of goods, persons, services and capital and on competition the machinery of courts provided for in the agreement conflicts with Art 164 of the EEC Treaty and, more generally, with the very foundations of the Community. As a result, it is incompatible with Community law.

[2] Source: ECJ Annual Report 2003, Table 15 p 229.

[3] U Sverdrup, 'Compliance and Conflict Management in the European Union: Nordic Exceptionalism' (2004) 1 *Scandinavian Political Studies* 23–43.

[4] Figures computed from ECJ Annual Report 2003, Table 16 (p 230) and 18 (p 232).

In comparing the first 10 years of the EFTA Court with the first 10 years of the ECJ, we find that the case load of the ECJ was greater and increased more rapidly. Starting with the entry into force of the EEC treaty in 1958, the ECJ received a total of 464 cases, which is 77 per Member State, compared to the 18 per Contracting Party received by the EFTA Court.[5] A vast majority of the ECJ cases were direct actions, many probably connected with the ECSC Treaty. As mentioned above, it has been shown in other studies that very few cases from the Nordic States end up being settled in the courts. There were only, in total, 19 actions for failure to fulfil an obligation against Denmark, Finland and Sweden in the time period 1995–2001, which is less than for Italy alone for a single year! On this account, we get a better comparison of the two courts if we leave the direct action cases aside. If we only compare requests for preliminary rulings/advisory opinions, the picture is different. The EFTA Court received 37 requests from the three present EFTA States, the ECJ 49 requests from the six Member States in the period from 1958 to 1967, meaning that the EFTA Court received slightly more requests from each participating state in its first 10 years than the ECJ.

It could be argued, however, that also such a comparison is misleading since the system of preliminary rulings was a novelty to most jurisdictions in 1958, whereas it was well established and known as an institution of law also in the EFTA countries in 1994. A closer look at the figures seems to confirm this. The ECJ had absolutely no requests in the first three years after the institution was established compared to the EFTA Court which received 14 requests. In this respect, one may say that the EFTA Court was given a 'flying start'.

On this basis, more information can probably be had by comparing the situation for the ECJ regarding the old EFTA States that joined the EU in 1995. Sweden and Finland are part of the Nordic states and are similar to Norway and Iceland in legal culture and structure.

	1994	1995	1996	1997	1998	1999	2000	2001	2002	2003	1994–2003
Iceland				1	2		2	3		1	9
Liechtenstein					1		3	1			5
Norway	2	2	5	5	2	1	2	3	1		23
Austria		2	6	35	16	56	31	57	31	15	249
Finland	1		3	6	2	4	5	3	7	4	35
Sweden	3	7	4	7	6	5	4	4	5	4	49

Requests for advisory opinions/preliminary rulings (Source EFTA Court and ECJ).

[5] Austria, Finland and Sweden have been omitted in this figure.

What is striking in this table is not a difference in the supply of cases to the two courts, but the way Austria differs from the other countries for the amount of requests for preliminary rulings. Although there seems to be a correlation between the number of requests and the population of a country, the number of requests from Austria far exceeds what can be explained by differences in the size of the population alone.

If we look at the other countries of the EU, we see that the number of preliminary rulings lodged before the Court, is not by any means evenly distributed between the Member States.[6] Big players are above all Germany, but also the rest of the original six. Austria certainly belongs to this league although its total number of cases is low due to the small number of years it has been a member. On the other hand, Denmark has a very low rate, averaging three cases a year, without any tendency pointing towards an increase in this rate in the latest years. Britain must be put in the same league with a very low number of cases when the size of the population is taken into account.

If we look at the EEA as a whole, we see clearly that the different states fall in different groups with one group characterised by a large and increasing number of requests from the national courts, and another group with a constant low number of requests. All the Nordic countries fall in the latter group. This conforms to what has been observed regarding the divergence in how the various EEA countries resolve conflicts with the Commission and the EFTA Surveillance Authority. In general, the larger Member States have more conflicts and they use court rulings more frequently than the EU average in settling these conflicts. By contrast, the smaller states in general and in particular the Nordic States, have fewer conflicts and they resolve them at an earlier stage and less frequently through the use of court rulings.[7] The findings also conform with previous studies on variations in the patterns of references to the ECJ form different Member States.[8]

The findings seem to suggest that differences between the two courts regarding matters like legal basis, history, recruitment, workload and duration of proceedings, at least taken together, do not seem to influence the supply of referrals from national courts. One could, for example expect that differences in legal

[6] I use data from the ECJ 2003 Annual Report and not the data of Stone Sweet and Brunell (n 302 below) to include the five years from 1998 to 2003. The last five years show that the increase in cases from UK and Denmark seen in their data has not continued. The annual number therefore stabilized. These developments remind us of the need for caution in making firm conclusions without very long time-lines, which of course, are lacking for the EEA.

[7] U Sverdrup, 'Compliance and Conflict Management in the European Union: Nordic Exceptionalism' (2004) 1 *Scandinavian Political Studies* 25.

[8] AS Sweet and TL Brunell, 'The European Court and the National Courts: A Statistical Analysis of Preliminary References, 1961–95' (1997) *Jean Monnet Working Paper* No 14/97, http://www.jeanmonnetprogram.org/papers/97/97–14–html; and A S Sweet, 'Integration and the Europeanisation' (2002) *Law Queen's Papers on Europeanisation* No 2/2002. Stone Sweet and Brunell found in their studies a high correlation between levels of transnational exchange and references. Inclusion of the Nordic States may give a more nuanced picture as to the causes of the patterns in variations that can be observed.

rules such as the obligation of court or tribunal of a Member State, against whose decisions there is no judicial remedy, to refer a case to the ECJ, where no such obligations exists before the EFTA Court, would lead to a higher number of cases before the ECJ. On the other hand, with the differences in the duration of the procedure vastly in favour of the EFTA Court, one could expect national courts to be more inclined to refer cases to this court than to the ECJ. It could be argued that differences among such variables cancel each other out, and that institutional differences between the courts after all are important factors for the supply of cases. But this explanation cannot account for the similarities to be seen between the Nordic States across institutional boundaries, and the differences between the Nordic States and other States within the same institutional settings. The data from the courts support conclusions that have been drawn from data from the implementation phase of community legislation:

The data analysis shows that the Nordic states are performing more or less at similar levels regardless of their formal organisational ties to the EU (member or non-member) and regardless of the fact that some states have more experience as member states than others (Denmark versus Sweden and Finland). These findings indicate that there is a distinct Nordic exceptionalism in the implementation of legislation.

These observations support the conclusion that distinct institutional traditions and styles of decision making are important in accounting for variation in conflict resolution; more so than the enforcement capacity of the European regime and the voting powers of the Member States in shaping Community legislation.[9]

To the extent that the explanations can be found in social and institutional characteristics of the Nordic States, it should not be expected that the next 10 years of the EFTA Court in figures and composition of cases will differ much from its first 10 years.

It is also interesting to see more specifically, from which level of national courts requests for preliminary rulings/advisory opinions come. Whereas 29 percent of all cases referred to the ECJ come from courts or tribunals against whose decisions there is no judicial remedy, the equivalent figures from Norway and Iceland are 17 and 19 percent respectively. Broken up on different states, the figures are more nuanced:

	Denmark	Finland	Iceland	Norway	Sweden	Germany	UK	EU total
Court of last instance	19	44	10	17	44	42	16	29
Other Courts	81	66	90	83	66	68	84	71

[9] U Sverdrup, 'Compliance and Conflict Management in the European Union: Nordic Exceptionalism' (2004) 1 *Scandinavian Political Studies* 39 and 25.

Referrals from courts or tribunals against whose decisions there are no judicial remedies and from other courts or tribunals. Percentage of total. (All referrals from Liechtenstein are from a court of last instance. EFTA cases from Austria, Finland and Sweden not included.)

A closer examination shows that there are no consistent differences between EU countries and EFTA countries. However, here the picture of the Nordic States as a separate, coherent group does not fit. A pattern that seems to emerge, however, is that there are a higher number of referrals from courts or tribunals against whose decisions there is no judicial remedy from countries whose legal systems operate with specialised courts and courts of last instance. In general, features of the national legal culture and structure of the court system condition the relationship between national courts and a supra-national tribunal.[10] The pattern we see in the referral ratio between higher and lower courts therefore fits well into the more general picture of factors determining the role of national courts in European integration.

From countries with a unified court system with only one court of last instance, like Denmark, Iceland, Norway and UK, the number of references from the court of last instance is lower. This does not necessarily mean that these courts take their obligation to refer less seriously than more specialised appeal courts. It is likely that the total number of cases reaching a court of last instance is higher in a country with several, specialised appeal courts than in a country with only one, general Supreme Court. This is consistent with the thesis of Stone Sweet and Brunell: The more any given court deals with questions of EC law, the more that court is likely to interact with the ECJ in a constructive manner.[11] There are simply more high-level courts dealing extensively with community law in a specialised court system than in a unitary court system. Comparisons should therefore be made between courts in similar institutional arrangements. From this point of view, it is not surprising that the Norwegian *Høyesterett* (Supreme Court) has as a large proportion of the total number of Norwegian referrals as the Danish *Høiesteret* (Supreme Court) has of the Danish cases and the House of Lords and Court of Appeal of the British cases. Differences in the legal obligation to refer a case to the European courts do not seem to have much influence on the actual behaviour of the highest courts.

[10] See W Mattli and AM Slaughter, 'Role of National Courts in European Integration' in Slaughter, *et al* (eds), *The European Court and National Courts—Doctrine and Jurisprudence* (Oxford, Hart Publishing, 1998) 272.

[11] AS Sweet and TL Brunell, 'The European Court and the National Courts: A Statistical Analysis of Preliminary References, 1961–95' (1997) *Jean Monnet Working Paper* No 14/97, http://www.jeanmonnetprogram.org/papers/97/97–14–html.

E. THE NORWEGIAN RECEPTION

1. In Numbers

The Supreme Court of Norway has mentioned the EFTA Court in its judgments in 21 cases.[12] In 14 of these cases, the EFTA Court is mentioned in relation to procedural matters in internal Norwegian law (mostly legal standing, non-referral of injunctions for interim protection and awarding of costs). This means that the Supreme Court refers to the jurisprudence of the EFTA Court as a source of law in seven cases. In three of these, the EFTA Court had given an advisory opinion in the case.[13] Of the remaining four, three concern transfer of undertakings, where there is an extensive jurisprudence from both the EFTA Court and the ECJ to which the court refers.[14] The last case is a case of the right of compensation of a commercial agent after termination of the contract of agency.[15] The legal question involves interpretation of Council Directive 86/653/EEC of 18 December 1986 on the coordination of the laws of the Member State relating to self-employed commercial agents. The Supreme Court states that there is no relevant jurisprudence from the EFTA Court or the ECJ, and goes on to interpret Norwegian law on the background of Article 17(2) of the Directive. The Court has dealt with similar issues in two previous cases, without any mention being made of the two EEA courts at all.[16]

We can compare these figures with the way in which the Supreme Court deals with the jurisprudence of the ECJ, which can be found in a total of 27 cases.[17] In all cases where use is made of jurisprudence from the EFTA Court, reference is also made to jurisprudence of the ECJ.

In 6 of the 27 cases, parties have argued from the jurisprudence on protection of fundamental rights that similar protection should be given within Norwegian law.[18] The legal issues in these cases fall outside the scope of the EEA Agreement, and the argument has been that Norwegian courts should recognise similar rights in Norwegian law to what the ECJ has recognised in Community law. So far, the Supreme Court has not been open to such arguments, and has dismissed them without a closer examination of the jurisprudence of the ECJ. In

[12] Based on searches made in the *Lovdata* data base September 2004 with search words 'EFTA domstol', 'EF domstol', 'EØS', 'rådsforordning' and 'rådsdirektiv'.

[13] Case E–3/02 *Paranova*; Case E–1/99 *Finanger;* and Case E 2/95 *Eidesund*, see Rt 2004 p 1474, Rt 2000 p 1811, and Rt 1997 p 1965.

[14] Rt 1997 p 1954; Rt 1999 p 977; and Rt 2001 p 248.

[15] Rt 2001 p 1390.

[16] Rt 1999 p 569 and p 579.

[17] Here excluded 12 cases concerning the Lugano Convention which is outside of the jurisdiction of the EFTA Court, bringing the comparable number to 27.

[18] Rt 1983 p 430 and 2000 p 2167 (legal privilege), Rt 1994 p 610 (self-incrimination in competition law procedure), Rt 1994 p 610 (proportionality review of administrative decisions), Rt 1996 p 624 (discrimination and mandatory requirements), Rt 2003 p 359 (retroactive effect of court rulings on individual rights).

three cases, the ECJ is referred to as a source of Community law as foreign law.[19]

The number of cases where the Supreme Court refers to the ECJ as a source of interpreting EEA law is therefore 17. As mentioned above, reference is also made to the jurisprudence of the EFTA Court in 7 cases, bringing the number of cases where the ECJ is the sole reference to 10. Most of these cases concern the interpretation of various pieces of secondary legislation.[20] Two cases concern free movement of goods and services, and one case concerns competition rules (Article 53).[21] All these three cases concerning rules of the main agreement were interim protection cases, where the Supreme Court held that a reference to the EFTA Court was unnecessary due to the time constraints and the preliminary nature of court decisions in such cases.

A closer examination of some of these cases reveals the approach taken by the Supreme Court towards the jurisprudence of the ECJ Report 2004 page 122 raised the question of interpreting the Norwegian Product Liability Act § 2–1(1) implementing Article 6 of the Product Liability Directive. There is no jurisprudence from the ECJ concerning the interpretation of this provision, and the Supreme Court decided the matter based on internal Norwegian sources. This case would evidently not satisfy the *acte claire* criteria of the ECJ.[22] In Report 2002 page 391 the issue was registration of a trademark. The Supreme Court stated on the basis of homogeneity that rulings of the ECJ on the Directive and Council Regulation (EC) No 40/94 on the Community trademark are of great importance when interpreting Norwegian law. Despite the fact that the Court found no directly relevant ruling from the ECJ, the issue of referring the case to

[19] Rt 1996 p 433 (Spain's Accession Treaty); Rt 2002 p 618 (recognition of movement and phytosanitary certificates originating from the part of Cyprus to the north of the United Nations Buffer Zone); and Rt 2003 p 223 (binding effect of a Norwegian interim decision within the EU).

[20] Directive 85/374/EEC on the approximation of the laws, regulations and administrative provisions of the Member States concerning liability for defective products (Rt 2004 p 122); Directive 89/104/EEC to approximate the laws of the Member States relating to trademarks (Rt 2002 p 391); Directive 86/653/ on the coordination of the laws of the Member States relating to self-employed commercial agents (Rt 1999 p 569); Directive 77/187 on the approximation of the laws of the Member States relating to the safeguarding of employees' rights in the event of transfers of undertakings, businesses or parts of businesses (Rt 1995 p 270 and p 1625 and 1999 p 989); public procurement (Rt 2004 p 351); and Regulation (EEC) 3820/85 on the harmonization of certain social legislation relating to road transport (Rt 1999 p 393).

[21] Rt 1996 p 1569; Rt 1995 p 1789; and Rt 1977 p 1859.

[22] Case 283/81 *Srl CILFIT and Lanificio di Gavardo SpA v Ministry of Health* [1982] ECR 3415:

> A court or tribunal against whose decisions there is no judicial remedy under national law is required, where a question of Community law is raised before it, to comply with its obligation to bring the matter before the Court of Justice, unless it has been established the question raised is irrelevant or that the Community provision in question has already been interpreted by the Court of Justice or that the correct application of Community law is so obvious as to leave no scope for any reasonable doubt. The existence of such a possibility must be assessed in the light of the specific characteristics of community law, the particular difficulties to which its interpretation gives rise and the risk of divergences in judicial decisions within the Community.

the EFTA Court was not raised in the premises of the Court's ruling.[23] In Report 1999 page 569 there was no jurisprudence from the ECJ to refer to when interpreting the Commercial Agents Directive. Instead, the Court relied on the Norwegian *travaux preperatoires* and on German law as described in a report from the Commission. In Report 1999 page 393 the Supreme Court cited a judgement from the ECJ and stated that even though the ruling did not cover the same matter as the case before the Supreme Court, it should have a 'certain influence' on the deciding of the case.[24]

Based on these examples, it seems that the Supreme Court takes the same approach to cases from the ECJ as to its own precedents according to the Norwegian theory of sources of law. If precedents are lacking, it investigates whether there are cases in issues similar to the one at hand, and seeks whatever guidance these give on aims and concepts of the relevant rules. In the total lack of cases, the issue is decided by reference to other national sources. Judged at face value, this seems to be an approach far from the one expected by a court of last instance under Community law. It would in my view, not be unfounded to claim that the Supreme Court has shown a certain reluctance to refer issues to the EFTA Court under the advisory opinion procedure.[25] On the other hand, as seen above, the statistics show that the Norwegian Supreme Court is no more reluctant in its referrals than comparable courts in the EU Member States. Regarding the situation in Sweden, the Commission has, in a recent reasoned opinion, stated that the country is in breach of Community law due to the reluctance of the Supreme Court to refer cases to the ECJ.[26] The Commission refers to a case involving civil law consequences of an infringement of Article 82 EC, where the Supreme Court refused to hear the case without referring the case to the ECJ as proof of a breach of Article 234 by Sweden. Most probably, it is a general trait within the EU that national courts interpret and apply Community law more often than the two Community courts themselves.[27] Such proof could therefore most likely be found in the court practise of many Member States.

[23] 'Som jeg skal komme tilbake til, foreligger det i EF en omfattende praksis om vilkårene for registrering av varemerker, men det foreligger ingen avgjørelse fra EF-domstolen som direkte gjelder det tolkningsspørsmål som foreligger til avgjørelse i vår sak. Det blir derfor et spørsmål hva man kan slutte seg til ut fra avgjørelser og premisser i saker som gjelder mer eller mindre likeartede spørsmål.'

[24] 'Selv om problemstillingen i saken for EF-domstolen var en annen enn i den sak Høyesterett her har til behandling, har dommen etter min oppfatning likevel en viss betydning for vår sak, idet EF-domstolen forutsetter at 24–timers perioden vanligvis løper fra det tidspunkt føreren aktiverer fartsskriveren.'

[25] In his opening address, President Baudenbacher formulates the same point in this manner: 'It appears that in particular the Norwegian Supreme Court follows some sort of an extended *acte claire* doctrine which includes to a certain extent the jurisprudence of the ECJ'.

[26] Reasoned opinion delivered to Sweden in accordance with Art 226 of the EC Treaty due to a breach by that State of Art 234 of the EC Treaty, Brussels, 13 October 2004 C(2004) 3899.

[27] See J Temple Lang, 'The Duties of National Courts under Community Constitutional Law' (1997) 22 *European L Rev* 3–18.

2. In Law

It has been shown above that the EEA Agreement has obligations directed towards the national courts of the EFTA States regarding their relations to the EEA courts. It has been explicitly accepted by the unanimous Supreme Court in *Finanger* that the Agreement addresses directly the courts, and that the Courts of the EFTA States under Article 3 EEA are under the obligation to 'take all appropriate measures, whether general or particular, to ensure fulfilment of the obligations arising out of this Agreement' and to 'abstain from any measure which could jeopardise the attainment of the objectives of this Agreement'.[28]

Following this obligation, the Court has taken steps to strengthen the cooperation between national courts and the EEA courts further if seen in relation to the more modest obligations entailed in the EEA Agreement. This can be seen in relation to both the EFTA Court and the ECJ.

A main feature of the legal situation of the EFTA Court is that it is not provided with exclusive rights to interpret the EEA Agreement in relation to the EFTA States. As we have seen from the review of EEA cases by the Supreme Court, the Court regards itself both formally competent and substantially qualified to interpret provisions of EEA law. On the other hand, although not under a strict obligation to follow the advisory opinions of the EFTA Court, the Supreme Court has set the requirements to diverge from these opinions so strictly, that it in practise amounts to an obligation to follow them. After stating that national courts have a duty to asses independently whether or not to follow the opinion of the EFTA Court, the Court in *Finanger* establishes that the opinion must have considerable persuasive effect, and the EFTA Court have significant authority.[29] In the recent judgment in *Paranova* the Court, with reference to *Finanger,* states that 'in my opinion it should take a lot for the Supreme Court to depart from the EFTA Court's understanding of the EEA provisions, especially in a matter like this where Community law/EEA law is both specialised and developed.'[30]

A similar approach has been taken towards the jurisprudence of the ECJ. As stated above, Article 6 EEA obligates the Courts to interpret the Agreement in conformity with the relevant rulings of the Court of Justice of the European

[28] Rt 2000 p 1811.

[29] The Court held:

> Men jeg finner samtidig at uttalelsen må tillegges vesentlig vekt. Dette følger etter min mening allerede av den omstendighet at EFTA–statene i samsvar med EØS–avtalen artikkel 108 nr. 2 ved inngåelsen av ODA–avtalen har funnet grunn til å opprette denne domstolen, blant annet for å nå frem til og å opprettholde en lik fortolkning og anvendelse av EØS–avtalen. Også reelle grunner taler for dette. Rettskildebruken innen EØS–retten kan avvike fra den nasjonale. Dette gjør at EFTA–domstolen med sin særlige kunnskap bør kunne uttale seg med betydelig autoritet.

[30] 'Etter min mening skal det meget til for at Høyesterett skal fravike det (EFTA)domstolen uttaler om forståelsen av de EØS–rettslige bestemmelsene, og ganske særlig på et område som det foreliggende, hvor EU/EØS–retten er spesialisert og utviklet', Rt 2004 p 1474. The case concerned parallel imports and trademarks.

Communities given prior to the date of signature of the Agreement. Case-law from after this date is not binding on the Courts of the Contracting Parties. The Supreme Court, however, in one of its first cases where it had to decide on the interpretation of an EEA provision, relied on the judgement of the ECJ in *Keck*[31] when interpreting Article 11 EEA (Article 28 EC) without any discussion of the relevance of this judgement in the light of Article 6 EEA.[32] This approach has later been confirmed in a consistent line of cases. It must on this background, be correct to state that in Norwegian law the distinction drawn in Article 6 EEA has lost its meaning as Norwegian courts are instructed by the Supreme Court to interpret the provisions of the Agreement in conformity with *all* relevant rulings of the ECJ.

Methodologically, this entails that provisions of the EEA Agreement should be interpreted by Norwegian courts according to the approach and method utilised by the ECJ when interpreting and applying community law. This is in conformance with the line which the Court has taken to interpret international obligations more generally, in several plenary judgments on the interpretation of the European Convention on Human Rights.[33]

F. EFFECTS ON THE LEGAL ORDER

Initially, the EEA Agreement was concluded as an agreement under international law. One of the basic aims of the Agreement was to connect the EFTA States to the Single European Market without constructing supranational institutions and rules.[34] The way the Agreement has been developed both by the EFTA Court and national courts has caused the differences between the EEA solution and Community law in this respect to be more of degree than of a qualitative nature. One aspect of this is the relations of the national courts to the EEA courts, where we see that there are no great differences in the approach of the national courts.

The jurisprudence of the EFTA Court, however, also affects the legal order of the EFTA States in other ways. According to the EFTA Court, the EEA Agreement is not merely a regional treaty under international law. The Court stated in *Sveinbjörnsdóttir* 'that the EEA Agreement is an international treaty *sui generis* which contains a distinct legal order of its own . . . less far-reaching than under the EC Treaty, but the scope and the objective of the EEA Agreement goes beyond what is usual for an agreement under public international law.'[35] This legal order 'is characterised by the creation of an internal market . . . the

[31] Joined Cases C–267/91 and C–268/91 Criminal proceedings against Bernard Keck and Daniel Mithouard [1993] ECR I–6097.

[32] Rt 1996 p 1569.

[33] See for instance Rt 2003 p 359.

[34] See HP Graver, 'Mission Impossible: Supranationality and National Legal Autonomy in the EEA Agreement' (2002) 1 *Eur Foreign Affairs Rev* 73–90.

[35] Case E–9/97 *Erla María Sveinbjörnsdóttir v The Government of Iceland* [1998] EFTA Ct Rep 97.

protection of the rights of individuals and economic operators and an institutional framework providing for effective surveillance and judicial review.'[36] The EFTA Court has developed general principles of EEA law. When interpreting the Agreement the objective of homogeneity must be borne in mind. For all practical purposes this interpretive principle eliminates the differences that could arise from the fact that Community law must be interpreted with the aim of integration in mind.[37] The provisions of the Agreement are to the benefit of individuals and economic operators who must be able to rely on the rights before the courts. The national courts must consider any relevant element of EEA law, whether implemented or not when interpreting national law. The states are liable for damage suffered by individuals for breach of the state's obligations under the Agreement. The Agreement also contains other principles such as protection of fundamental rights and the principle of proportionality.[38] When the EEA Agreement was new, it was debated whether the Agreement could be characterised differently from a normal international treaty and whether it could be seen to include general principles not entailed by its express provisions.[39] Many of these questions may now be regarded as settled by the jurisprudence of the EFTA Court and by the Norwegian Supreme Court in *Finanger*. In that case, the Court stated that the principle of loyalty in Article 3 EEA is applicable to the courts and that Norwegian courts should use the principle of presumption in a way 'not less far-reaching' than the Community interpretation obligation.[40] The majority of the Court in *Finanger* rejected the

[36] Case E–2/03 *Ákæruvaldid (The Public Prosecutor) v Ásgeir Logi Ásgeirsson, Axel Pétur Ásgeirsson and Helgi Már Reynisson* [2003] EFTA Ct Rep 187, para 28.

[37] As stated by the ECJ in Case C–286/02 *Bellio Flli Srl v Prefettura di Treviso* (1 April 2004) para 34:

> It should be emphasised in this connection that, as Art 6 of the EEA Agreement states, the provisions of the agreement, in so far as they are identical in substance to corresponding rules of the EC Treaty and to acts adopted in application of that Treaty, must, in their implementation and application, be interpreted in conformity with the relevant rulings of the Court given prior to the date of signature of the EEA Agreement. Furthermore, both the Court and the EFTA Court have recognised the need to ensure that the rules of the EEA Agreement which are identical in substance to those of the Treaty are interpreted uniformly (Case C–452/01 *Ospelt and Schlössle Weissenberg Familienstiftung* [2003] ECR I–9743, para 29, and Case E–1/03 *EFTA Surveillance Authority v Iceland* [2003] EFTA Ct Rep 145, para 27).

[38] For more details and references to relevant cases see The EFTA Court, *Legal Framework, Case Law, and Composition 1994–2003* (Luxembourg, 2004) 23–40.

[39] See for instance, PC Müller-Graff, 'EEA Agreement and EC Law: A Comparison in Scope and Content' in PC Müller-Graff and E Selbig (eds), *The European Economic Area—Norway's Basic Status in the Legal Construction of Europe* (Berlin, Berlin Verlag Arno Spitz GmbH, 1997) 17; and F Sejersted, 'Between Sovereignty and Supranationalism in the EEA Context–On the Legal Dynamics of the EEA Agreement' in PC Müller Graff and E Selvig (eds), *The European Economic Area–Norway's Basic Status in the Legal Construction of Europe* (Berlin, Berlin Verlag Arno Spitz GmbH, 1997) 43.

[40] For an overview of the principle of presumption also covering basic parts of Norwegian law, see SS Jensen, *The European Convention on Human Rights in Scandinavian Law* (Copenhagen, Jurist-og økonomforbundets Forlagm, 1992). For an overview of the Community interpretation obligation, see T Ojanen, *The European Way: The Structure of National Court Obligation under EC Law* (Helsinki, Gummerus Oy, 1998).

claim to give the Directive direct effect contrary to the express wording of a Norwegian statute. But it is important to stress that the issue was one of horizontal effect between two private parties, which does not fall under the obligation to give direct effect in Community law. Even under these circumstances a large minority was of the opinion that the Directive should prevail over national law, and the majority made it part of their reasoning that the facts were not a case of giving an individual rights in a claim against the state.

In the subsequent *Finanger II* case regarding the liability of the Norwegian State for incorrect transformation of the Motor Vehicle Insurance Directive, the State as defendant has admitted that the principle of state liability is part of the Agreement and as such directly applicable before the Norwegian courts. In my view, it is still open to question whether direct effect of a Directive will be accepted in a 'proper' Community setting, that is in a case where an individual claims the rights of the Directive in an action against the state. Direct effect and supremacy of the main part of the Agreement is already established by the act implementing the Agreement, and by the interpretive principles established in *Finanger*. If there is no open and clear legislative intent of non-compliance, a strong case could be made that an individual must be able to rely on obligations undertaken by the state in directives that have been become part of the Agreement.

The fact that the Supreme Court has accepted that the loyalty obligation also applies to the courts is of crucial importance. This duty entails a duty to cooperate with the EFTA Court, to apply EEA rules in a loyal manner and, when necessary to ensure that other national authorities apply the Agreement and comply with it. In Community law it can be held that basic features such as disallowing state authorities to rely on national laws which are inconsistent with Community obligations (direct effect and supremacy), the interpretation obligation and the duty to give effective remedies to breach of Community law all stem from the duties of national courts under Article 10 EC.[41]

The approach taken by the Supreme Court in *Finanger* is very similar to the approach the House of Lords took on the sovereignty issue prior to *Factortame* by reading national provisions not by reference to ordinary rules of construction, but in a manner designed to effectuate the dictates of Community law.[42] The House of Lords, later in *Factortame* gave a general statement concerning the priority of Community law over national law in the event of a clash between the two. The facts here concerned the relations between new requirements of registration in the Merchant Shipping Act of 1988 and primary rules of freedom of establishment. This conflict would in Norwegian law already have been solved in favour of the EEA rules by reference to § 2 of the EEA Implementing

[41] J Temple Lang, 'The Duties of National Courts under Community Constitutional Law' (1997) 22 *European L Rev* 3–18.

[42] See PP Craig, 'Report on the United Kingdom' in Slaughter, *et al*, (eds), *The European Court and National Courts—Doctrine and Jurisprudence* (Oxford, Hart Publishing, 1998) 198–200.

Act which states that legislation implementing EEA rules has priority over other acts of legislation. There is therefore no need for a judicial construction to reach this result in Norwegian law.

It has been argued by president Baudenbacher of the EFTA Court that the described features form facets of an EEA constitutional order.[43] It can certainly be argued that together with the surveillance powers of the EFTA Surveillance Authority and the fact that the main part of the Agreement is transformed into national law, the supranational qualities of the EEA do not lag far behind the EU in features, albeit quite different in scope. Supremacy of implemented rules is secured in accordance with Protocol 35 to the Agreement by the EEA Implementation Act. Supremacy of *non-implemented* rules follows from the solution of the question of direct effect. In Norwegian law, this question is more correctly framed as a question of supremacy, as there is no doubt that non-implemented rules are a basis for valid legal arguments and will be followed by the courts in the absence of national rules barring such a result. As mentioned above I believe it is not unlikely that rights will be granted to individuals according to non-implemented EEA rules in a case against the state, even in contradiction to national legislation if the conditions for direct effect are met. Economic rights follow from the fact that the obligation of state liability has been accepted. It is difficult to see what kind of arguments the government could use for not granting a right, apart from a general and principled argument of sovereignty and the fact that the Agreement does not entail a transfer of legislative powers. Such arguments however, are of a very formal kind, when it is clear in law that the individual will be compensated for the non-fulfilment of the obligation in any case. It is highly unlikely that a situation can arise, where the conditions for direct effect under EEA law are met in relation to a specific person, without the conditions for state liability also being met.

The crucial test, however, is how EEA rules fare in conflict with legislative acts of the Storting, where there is a clear legislative intent that the act shall prevail over an EEA obligation. In the Community context, the House of Lords has made a contractual argument towards Community law: Joining the EU means joining on the terms that are made, and supremacy and exclusive competence of the ECJ are parts of these terms. This must entail that the State, also in the capacity of legislator is bound by the terms, and therefore cannot pick and choose to which obligations to subscribe while still remaining in the Community.[44] A similar argument could be made in Norwegian law in relation to the EEA Agreement. There is a clear obligation under the Agreement to give effect and supremacy to EEA obligations. This follows from Article 7 and Protocol 35. There is no option under the Agreement for the national legislator to pick and choose among the obliga-

[43] C Baudenbacher, 'Facets of an EEA Constitutional Order', in N Colneric, *et al* (eds), *Une communauté de Droit, Festschrift für Gil Carlos Rodríguez Iglesias* (Berlin, Berliner Wissenschafts Verlag, 2003) 343–59.

[44] See PP Craig, 'Report on the United Kingdom' in Slaughter, *et al* (eds), *The European Court and National Courts–Doctrine and Jurisprudence* (Oxford, Hart Publishing, 1998) 200.

tions. It is true that the Agreement is implemented into Norwegian law by a legislative act by the Storting, and as such, according to Norwegian constitutional law may be 'unimplemented' by a simple legislative act. However, by implementing the Agreement, also Article 7 and Protocol 35 are Norwegian law. The Storting is not bound by the Agreement to give up its legislative freedom to revoke its obligations. The Agreement provides in Article 127 for a right to withdraw from the Agreement. It could be argued that the Storting, by implementing the Agreement has accepted the obligation to legislate according to its obligations, and must follow the provisions of the Agreement provided to exercise its sovereignty. This would mean that, apart from safeguard and emergency measures, contrary legislation could only be passed after a withdrawal and twelve months' notice in writing to the other Contracting Parties according to Article 127.

The traditional argument in Norwegian doctrine is different. Since the acceptance and implementation of the EEA Agreement has been made according to provisions empowering the state to conclude such agreements and undertake such legislation in the Norwegian constitution, it must follow from a normal application of the Constitution that the courts are bound by later decisions of the Storting revoking these acts, in part or fully. What will Norwegian courts do should a question like this arise? It is in my opinion difficult to predict. Should the courts protect the sovereignty of the Storting to legislate in contradiction to its clear obligations under the Agreement? It would be clear that by doing so, the Storting would be breaking the law. And since the Agreement has been made part of Norwegian law, not only would it be an international obligation broken, but also an obligation under Norwegian law. And is it not the duty of the courts to uphold the law also in the face of unlawful acts by the legislator?

The Court could of course take the more withdrawn position indicated by the majority of the Supreme Court in *Finanger*; it is up to the legislator to fulfil its obligations to implement EEA rules and it must therefore also be up to the legislator to sort out any difficulties that may arise. In *Finanger*, this was a viable position because no court is under the obligation to give horizontal effect to directives contrary to provisions under national law. Would it be viable in a case of express legislative disobedience? I believe it would. Under Community law, national courts are under the obligation to give effect to Community law, under certain conditions also in cases directly against the national legislator. Accepting this is part of the deal when joining the Community and the contractual argument applies. Under the EEA Agreement, no such obligation on the courts exists. The national courts are therefore not under an EEA obligation to correct violations by the legislator. This is, in my view, the main content of the claim that the Agreement does not entail direct effect in the Community law sense. An obligation therefore must be constructed under national law, and here the traditional view will be powerful. The conservative prediction would therefore be that the courts would apply legislation that expressly contradicts EEA rules.

Also on this point there is correspondence between the Norwegian situation and the situation in the Member States of the EU. It seems to be a general trait that the courts are constrained in their relation to the Community by the shape and specific form of national law.[45]

Perhaps the area where the situation within the Member States differs the most is on the question of *kompetenz-kompetenz*. This is not a difficult issue in the EEA, since there is no provision on an exclusive competence for an EEA Court to rule on the validity of an EEA rule. Nevertheless, it is not likely that Norwegian courts will find an EEA rule invalid based on a test of the validity of the underlying Community rule or on the provisions of the EEA Agreement without requesting an opinion from the EFTA Court. Questions of limiting the scope of the Agreement are in my opinion another matter. The EFTA Court has already twice defined limits to the scope of the Agreement—in relation to the common commercial policy towards third countries and in relation to measures to the maintenance of the national identity of a State.[46] Where the role of the *kompetenz-kompetenz* issue in the EU is mostly theoretical due to the breadth of areas over which the Union institutions have power, it is of a highly practical nature within the EEA. Here therefore lies a field where national courts can assert their independence and powers without seriously impairing the functioning of the Agreement.

G. ASSESSMENT

Looking back 10 years, the EEA Agreement has elements today, which were lacking, or even rejected at the moment of its inception. The Agreement was created as an instrument under international law, and as a clear alternative to the supranational arrangement of the, at that time, European Communities. Basic elements of Community law as a legal order, the subjects of which comprise not only Member States but also their nationals, with main characteristics such as the overall aim of integration, direct effect, state liability and the obligatory leading interpretive role of the ECJ, did not form part of the agreement.[47] Today the individuals and economic operators are able to rely on their rights before the courts, the aims of interpretation identical through the EEA aims of homogeneity, direct effect, supremacy and state liability established through interpretation and the leading role of the ECJ and the EFTA Court accepted through the conduct of national courts.

Attaining the aims of the Agreement, equal conditions of competition, and the respect of the same rules, with a view to creating a homogeneous European

[45] W Mattli and AM Slaughter, 'Role of National Courts in European Integration' in Slaughter, *et al*, (eds), *The European Court and National Courts—Doctrine and Jurisprudence* (Oxford, Hart Publishing, 1998) 274.

[46] Case E–2/97 *Mag Instrument Inc and California Trading Company Norway, Ulsteen* [1997] EFTA Ct Rep 129; and Case E–1/01 *Hördur Einarsson v The Icelandic State* [2002] EFTA Ct Rep 3.

[47] See in this respect Opinion 1/91 [1991] ECR I–6079 and PC Müller-Graff and E Selbig, (eds), *The European Economic Area—Norway's Basic Status in the Legal Construction of Europe* (Berlin, Berlin Verlag Arno Spitz GmbH, 1997).

Economic Area, was probably impossible within the political constraints given at the time of the negotiations. The provisions included in the Agreement to secure homogenous interpretation have the form of a request, rather than an obligation on the cooperating national and international courts.[48] The response has been positive. The two EEA courts have actively been cooperating in forming a uniform legal order. National courts have by no means been passive recipients, but have actively participated by making references at the same level as courts in the EU Member States, by adhering to the interpretations of the ECJ, taking no notice of the distinction made in Article 6 EEA, and by setting the conditions for disregarding the advisory opinions of the EFTA Court so strictly that following them amounts to an obligation. In this way, the development of the EEA Agreement mirrors the development of Community law where the 'rules of the game' for the courts to play have largely been developed by the ECJ and the national courts in concert.[49]

Above it was shown that on the level of statistics, the role of the EFTA Court and its relation to national courts is comparable to the situation within Community law. The variations one can see cannot be explained so much by formal differences in obligations and norms between Community law and the EEA Agreement, as by other factors such as differences in social, cultural and legal structures among the different countries. The same can be said on the level of legal norms and doctrines. Although, here one would expect legal differences between the two instruments of law: Community law and the EEA Agreement, to play a more significant role. After all, Community concepts of direct effect, supremacy etc, are required by law in the Community legal order, whereas they are not by the EEA Agreement. The most basic explanation as to why the ECJ's vision of an integrated legal Community has prevailed in the Member States is: It is the law.[50] How can then the seeming lack of difference between the situation in the EU and the EEA be explained?

Direct effect of primary law, state liability and the duty of the Courts to interpret national law in light of EEA obligations, have been clearly and firmly accepted in national law by Norwegian courts.[51] The same is the case with the principle of homogeneity as a leading interpretative aim, and the role of the ECJ

[48] In the words of PC Müller-Graff, 'EEA Agreement and EC Law: A Comparison in Scope and Content' in PC Müller-Graff and E Selbig, (eds), *The European Economic Area—Norway's Basic Status in the Legal Construction of Europe* (Berlin, Berlin Verlag Arno Spitz GmbH, 1997) 17, 38.

[49] See T Ojanen, *The European Way, The Structure of National Court Obligation under EC Law* (Helsinki, Gummerus Oy, 1998) 326–27.

[50] AS Sweet, 'Integration and the Europeanisation of the Law' (2002) *Queen's Papers on Europeanisation,* No 2/2002, p 15.

[51] Direct effect of the main part of the EEA Agreement was established by the EFTA Court in its first advisory opinion in Case E–1/94 *Restamark* [1994] EFTA Ct Rep 15, and has been applied without discussion in Norwegian courts. State liability was established in Case E–9/97 *Sveinbjörnsdóttir* [1998] EFTA Ct Rep 97, and has been accepted by the Supreme Court in Iceland and by the Norwegian Government. It is therefore highly unlikely that the Norwegian Supreme Court will reject this in principle in defence of the State. The interpretation obligation is established clearly in Case E–4/01 *Karlsson* [2002] EFTA Ct Rep 242, and by the Supreme Court in *Finanger.*

and the EFTA Court as the proper courts to establish precedents on the interpretation of Community and EEA law.[52] This development is despite the fact that the EEA Agreement was conceived as a political alternative to the supranational arrangement of the European Communities. Again, if we compare with the Community situation, what needs explanation is the degree of smoothness which characterises the acceptance of these supranational traits into the EEA Agreement. After all, the Community experience shows a certain degree of correlation between the rate of acceptance of core supranational features of Community law and national attitudes toward European integration.[53] Based on this, one would maybe expect a higher degree of reluctance in Norwegian courts.

One factor in the explanation is probably the traditional strong loyalty Norwegian courts have towards the legislation of the Storting and the expressed will of the legislator. Paradoxically, this has brought the courts into a position where they may question, and even disapply legislation passed by the same Storting. In *Finanger*, the Court referred to the will of the legislator in the passing of the EEA Implementation Act as a strong argument for the duty of the courts to interpret Norwegian law in conformity with EEA obligations. Homogeneity is a strong legislative and political aim, and the EEA Agreement the only viable alternative to achieve this. This places a responsibility also on the courts to ensure that this alternative functions.

Another factor is the familiarity of the Norwegian legal culture to the doctrine of precedents and to defining law according to the methods and reasoning of a court empowered to have the last word in a legal matter. It is a basic characteristic in the Norwegian theory of sources of law and legal methodology that the jurisprudence and mode of reasoning of the final court should be paradigmatic to other lawyers. Since the development of Community law and EEA law, despite formal bindings or non-bindings in the EEA Agreement inevitably is performed by the courts in Luxembourg, these courts take the place of the paradigmatic court in matters on EEA law. The same pattern is formed in the relation to the European Convention for Human Rights, where the Supreme Court in several rulings has stated that the method of interpreting the convention must be based on the case-law and method of the Human Rights Court.[54] Based on this, it is no great step in legal thinking to surpass the distinction made in Article 6 EEA and treat the case-law as such of the EEA courts as sources of law with the greatest authority.

A third factor that may have been playing in the *Finanger* reasoning is a desire to regain control over the legal relations between national law and the EEA Agreement. The way the argument is framed in this case, the very strong

[52] See the review of Norwegian Supreme Court cases above.

[53] W Mattli and AM Slaughter, 'Role of National Courts in European Integration' in Slaughter, *et al*, (eds), *The European Court and National Courts—Doctrine and Jurisprudence* (Oxford, Hart Publishing, 1998) 274.

[54] See notably Rt 2000 p 996 and 2002 p 557.

compulsion to interpret, and even bend national law according to EEA obligations, follows from a doctrine of presumption in national law, and not from a Community law or EEA law obligation of interpretation.

Finally, account must be taken of the more general picture under which the reception of the EEA Agreement has taken place within the Supreme Court. In the last decade the Supreme Court has been called upon to reformulate the relations between national law and international law more generally and specifically in relation to human rights. No less than three times did the Supreme Court meet in plenary sessions over the effects of the European Convention on Human Rights in 2000–02 in addition to the plenary treatment of the EEA in *Finanger*. There had been much uncertainty and disagreement, also among the judiciary itself, on the effects of international obligations in Norwegian law and the method to construct and interpret both national and international rules in the event of a potential conflict. Strong voices, among them several former presidents of the Supreme Court, had over the past decades propagated for leaving the traditional concept of dualism behind and for applying international fundamental rights directly in Norwegian law without any legislative implementation. Seen on this background, the result in *Finanger* can be seen as a middle-of-the-road compromise, which is not very far reaching. It must be recalled that a large minority of the Court supported a result that would have amounted to giving the directive horizontal direct effect and supremacy over contradicting Norwegian legislation.

H. DISCUSSIONS

THORGEIR ÖRLYGSSON

Thank you, Dr Graver, for your very interesting and informative contribution. Now, the former President of the EFTA Court, Bjørn Haug, has asked for the floor. The floor is yours, Mr Haug.

BJØRN HAUG

Mr Chairman, Mr President, Your Excellencies, Ladies and Gentlemen,

I had the mixed pleasure of being a Judge in the EFTA Court for the first six years, five of them as President of the Court.

I would like to make a few comments on two points. One is about the short and turbulent history of the EFTA Court. The other is about the legal framework under which the Court is acting under the Treaty.

First, the history. You will recall that when the Agreement on the European Economic Area was signed in May 1992 there were six states participating on the EFTA side. But after a referendum, Switzerland opted out even before we got started. So we started on 1 January 1994 with five EFTA states, Austria, Finland, Sweden, Norway and Iceland. But already after a couple of months, four of those states had signed membership agreements with the European Community subject to referendums. The result was that already after one year, on the 1 January 1995, three of the five EFTA states opted out to become full members of the European Community. So there we were, left after one year with two EFTA states, Iceland and Norway. A little later Liechtenstein was also allowed by the Community to join us, and we were joined in the Court by Mr Baudenbacher, now the President of the Court, as a part of the team of judges.

While the number of EFTA States was diminishing, the Community in many ways was growing tremendously. The Community members grew from the 12 states in May 1992 to 15, and now recently up to 25 states. And there has been a development of integration and a development into new areas of co-operation which has given the other party to the EEA Agreement quite another dimension.

So my first point is that the brief but turbulent history of 10 years has made the future for the EFTA Court look quite different from what it did when the Treaty was signed.

My second point is a few remarks on some aspects of the Treaty structure and the framework under which the EFTA Court is working.

The main task of the EFTA Court and the EFTA Surveillance Authority is to ensure a parallel interpretation and application of the agreed set of rules and principles developing in the European Economic Area. There are two important limitations in the way such parallel interpretation and application may be achieved. First, I would like to remind you that the EFTA Court has a mandate, in certain cases, to make rulings on rights and obligations of the EFTA States under the EEA Agreement. But there is no mandate for the EFTA Court to act as a supranational court handing down decisions legally binding on national courts or on nationals or corporations within the EFTA States. It may only act by giving advisory opinions which ideally should be convincing and persuasive, but they are not legally binding. This was an important peculiarity at the time when the Treaty was signed in 1992, and I believe it is still an important aspect today, both legally and politically.

Second, the EEA Agreement did not establish the EFTA Surveillance Authority or the EFTA Court, as supranational legislative bodies, with powers to issue legislative decrees with a legal effect of legislation on the national level within the EFTA States. What the EFTA States undertook was an obligation to implement the relevant rules into their national systems. The EFTA States may well breach their Treaty obligations to make such implementation or they may breach their Treaty obligations by inadequate implementation. But neither the EFTA Surveillance Authority nor the EFTA Court have the mandate to by-pass the national legislative bodies and issue legislative decrees with direct national effect. Thus, the mandate of the EFTA Court is restricted to the interpretation of the Treaty provisions and the Community legislation referred to in the Treaty.

It may also be worthwhile to point out the difference between the relevant substantive provisions of Community law and the Treaty provisions setting out the legal framework for the EFTA Court and its work.

It is clear that the substantive provisions of Community law are under constant development and clarification. It is the obligation of the EFTA Court to follow this development of the relevant substantive body of law and reflect it in its advisory opinions. In this connection, in practical terms, there is little difference between the developments in decisions in the Community before and after the signing of the EEA Agreement in 1992.

But another matter, are the Treaty provisions laying down the mandate of the EFTA Court. The EFTA Court, in my opinion, has no authority to expand its own mandate for instance in the direction that its advisory opinions should take on the character of decisions legally binding on the national level. It is in case for the Contracting Parties to amend the Treaty provisions, not for the Court to do so. I believe that both national courts and legal scholars who are explaining and analysing the Court's pronouncements, should keep this fundamental point in mind. It is, of course, the aspiration of the EFTA Court to deliver convincing legal arguments on the substantive issues placed before it, but the persuasive power of the Court's opinion should not be confused with a development into legally binding decisions.

In this connection, I think of professor Graver's remarks concerning the Norwegian Supreme Court's pronouncement that the persuasion and the authority of the EFTA Court should make the national courts follow the legal opinions of the EFTA Court. The Supreme Court's support of the EFTA Court's expertise is of course appreciated. But to suggest that national courts should have come under any legal obligation to follow the EFTA Court's opinions, has in my opinion no basis in the Treaty nor in the Supreme Court's remarks. I think this is a point to keep in mind.

Finally, there are other border lines to be aware of as well, for instance when or if the EFTA Court makes assumptions concerning the contents of national legislation implementing Community laws and regulations. Of course, the EFTA Court may have assumptions in this respect, but it is not for the EFTA Court to pronounce any binding interpretation of national laws.

Thank you.

THORGEIR ÖRLYGSSON

Thank you, Mr Haug. Are there any questions to Dr Graver? Yes, would you please tell your name?

INGE LORANGE BACKER

I am Inge Lorange Backer from the Norwegian Ministry of Justice, former professor of law and a colleague of Professor Graver some years ago. I would like to make a few comments concerning the question of direct effect. As I understood Professor Graver, that doctrine would certainly not apply where there is clear legislative intent of non-compliance. That is a situation, I believe, where examples will be few and very far between, especially as regards non-compliance with secondary legislation. Concerning directives (or regulations), the matter will in fact be decided when making the decision of whether to include the directive in the EEA Agreement or not.Once that decision has been made, as was the case regarding the Patent Directive, to take one famous example, it is by all means to be expected that it will be properly implemented in the national legislation.

So, I think there are other situations which deserve our particular interest, one of which is where the national parliament has a clear intent of upholding a specific policy in a matter where the legal situation under EEA law may be unclear. It may turn out here that upholding this national policy will in fact be a breach of EEA law. I submit it should be treated as such, and that there is a vital difference between this and allowing for direct effect. I see at least two arguments against direct effect in these circumstances. One has to do with the question of foreseeability. It seems, I submit, fairly clear that one could hardly predict a doctrine of direct effect at the time when the EEA Agreement was concluded, rather the contrary. I am referring now to what Attorney General Bjørn Haug just said. Moreover, there are constitutional limits in national jurisdictions. Surely, it would raise a question of constitutional authority if the national courts in the case of Norway would apply a doctrine of direct effect. I would like to ask Professor Graver for his comment on the observation that where there are constitutional boundaries of that kind in States Parties to the Treaty, they should be taken into account as an important argument when deciding the obligations of the Treaty, insofar as the question of direct effect is concerned. Thank you, Mr Chairman.

PROFESSOR GRAVER

Thank you very much for your question. In my view, the use of the term direct effect to analyse these problems is misconceived, because as I said, I think this is more a question of supremacy than direct effect, because even under such a situation which you described with an *unclear obligation* and a *clear legislative intent* the obligation, as such, being unclear, would be a source of legal arguments to evaluate the legal situation also under Norwegian law. So it is more a question of supremacy and I agree, it is an open question on the traditional scope of direct effect of directives being the vertical direct effect of non-implemented or wrongly implemented directives. I think it is an open question what Norwegian courts would do and I don't think they will go as far as Community courts have to go under Community law, so I think there is a difference, but there is a small scope of difference when you compare to the whole picture of relations between Community law and national law. I also think that it is another aspect which is common across the boundaries of Community membership or not, is that national courts do reflect such issues on the basis of their constitutional obligations. This is illegal under Community law, it is also illegal under EEA law, because EEA law does not entail any provision saying that the national constitution's exempt from the obligations under EEA law, but I think it is an established fact which is in this respect, Norway's situation does not differ much from the situations of the members states of the EU. I think, may be, if one should use sort of a characterization of these issues, I think that the main difference between the EU situation and the EEA situation is that within the EU a breach of the obligations by national courts is unthinkable. It is unthinkable because it is not regulated in the Treaty, so legally it is unthinkable. Under the EEA Agreement, breach is thinkable, because it is regulated, but it is still a breach.

THORGEIR ÖRLYGSSON

One final question for Dr Graver? Since not, I just want to thank you once again, Dr Graver for your contribution. I then have the pleasure of introducing to you our third speaker this morning, Dr Marco Bronckers. His topic is 'Exceptions to liberal trade in foodstuffs: The precautionary approach and collective preferences'. Dr Marco Bronckers holds a PhD in law from the University of Amsterdam. He is a member of the Dutch Bar and is a partner in the Brussels office of Wilmer, Cutler and Pickering. His legal specialities are EU law, competition law and WTO law. Mr Bronckers is a professor of law at the University of Leiden, he speaks and writes regularly on trade and competition law. Dr Bronckers, the floor is yours.

Exceptions to Liberal Trade in Foodstuffs: The Precautionary Approach and Collective Preferences

MARCO BRONCKERS

TODAY IS A happy occasion, where we celebrate the anniversary of a relatively young, small but influential international Court. When its President, Carl Baudenbacher, asked me about a year ago to speak at this event, he suggested I address the precautionary principle. I was happy to do so, as the EFTA Court's case law in this area has been path-breaking. It even inspired the Court of Justice of the European Communities, the neighbouring European Court, to reconsider its jurisprudence.

A. THE EFTA COURT'S *KELLOGG'S* JUDGMENT

I am referring of course to the EFTA Court's *Kellogg's* judgment of April 2001.[1] In this landmark case, the EFTA Surveillance Authority challenged a Norwegian ban on cornflakes, fortified with certain vitamins and iron. These cornflakes had been lawfully manufactured and marketed by Kellogg's in other EEA Member States. According to Norway, there was no nutritional need for the addition of these nutrients to cornflakes. When challenged by the EFTA Surveillance Authority, that this prohibition constituted an unjustified import ban, Norway invoked the precautionary principle. Better safe than sorry, Norway argued: according to the present state of scientific research, when eaten in uncontrollable and unforeseen amounts nutrients such as those Kellogg's added to its cornflakes might create a health hazard.

The EFTA Court rejected Norway's plea, and condemned the import ban on Kellogg's cornflakes. According to the Court:

[1] See Case E–3/00 *EFTA Surveillance Authority v Norway* [2000–01] EFTA Ct Rep 75.

The mere finding by a national authority of the absence of a nutritional need will not justify an import ban, a most restrictive measure, on a product which is freely traded in other EEA States.[2]

The Court held that Norway was at fault because it had confined itself to a hypothetical and conjectural projection of what might happen in the future, without having made a comprehensive assessment of the health risks posed by the fortified cornflakes.

Some two years after the EFTA Court's *Kellogg's* judgment, in September 2003, the ECJ rendered judgment in a similar case. At stake here were Danish restrictions on *Cranberry juice*. Like Norway in the earlier case, Denmark too only tolerated the addition of vitamins if there was a nutritional need for them. On these grounds, Denmark prohibited, for instance, the sale of a cranberry drink to which vitamin C had been added. In light of earlier case law of the European Court, which Denmark invoked, one might have expected the ECJ to uphold the ban.[3] Yet the European Court struck down the Danish restrictions, which it found disproportionate.[4] In distancing itself from earlier case law, the ECJ several times cited approvingly the EFTA Court's judgment in *Kellogg's*.[5] The Danish *Cranberry juice* judgment is an important judgment too, showing that the European Court of Justice envisages a more rigorous application of the precautionary principle as well.[6]

The precautionary principle therefore seemed an ideal subject for this occasion to pay tribute to the contributions of the birthday Court, the EFTA Court. This tribute I still would very much like to pay today. Yet I want to approach the precautionary principle in a slightly different way, looking beyond European case law, and placing it in a broader setting.

[2] Judgment, *ibid*, at Rec 28.

[3] See notably, Case 174/82 *Sandoz* [1983] ECR –2445. That the outlook of the ECJ in *Sandoz* differed from the EFTA Court in *EFTA Surveillance Authority v Norway* (and from the relevant WTO rules on the precautionary principle, embodied in the SPS Agreement), was highlighted in M Slotboom, 'Do Public Health Measures Receive Similar Treatment in European Community and World Trade Organization Law?' (2003) 37(3) *Journal of World Trade* 553, 584–85. Slotboom noted that the discrepancy between the EFTA Court's judgment and the previous case law of the European Court of Justice was striking. Both courts were interpreting similar Treaty principles, and the EFTA Court pursuant to the homogeneity rules of Art. 6 EEA Agreement was bound to interpret the EEA Agreement in accordance with the relevant case law of the ECJ of corresponding provisions in the EC Treaty given prior to signature of the EEA Agreement. *Ibid* at 585. However, as President Baudenbacher notes in his contribution to this volume, 'The EFTA Court Ten Years On': 'as far as law in action is concerned, homogeneity in the EEA is not a one-way street.' See above.

[4] See Case C–192/01 *Commission v Denmark* [2003] ECR I–9693.

[5] Judgment, *ibid*, at recitals 47, 49, 50, 51, 52, and 53. See also Case C–236/01 *Monsanto* [2003] ECR I–8105 at Rec 106. The CFI had cited *Kellogg's* approvingly on two earlier occasions, in Case T–13/99 *Pfizer* [2002] ECR II–3305; Case T–70/99 *Alpharma* [2002] ECR II–3495.

[6] See more recently Case C–24/00 *Commission v France* (5 February 2004) (*Red Bull*).

B. THE PRECAUTIONARY PRINCIPLE IN THE WTO

Now where did the EFTA Court get its inspiration from for its *Kellogg's* judgment on the precautionary principle? While there may have been other sources, I am very much reminded of a package of treaties that was signed about 10 years ago, the WTO agreements. This package includes a treaty called the Agreement on Sanitary and Phytosanitary Measures. Very briefly, this agreement prescribes that when a WTO member decides to restrict imports of foodstuffs to protect the safety of its citizens, it has to make a careful risk assessment, it has to look at scientific evidence, and it cannot just rely on mere hypothesis about risks.[7]

This agreement has spawned several well-known cases in the area of food safety in the WTO. You will recall, for instance, the ban on hormone treated beef instituted by the European Union and struck down by the WTO.[8] Presently, litigation is pending in the WTO as to whether the EU has maintained a WTO-illegal moratorium on the approval of GMOs (genetically modified organisms).[9]

At first blush this may look a like a parallel development. A stricter application of the precautionary principle regarding the marketing of foodstuffs originates with the WTO, at the international level. Then the international rule inspires similar developments at the regional level, by the EFTA Court and the European Court of Justice. So all seems fine and well. Yet if you scratch this surface view a little bit then you quickly realize that not all is well. For one thing, the European Court of Justice earlier on had ruled that the EC's ban on hormone-treated beef was *compatible* with EC law.[10] The WTO's subsequent critical ruling on this ban, came as a rather unwelcome surprise to many in the EC, and still has not been fully digested.[11] This again became quite clear

[7] WTO Agreement on the Application of Sanitary and Phytosanitary Measures, Arts 2.2 and 5.2. See generally D Prevost and P van den Bossche, 'The Agreement on the Application Sanitary and Phytosanitary Measures' in Appleton and Macrory, (eds), *The World Trade Organization: Legal, Economic and Political Analysis* (New York, Springer, 2004).

[8] *EC Measures Concerning Meat and Meat Products (Hormones)*, WT/DS26, 48/AB/R, 13 February 1998 (hereinafter: *EC—Hormones*). Other WTO cases involving the SPS Agreement and the issue of scientific evidence include *Australia—Measures Affecting Importation of Salmon*, WT/DS18/AB/R, 6 November 1998; *Japan—Measures Affecting Agricultural Products*, WT/DS76/AB/R, 19 March 1999; and *Japan—Measures Affecting the Importation of Apples*, WT/DS245/AB/R, 10 December 2003.

[9] *European Communities—Measures Affecting the Approval and Marketing of Biotech Products* (WT/DS291, 292, 293, brought by US, Canada and Argentina). The final Panel report is expected later in 2005.

[10] Case C–331/88 *Fedesa* [1990] ECR I–4023. These different hormone beef-rulings are analysed comparatively by Slotboom, above, n 351.

[11] The EC recently has enacted a new Hormones directive with a view to implement the WTO ruling, which effectively maintains the import ban on hormone-treated beef (Directive 2003/74/EC of the European Parliament and of the Council of 22 September 2003 amending Council Directive 96/22/EC concerning the prohibition on the use in stockfarming of certain substances having a hormonal or thyrostatic action and of beta-agonists, OJ L 262/17, 14 October 2003). The EC is now seeking a ruling from the WTO that this new Directive is WTO-compatible, and that the United

earlier this year, when a draft paper that had been prepared within the Director General for trade at the European Commission was leaked to the Financial Times.[12]

As summarized by the Financial Times, the idea of Commissioner Pascal Lamy's advisers was that WTO Members, like the EU or the EFTA Member States, should be allowed to ban imports from countries with 'collective preferences' different from their own. This should not be seen as protectionism, these advisers argued, but rather as recognition of different social and cultural values that each Member State should be allowed to protect in an age of globalisation. The prime examples given of trade restrictions justified by collective preferences were: the EU's import ban on hormone-treated beef, and the EU's *de facto* ban or moratorium on biotech (GMO–) foods. In other words, these are examples of government intervention implicitly or explicitly based on the precautionary principle.

The FT warned immediately that acceptance of this notion of collective preferences would have dire consequences. It could declare 'an open season' for special interest lobbying on the part of industrial and agricultural sectors that seek protection, under a new name.[13] This concern was echoed, and amplified elsewhere. One commentator noted: 'public opposition to globalisation is likely to grow, as people are asked to sacrifice to economic efficiency their opposition to child labour or their desire to spend their tax dollars in an environmentally friendly manner. If trade debates are framed in that manner, free-trade advocates will lose.'[14]

After much speculation and rumour, Commissioner Lamy finally articulated his thinking in public at a conference in September 2004, where he released a paper on collective preferences.[15]

C. COMMISSIONER LAMY'S PROPOSAL ON COLLECTIVE PREFERENCES IN THE WTO

When national trade barriers were high, international trade did not flow that easily. As a result, the 'ideological content' of goods and services, that is to say

States and Canada are maintaining illegal restrictions on imports from the EC in response to the beef hormone ban (see *Canada—Continued Suspension of Obligations in the EC—Hormones Dispute—Request for Consultations by the European Communities*, WT/DS321/1, G/L/714, 10 November 2004).

[12] G de Jonquières, 'Europe Studies Radical Trade Veto Proposal', *Financial Times*, 5 February 2004.

[13] See Leader, 'Lamy's Big Idea', *Financial Times*, 10 February 2004.

[14] See Stokes, 'New Trade Barriers: National Preferences', *National Journal*, 24 April 2004, p 1276–77.

[15] Lamy, 'The Emergence of Collective Preferences in International Trade: Implications for Regulating Globalisation', paper presented at the conference *Collective Preferences and Global Governance: What future for the Multilateral Trading System*, organized by the European Commission (Brussels, 15 September 2004) [hereinafter: Lamy paper]. http://trade-info.cec.eu.int/doclib/docs/2004/september/tradoc_118,929.pdf (last visited 9 December 2004).

the difference in values they represented was less visible, according to Commissioner Lamy. Now, with lower trade barriers, and increased trade activity, clashes between different values, between different collective preferences occur more frequently and intensely. Differences in values are normally not a problem. They can actually stimulate trade. Yet these differences in values sometimes create tensions that one has to address, that politically cannot remain unresolved. In those circumstances, a country should be entitled to impose trade restrictions and it should not then be accused of protectionism. That country would be trying to reconcile different ideologies.

Again, Commissioner Lamy cited the EC's bans on hormone treated beef and on GMOs as examples of collective preferences. He argued that collective preferences may develop over time, and conceded that they are also not always rational. As an example of a collective preference, he cited food safety: food scandals that occurred in Europe during the last two decades (eg, dioxin, BSE) have influenced European attitudes to food safety. Europeans may well be more cautious about what they eat than, say, North-Americans.

1. The Proposal in Legal Terms

If we translate Commissioner Lamy's thesis into legal terms, he is saying that the WTO agreements did not leave sufficient room for the cautionary approach towards food safety favoured by the EU in the *EC Hormones case*,[16] and that conceivably the EU may yet again draw the short end of the stick in the now pending *GMO* cases. Commissioner Lamy added that he did not want to be misunderstood. With his proposals, he did not seek to upset the liberal trading system. What he was trying to do was to create more support for this system amongst the public at large. To summarize his plea to the public: liberal trade as such is a fine principle, but when we really feel strongly about something, we can still intervene and restrict trade and protect our social choices, our collective preferences.

How does Commissioner Lamy want to do that? He proposes that the WTO should accept the introduction of a new safeguard clause, which would allow a country to restrict trade in order to protect or express deeply held collective preferences. This clause should allow any importing WTO member like the EU to restrict trade unilaterally, in the event the importing country believes that the exporting country in producing the goods adopts public policies that are different from, and unacceptable to, the importing country. Thus, the EU might impose unilateral safeguard restrictions on imports from countries that condone production methods of goods, which the EU considers harmful to health (eg,

[16] One will recall though, that the EU chose not to raise the precautionary principle explicitly provided for in the SPS Agreement (Art 5.7 SPS) in the first Hormones case. Accordingly, the WTO Appellate Body did not reach that issue, although it pointed out that the precautionary principle was implicitly reflected in other SPS provisions as well. See *EC—Hormones*, above, n 356, para 124.

hormone-treated beef) or to the environment (eg, biotech seeds). Whenever an importing country would use this safeguard clause to protect collective preferences through additional trade restrictions, Commissioner Lamy envisages that this country would pay compensation. This proposal should assuage the concerns of the EC's trading partners, by reducing the damage suffered by the exporters concerned.

However, while I appreciate the political concern of Commissioner Lamy, I happen to think that the remedy he proposes, this additional safeguard clause, is misguided. Commissioner Lamy recognized that the 'range of areas in which collective preferences' could trigger the application of a safeguard clause is 'immense'.[17] Yet he submitted that this is no reason for concern as 'different collective preferences usually pose no problem', and that in any case 'it all depends on the conditions attached to the use of the clause'.[18] In his view, the first such condition would be that the country proposing to adopt a safeguard measure conducts an internal review ensuring that (i) the collective preference is well founded rather than unwarranted,[19] (ii) and that the safeguard would not restrict trade more than other measures capable of satisfying the particular collective preference. The second condition, restricting the use of the safeguard clause, would be the obligation on its users to pay compensation to affected exporters.

2. Legal Concerns about This Proposal

My principal concerns about this proposal are threefold.

First, Pascal Lamy's safeguard clause opens the door for an importing country to force its social choices on an exporting country. This raises the prospect that a WTO member like the EU would take extra-territorial measures: measures that have no, or only a tenuous link with the EU's own territory, but that rather seek to change behaviour on foreign markets. That is a very controversial proposition, especially in respect of developing countries that may find it difficult to stand up against such pressures. This concern is particularly acute in the event the values that a powerful importing country seeks to impose on another country are not affirmed in an international convention.

Second, it will be difficult for an international panel to review whether a collective preference espoused by a WTO member to restrict trade is 'well-founded'. This would put the international tribunal in an uncomfortable position, as it would require the tribunal to second-guess a domestically sensitive political judgment. As a result, and this leads me to a third objection, most of the emphasis to constrain the use of the safeguard clause would fall on the

[17] See Lamy paper, p 14.
[18] *Ibid.*
[19] *Ibid*, p 14–15.

compensation requirement. Yet if compensation is the only operational constraint on the exercise of collective preferences, that amounts to saying that countries can 'buy themselves out' of an international obligation. If that were accepted, it would undermine the tenets of a rules-based international trading system, which is based on predictability and equality. Again, developing countries may find it more difficult to 'buy themselves out' of an obligation than richer, more powerful countries. And private operators lose the benefit of a more predictable trading environment if counties can at any time unilaterally choose to deviate from WTO obligations.

Given the seriousness of these objections, I suggest that the proponents of collective preferences think again. They have not made a case that collective preferences necessitate a broad-based exception to liberal trade principles, such as a safeguard clause. If indeed they do no want to jeopardize the liberal trading system as we know it today, but merely seek ways to address certain particularly nettlesome political issues, one can and should think of different, less far-reaching solutions.

3. Alternative Proposals

For example, if the EU is particularly concerned about food safety, and wants to pursue a policy that deviates from agreed WTO principles, then the EU could seek a targeted solution, ie, a waiver from its WTO obligations specifically in respect of its new Hormone—or GMO *régimes* in the event both were held to be WTO—inconsistent in dispute settlement. In other words, if the EU is concerned about a limited number of issues, then a multilateral, tailor-made solution for those issues is preferable to a relatively open-ended, unilateral exception like a safeguards clause.[20]

One other idea would be to make explicit provision that the WTO panels and the Appellate Body cannot only review the WTO agreements (the so-called 'covered agreements'), but also other international agreements that are relevant to a resolving a claim brought under WTO law.[21] This would alleviate political concerns that the WTO is biased in favour of liberal trade, subjugating other

[20] See Art IX3, WTO Agreement. Waiver requests are generally subject to review and approval by ¾ of the WTO membership. Waivers are supposed to be temporary, and are subject to periodic review by the WTO membership, but can remain in existence for quite a long time. For examples of waivers see General Council—Annual Report (2003), 6 January 2004, WT/GC/76, p 6–7. In practice, compensation may have to be offered by the waiver-seeking country in order to obtain sufficient support amongst the WTO membership.

[21] This would require an amendment of Art 3.2 DSU. Some have argued forcefully on technical grounds that other international agreements can already be taken into account in WTO dispute settlement. See, notably, J Pauwelyn, *Conflict of Norms in Public International Law—How WTO Law Relates to other Rules of International Law* 440 *et seq* (Cambridge, CUP, 2003). Yet an amendment to the DSU is preferable, if only because it inspires more confidence amongst the general public than technical solutions proposed by experts that are more difficult to verify and that would need to be tested in a series of cases.

values. The challenge here would be to verify that the international agreements in which such other values have been incorporated (eg, labour and environmental agreements) can be considered to be as binding and enforceable as the WTO obligations that would arguably oppose them. In other words, it may well be that governments (or certain ministries) have found it relatively easy to enter into a number of international conventions as they anticipated that any obligations flowing from these rules would never be enforced as rigorously as WTO obligations are.

Admittedly, these two particular solutions do not expand the possibilities a WTO Member already has to take unilateral action to pursue public policies under the WTO agreements.[22] Indeed, my preference would be to look for additional, multilateral solutions first. I have indicated just two examples. There may well be other, legally manageable, solutions to address the political concerns about collective preferences raised by Commissioner Lamy.

4. Are Collective Preferences a Temporary Phenomenon?

Rather than addressing Mr Lamy's proposals, however, one might also choose to sit back and wait, hoping that this problem of collective preferences will simply blow over. Yet I do not think that this problem will disappear.

Not only Pascal Lamy, but also his predecessor Sir Leon Brittan, expressed the political need for something 'extra' to persuade European citizens that the liberal trading framework is still a good idea. Sir Leon did so already some 10 years ago. He felt then that there was a need to show to the general public that open trade policies are fair, notably by addressing the exploitation of child labour.[23] Commissioner Lamy arrived at a similar conclusion by calling attention to collective preferences, although he emphasized different examples, notably in the food safety area. If Pascal Lamy, and his predecessor, Sir Leon Brittan, who each have come from a different political spectrum, see the need to improve the appeal of liberal trade based on their hard won experiences as trade negotiators, their plea cannot be easily dismissed. What we have to take on board as lawyers is that people who have to sell the message of liberal trade come back to us and say: we cannot do it on the basis of the rules that we have here, we need something extra.

Therefore, my submission to you is that this debate on collective preferences will not go away. The new European Commissioner for External Trade, Peter

[22] For an example of such a unilateral action in the environmental area against other WTO Members, see the ultimate approval by the WTO Appellate Body of a US measure restricting imports of shrimp caught by third countries with nets that killed sea turtles too. See *United States—Import Prohibition of Certain Shrimp and Shrimp Products*, Recourse to Art 21.5 of the DSU by Malaysia, WT/DS58/AB/RW, 21 November 2001.

[23] See L Brittan, 'How to Make Trade Liberalisation Popular' (1995) 18(6) *World Economy* 761–67.

Mandelson, may come up with a new term, but the concern of his predecessors will probably remain with him.

D. HOW ABOUT INTRA-EUROPEAN COLLECTIVE PREFERENCES?

This brings me to my final point. I have tried to give you a window on the world, by calling attention to a debate the EU has launched in respect of its trading partners in the WTO, which implicates the precautionary principle. Yet I believe this debate, about what are more broadly referred to as collective preferences, can also be relevant to the more European-oriented debate at this symposium.

One of the other earlier speakers today, Professor Müller-Graff, has argued that more respect for diversity may create more homogeneity, more mutual understanding. Professor Müller-Graf was speaking about intra-European trade relations. Set in the key of Pascal Lamy's proposals, this almost sounds like a plea to recognize collective preferences as grounds for additional (trade) restrictions within the European Union. Yet the concern about collective preferences within the EU has not led to the same level of political controversy as it has within the broader framework of the WTO.

We have had concerns in the past, notably when the EU enlarged, that the new member states were working with different standards, different social standards (consider the accession of Portugal for instance), and that the existing Member States needed some extra protection within the European integration model.[24] What I find interesting is that we have not heard that so much in connection with the most recent enlargement of the EU to 25 countries. Why is it that in the Union of 25, with undeniable differences in values, we do not see a similar, focused demand for exceptions to liberal trade to protect these differences?

While the key EU Treaty rules about liberal trade are very similar to the provisions of the old GATT agreement, both systems have developed into different institutions. In the EU, for instance, we have harmonization instruments, legislative measures, at our disposal to iron out divergences between collective preferences.[25] Furthermore, the EU courts are quite creative, and have come up with so-called 'mandatory requirements' as unwritten, judge-made exceptions to liberal trade principles to which an EU member can appeal to protect its

[24] See A Sapir, 'Trade Liberalization and the Harmonization of Social Policies: Lessons from European Integration' in JN Bhagwati and RE Hudec (eds), *Fair Trade and Harmonization: Prerequisites for Free Trade?* (Cambridge, MA, MIT Press, 1996) 543–70.

[25] Note that the EC Treaty (in Art 95.5) allows individual Member States to take additional restrictions in the areas of the environment, if they have science-based concerns that go beyond harmonizing measures at the EU level. See more generally on the role of science in EC risk regulation T Christoforou, 'The Precautionary Principle and Democratizing Expertise: A European Legal Perspective' (2003) 30(3) *Science & Public Policy* 205–11; and IS Forrester, 'The Dangers of Too Much Precaution' in Hoskins and Robinson (eds), *A True European, Essays for Judge David Edward* (Oxford, Hart Publishing, 2003) 203–31.

collective preferences in the absence of EU harmonization measures. One might also expect fewer concerns about differing social values, different collective preferences, amongst the EU of 25, or the EEA of 28, because politically these blocs of countries constitute a more cohesive group.

Contrast this with the WTO. In the WTO there is no legislative instrument, other than new treaties, that could help to harmonize differences between collective preferences. Furthermore, the jurisprudence of WTO panels and notably of the WTO Appellate Body has shown that these tribunals are very much text-oriented. Accordingly, the idea that the WTO Appellate Body might create a 'mandatory requirement' to justify trade restrictions that cannot be found in the text of the WTO agreements would strike many people with horror. At the same time, the WTO currently numbers 148 members amongst whom the social values or collective preferences probably diverge more widely than amongst the EU or EEA-countries.

Do these differences between the EU and the WTO fully explain why the precautionary principle, as it was adopted by the EFTA Court and later on by the European Court, in the area of food safety, has created less resistance? I doubt it.

When we talk about food safety and the precautionary principle, we are talking about an area where there is no harmonization, either within the EU or within the EEA. Furthermore, as illustrated by the cases I have discussed in the beginning, the European courts have not introduced new flexibilities in the area of food safety. On the contrary, starting with *Kellogg's*, the European courts have been saying to Member States that they have to be more careful before they introduce trade restrictions when they want to take precautionary measures. And what about political cohesion? You will recall that the debates that we are having on the precautionary principle within the WTO are debates notably with our transatlantic partner the United States. Is it really true that we, for example here in Luxembourg, are less trustful about the food that is coming from the United States, than about the food which is coming from the new EU Member States?

Another explanation of why the precautionary principle as applied to food safety has created less controversy within the EU than within the WTO is probably the type of issues that were before the European Courts: cornflakes fortified or cranberry juice enriched with vitamins, compared to hormone treated beef or biotech food in the WTO. The WTO has had to deal with politically more explosive issues than the European Courts.

I think there may be yet another explanation. One likes to say that politics is the art of the possible, but I also believe that judging is an art. It is an art for international judges to know when they can resolve controversial disputes, when to seize the right moment and the right case to enforce a new constraint on the autonomy of Member States. And I believe that the relatively smooth acceptance of the precautionary principle in the food safety area within the EU also reflects the talent of the courts that have pronounced themselves on this issue, to begin with the talent of the EFTA Court. For that reason as well, I join the ranks of those who have already congratulated the Members of this Court today.

E. DISCUSSIONS

THORGEIR ÖRLYGSSON

Thank you very much, Dr. Bronckers, for your excellent presentation. I have somewhat the feeling that Professor Müller-Graff wants to comment on some of your statements. Am I right?

PETER-CHRISTIAN MÜLLER-GRAFF

Only a very short remark on your comment on the relationship or comparison between WTO law on the one side, and European market law on the other side. One has always to keep in mind that these are two different normative frameworks. I concur that WTO law is not too rigid for taking up what is called mandatory requirements in EC law. This is true for provisions of the GATT, SPS and TBT. Problems can be handled, if one likes to handle them in this way, by panels and the Appellate Body. In this respect, my suggestion has always been to inspire the relevant GATT articles, SPS provisions and TBT rules by the jurisprudence of the European Courts in this matter, which, of course, also implies to inspire them to draw this distinction between economic and non-economic interests. When you mentioned this proposal concerning collective preferences, one gets the idea that perhaps a clear borderline between economic and non-economic interests is lacking, and this may have caused your mis-feelings about this proposal. However, one should always keep in mind the difference of the legal frameworks. On the WTO level no empowerment exists to approximate different national laws. This implies that there is no means available except a new treaty to overcome justified restrictions. If, in the interpretation of WTO articles, the conclusion is drawn that a measure constitutes a justified restriction, then it can be overcome only in the next Round of negotiations. One has to keep this in mind and this might perhaps generate a structural tendency in the WTO to be a bit more sceptical and strict towards accepting justifications and exceptions.

PROFESSOR MARCO BRONCKERS

Your comments are useful. I would only add one or two words of caution.

In my experience, pleading before GATT panels and the Appellate Body which consist primarily of non-Europeans, it is not necessarily viewed very well if you rely too much on European case-law to tell them what is what. Furthermore, if your clients are non-European governments they may not want you to rely too much on your European heritage either.

There is also a major difference between the interpretation of WTO law and European law. The people who sit on WTO tribunals are constrained in two important ways. Compared to European Courts' judgments one notices the almost fanatical devotion to textual arguments in WTO dispute settlement. Consequently, the idea of enlarging the public policy exceptions set forth in Article XX GATT, for example, by introducing unwritten 'mandatory requirements' would fill the WTO members with horror. Furthermore, according to the text of the WTO dispute settlement understanding, panels and the Appellate Body can only review claims on the basis of what are called the 'covered agreements'. This term of 'covered agreements', refers to the WTO agreements. As I have said in my presentation, I find this limitation unfortunate. It makes it difficult for WTO panels and the Appellate Body to look beyond the WTO agreements, to look at other international conventions. I therefore believe that those who are concerned about collective preferences have a point when they say we have to do something and improve the current framework, because this does not necessarily inspire confidence amongst NGOs, amongst the general public, that the WTO is able and willing to consider properly social choices that go beyond liberal trade.

THORGEIR ÖRLYGSSON

Somebody has raised his hand; would you please introduce yourself?

IAN FORRESTER

My name is Ian Forrester. I am a practitioner in Brussels, and a teacher. I would like to suggest that there is a spectrum of possibilities for a rule-making government agency. At one extreme it may say 'We wish to ban this product because we disapprove of it. We do not really like it, it is not quite natural and maybe it will do harm'. And at the other extreme, it may say 'We ban this product because it presents a guaranteed, certain danger to public health'. That is a very broad spectrum, yet European Union bans upon products have been initiated from various points along it. I think we are very fortunate that the Special K cornflakes case, a rather easy case, was the first to come to the EFTA Court. It is not difficult to see in a ban of Kellogg's cornflakes something a bit irrational and something a bit excessive. The greater challenge will come when the EFTA Court has to examine much more difficult questions which have to be examined on the basis of science, rather than emotion. And in that context, one question which is yet to be addressed by the EFTA Court, which has been addressed already by the Community Courts, is whether the setting of the acceptable standard of risk is a political act or a scientific act. Is it a matter of public policy or is it a matter of scientifically analyzed prudence? And I observe that we may see a contrast between what Europe does internally and what Europe says externally. So for international trade purposes Europe says, and I am grossly exaggerating and oversimplifying and being maybe unfair, we want to ban on moral grounds as opposed to the Americans, who say we should only ban on scientific grounds. So, I observe that if we look at the *internal* jurisprudence of the three courts in Luxembourg, we may detect a greater rigor in insisting that, with respect to food bans for example, governmental actions which hinder trade should be justified by verifiable scientific grounds, whereas in *external* matters we are ready to prohibit things which we basically do not like on grounds which are arguable morally, but are not arguable scientifically. And therefore it is intriguing, I submit, to consider the consequences, if I am right, of the fact that Europe is not doing internally what Europe is recommending externally.

PIERRE PESCATORE

I am quite surprised that whenever the discussion concerns the rules of GATT, everybody quotes Article XX and nobody ever takes note of the existence of Article III. The last intervention is liable to that remark and this brings me to the well known 'hormones litigation'. In this case, the US and Canada complained about restriction on marketing which had been indistinctly applied by the Community in its own market and on imports. It fell, therefore, under Article III of GATT the basis of which is national treatment. Article III of GATT does not require more than treating imports on the same footing as a country's own production. So, if there was an import ban on hormones, for whatever reasons—sanitary reasons or simply commercial reasons—the United States and Canada could not claim more than to be treated on the basis of the national treatment standard. In the adjudication of the GATT (WTO at panel level and also at level of the appellate body), this issue was completely dodged. They did not even take note of the existence of Article III, turning instead to a particular agreement on sanitary measures annexed to the GATT Agreement. To say it in other words, the ban on sale of hormone meat was a policy option established for anybody concerned on equal terms, ie, for domestic producers and for importers alike, and not a matter of undue discrimination.

PROFESSOR MARCO BRONCKERS

I am very appreciative of Professor Pescatore's remarks, but he has as we all know, contributed significantly to the European Court's development of the principles concerning free movement of goods. What may be less known to this audience is that he has also been a GATT panellist. In the late 1980s, he sat on a case, known as the *Section 337* case, which made an important contribution to the case-law on Article III GATT, the GATT's national treatment principle to which Professor Pescatore refers.

Professor Pescatore now calls attention to this principle of Article III, and its relevance to evaluating so-called 'indistinctly applicable' measures, of which the EC Hormones ban would be an example. He argues rightly that Article III itself may tolerate certain 'indistinctly applicable' measures, so that one would not have to reach the public policy exceptions of Article XX GATT. However, the rulings of the WTO panel and WTO Appellate Body only concerned the SPS Agreement, the WTO's Agreement on sanitary and phytosanitary measures.[26] The SPS Agreement contains an additional obligation beyond Article III GATT, which says that indistinctly applicable measures, falling within that Agreement's scope, still have to have some scientific justification. And if such scientific justification is lacking, then even an indistinctly applicable measure can be challenged. This, I submit, is the reason why the United States never brought the Hormones case in the 1980s when the ban was first introduced by the EC, but waited until after the negotiations on the SPS Agreement in the Uruguay Round had been concluded in 1994.With this agreement the United States had this additional standard that they could rely on, and which they ultimately successfully did.

INGE LORANGE BACKER

I am not going to engage myself in the last discussion, but otherwise my intervention is basically a follow-up of what has already been said. I think that there are two sides of the coin as regards the *Kellogg's* decision. One side, which I presume is the more important, is the legal recognition of the precautionary principle in EEA law. The other side, of course, is that the precautionary principle in the actual case did not justify the measures taken in the national jurisdiction. And from the latter point of view, of course, if the Danes could survive on fortified Kellogg's cornflakes, the natural hypothesis surely would be that Norwegians also could. But that is a kind of assessment which could easily be different with regard to the precautionary principle under other circumstances, if more unknown factors, novel substances or novel products are involved, or if more serious threats are involved than the one which was probably the case with regard to the cornflakes. And that brings me to conclude that the EFTA Court by this decision has taken the first, and only the first, but nevertheless an important step in developing the precautionary principle. It has to be supplemented by

[26] To be precise, the United States and Canada in their initial WTO-complaint against the EC Hormones ban argued that this ban violated both the SPS Agreement as well as Art III GATT. The WTO panel started its analysis with reviewing the ban under the SPS Agreement, and found that the ban violated this Agreement. Having found this violation, the panel exercised judicial economy and did not rule on the US and Canadian complaints under Art III. None of the parties appealed or cross-appealed the panel's refusal to rule on Art III. Accordingly, only the panel's interpretation of the SPS Agreement was before the WTO Appellate Body on appeal, and the Appellate Body report made only tangential reference to Art III GATT (in connection with its interpretation of the SPS Agreement).

future cases where one should also pay due regard to the use of the precautionary principle in various environmental treaties, where it has its foundation, as is well known. That is, I think, a necessary answer to the really big challenge facing us both at the European and at the global level, namely to bring about a sustainable development. For that reason, we do need a legal workshop, which gives room for jurisdictions to find the legal ways to bring about sustainable developments and accordingly, I would certainly subscribe to the final conclusion made by the speaker. Thank you, Mr Chairman.

THORGEIR ÖRLYGSSON

Thank you Mr Bronckers for your excellent presentation once again. Since we are a little bit behind the time schedule, we have to break now for lunch. I want to thank President Baudenbacher for his excellent introductory remarks; I want to thank our guest speakers for their contributions, and finally I want to thank the audience for its contributions to the discussions. Thank you.

II. Homogeneity as a Fundamental Principle of Economic and Legal Spaces

PER TRESSELT

Vassilios Skouris became President of the European Court of Justice after four years of service as a judge. We already know that he will be remembered as the President who effortlessly guided the Court through its breath-taking enlargement. He has formidable qualifications for that particular task. Firstly, his cultural formation is neither Roman-Catholic nor Protestant, secondly he has brilliant academic careers in two very different intellectual environments and thirdly he has twice served as his country's Minister of Home Affairs. We are much honoured that he will address us on the subject of the ECJ and the EFTA Court under the EEA Agreement and he has added an enticing subtitle, a paradigm for international cooperation between judicial institutions.

The ECJ and the EFTA Court under the EEA Agreement: A Paradigm for International Cooperation between Judicial Institutions

VASSILIOS SKOURIS

A. INTRODUCTION

ONE OF THE essential characteristics of the European continent at the beginning of the 21st century is the parallel existence of national states and supranational structures that are 'equipped' with systems of judicial enforcement. As far as the latter are concerned, I am referring principally to the European Union (hereinafter the 'EU'), the European Economic Area (hereinafter the 'EEA') and the European Convention on Human Rights (hereinafter the 'ECHR'). Indeed, one could even suggest that this is a worldwide trend, especially if we take a closer look at similar efforts in the African continent and Latin America. The inevitable result of the parallel existence of such systems is that national and international courts are quite often called upon to interpret similar or identical provisions of law. Although it is true that the development of conflicting case-law between judicial institutions functioning in distinct legal orders on the one hand, and judicial institutions operating within the same legal order on the other, is not equally problematic, it also clear that, especially in Europe, a certain degree of case-law uniformity is of the essence even at the international level.

When invited to address the conference on the occasion of the EFTA Court's 10th anniversary, I chose to view the ECJ and the EFTA Court from a more general perspective and to submit some thoughts on the international cooperation of judicial institutions by using the rapport between the ECJ and the EFTA Court as a paradigm.

It is a well-known fact that EU law to be interpreted by the ECJ and the EEA law to be interpreted by the EFTA Court are largely identical. In addition, given the two pillar structure of the EEA, the emergence of conflicting case-law between the ECJ and the EFTA Court could have disastrous consequences. Hence, a series of safeguards were put in place in order to ensure the principal objective of the EEA agreement: homogeneity. In the course of this short article, I will briefly outline these safeguards and attempt to illustrate, with a few examples, how they have worked in practice during the last 10 years. I will then focus my attention on the need for further international cooperation between judicial institutions in Europe and explain why, in my view, the relationship between the ECJ and the EFTA Court can serve as a good example of such cooperation.

B. THE ECJ AND THE EFTA COURT: ACHIEVING HOMOGENEITY

When seeking ways of achieving homogeneity and coherence in the case-law of two international courts one has to first explore whether it is possible to achieve that by statutory means. In the case of the ECJ and the EFTA Court that was possible since both the EU and EFTA countries are party to the EEA agreement. I am of course referring to Article 6 of the EEA Agreement and Article 3, paragraph 2, of the Surveillance and Court Agreement. According to these provisions, the EFTA Court is, on the one hand, bound to follow the ECJ precedents for the period prior to the signing of the EEA Agreement (2 May 1992) and, on the other hand, required to pay due account to the principles laid down by the relevant rulings by the ECJ rendered after that date. These provisions concern either the interpretation of the EEA Agreement itself, or of such rules of EU law in so far as they are identical in substance to the provisions of the EEA Agreement.

It is interesting to note that, according to the wording of these provisions, the duty of the EFTA Court with regard to respecting the ECJ case-law may be different based on whether that case-law was established before or after the signing of the EEA agreement. It can certainly be argued that an obligation to follow a precedent is not the same as the obligation to pay due account to a precedent. Nevertheless, it does not seem that the EFTA Court has treated the ECJ case-law differently depending on when the pertinent judgements were rendered.

The reasons are twofold, yet quite simple. First, jurisprudence is something dynamic and constantly evolving. Case-law on a particular issue of EU or EEA law often does not derive from one judgment only, but from a series of judgments rendered over a long period of time. Second, one has to take into account that the context in which the ECJ and the EFTA Court are interpreting identical provisions of law is not the same. Thus, the concepts of being bound by a precedent and having to take due account of a precedent automatically become relative. We can certainly imagine instances where pre-May 1992 ECJ case-law might have to be adapted in order to be applied in the EEA context. Conversely, there can also be instances where post-May 1992 ECJ case-law cannot but be considered as binding also in the EEA context.

These statutory provisions seem to impose one-sided obligations on the EFTA Court. This could be true in theory but in practice they have proven to provide an adequate framework in order to achieve a harmonious coexistence between the ECJ and the EFTA Court. In fact, avoiding conflicting case-law and developing coherent jurisprudence are tasks that require constant cooperation and vigilance from all institutions involved. The day-to-day practice of the ECJ and the EFTA Court clearly illustrates that statement.

As far as the EFTA Court is concerned,[1] few, if any, would disagree that it has fulfilled its statutory obligations and respected the ECJ precedents throughout its 10-year existence. However, it has done much more than that. Although its obligations with regard to respecting the ECJ case-law only concerned either the rules of the EEA Agreement or EU law provisions that find their identical counterpart within the EEA context, the EFTA Court was inspired by the fundamental doctrines of Community law, as developed in the ECJ jurisprudence, and established equivalent groundbreaking case-law within its area of competence. The celebrated *Sveinbjörnsdóttir*[2] judgment, where the EFTA Court recognised that the EEA agreement is a *sui generis* international treaty that contains a distinct legal order and, more importantly, ruled that the principle of State liability was an inherent part of EEA law, is a perfect example. It is noteworthy that this ruling was subsequently acknowledged by the ECJ in the *Rechberger* judgment.[3]

As far as the ECJ is concerned, I have already mentioned that it does not have a statutory obligation to follow or pay due account to the case-law of the EFTA Court. Nevertheless, ignoring EFTA Court precedents would simply be incompatible with the overriding objective of the EEA agreement which is homogeneity. Conscious of that fact, the ECJ has contributed to the fulfilment of that objective by taking under consideration the EFTA Court case-law although, in most cases, it has not done so expressly.

However, the ECJ was recently faced with a series of cases concerning the conditions under which Member States could prevent the production or marketing of enriched foodstuffs on the basis of public health concerns. To be more specific, in Case C–192/01, *Commission v Denmark*,[4] the Commission sought from the Court a declaration that, by applying an administrative practice which entailed that enriched foodstuffs lawfully produced or marketed in other Member States may be marketed in Denmark only if it were shown that such enrichment with nutrients met a need in the Danish population, the Kingdom of Denmark had failed to fulfil its obligations under Article 28 of the EC Treaty.

[1] For a detailed analysis of the EFTA Court's handling of ECJ precedents see, among others, C Baudenbacher, 'The EFTA Court and the European Court' in P-C Müller-Graff and E Selvig (eds), *EEA–EU Relations* (Berlin, Berlin Verlag Arno Spitz GmbH, 1999) 69.

[2] Case E–7/07 *Sveinbjörnsdóttir* [1998] EFTA Ct Rep 127.

[3] Case C–140/97 *Rechberger ea* [1999] ECR I–3499.

[4] Case C–192/01 *Commission v Denmark* [2003] ECR I–9693.

In a landmark judgment, the ECJ consolidated its previous case-law in that field and established a test in order to balance free movement of goods and public health concerns in the area of enriched foodstuffs where scientific data are mostly insufficient and inconclusive. In doing so, the ECJ cited no less than 6 times in its reasoning the EFTA Court's case-law on the issue as it results from Case E–3/00, *EFTA Surveillance Authority v Norway*.[5]

The ECJ does not of course always follow pertinent EFTA Court case-law and it is not supposed to do so. To cite one example, in *Silhouette*,[6] the ECJ did not follow the EFTA Court case-law on the exhaustion of trade marks under directive 89/104/EEC. In that case, Advocate General Jacobs explained quite convincingly in his opinion why the differences in scope between the EEA Agreement and the EC Treaty justified that result.

But achieving homogeneity requires much more than paying due account to case-law and precedents. It also requires taking under consideration the effective realisation of the EEA Agreement's objectives. The *Ospelt*[7] case is a perfect illustration. It concerned restrictions imposed by an Austrian law on real estate transactions relating to agricultural and forestry plots. The question was essentially whether EEA States were 'third countries' within the meaning of Article 73c of the EC Treaty and consequently whether such restrictions on the free movement of capital could be imposed on transactions involving nationals of EEA States. The ECJ first considered that

> one of the principal aims of the EEA Agreement is to provide for the fullest possible realisation of the free movement of goods, persons, services and capital within the whole European Economic Area, so that the internal market established within the European Union is extended to the EFTA States. From that angle, several provisions of the abovementioned Agreement are intended to ensure as uniform an interpretation as possible thereof throughout the EEA. It is for the Court, in that context, to ensure that the rules of the EEA Agreement which are identical in substance to those of the Treaty are interpreted uniformly within the Member States.

The ECJ then went on to state that

> [i]t would run counter to that objective as to uniformity of application of the rules relating to free movement of capital within the EEA for a State such as the Republic of Austria, which is a party to that Agreement, which entered into force on 1 January 1994, to be able, after its accession to the European Union on 1 January 1995, to maintain legislation which restricts that freedom vis-à-vis another State party to that Agreement by basing itself on Article 73c of the Treaty.

In conclusion, few would argue against the statement that ECJ and the EFTA Court have gone to great lengths in order to achieve homogeneity and ensuring the efficient coexistence of the EEA Agreement and the EC Treaty system. In

[5] Case E–3/00 *EFTA Surveillance Authority v Norway* [2000–01] EFTA Ct Rep 73.
[6] Case C–355/96 *Silhouette International Schmied* [1998] ECR I–4799.
[7] Case C–452/01 *Ospelt and Schlössle Weissenberg* [2003] ECR I–9743.

fact, they were quite successful in doing so and there is no reason to doubt that this form of cooperation will continue to function effectively in the future.

C. THE NEED FOR COOPERATION BETWEEN JUDICIAL INSTITUTIONS IN EUROPE

The European Union has just completed the most significant enlargement in its history. Another enlargement is set to take place most probably in 2007. The Council of Europe has relatively recently also experienced a significant enlargement. It now includes 46 Member States. As European integration progresses at the EU level and as European nations in general purport to establish closer links amongst them, cooperation at the judiciary level becomes all the more important. I would like to illustrate this with two examples.

The first one concerns the field of the protection of fundamental rights. As far as the 25 Member States of the EU are concerned, there are three parallel systems for the protection of fundamental rights which are applicable: national constitutions, the ECHR and the EU system of protection which soon, we hope, will include a legally binding Charter. It would probably be superfluous to elaborate on the fact that a multitude of sources of law with sometimes overlapping fields of application is certainly not efficient and can be the source of confusion for private individuals, lawyers and judges. The range of the protected rights and the level of protection can be different from one text to another. The risk of conflicting case-law between ECJ on the one hand and national supreme courts and the European Court of Human Rights (hereinafter the 'EurCourtHR') on the other is always present.[8]

Avoiding conflicting case-law, and different standards of protection of fundamental rights, will undoubtedly require vigilance and close cooperation between all the judicial institutions involved. The ECJ and the EurCourtHR have a few years ago embarked on such an effort by organising relatively frequent meetings and exchanges of view. An initiative was also taken recently in order to organise similar exchanges between the ECJ and the European Committee on Social Rights.

The second example concerns the EU alone. The Treaty establishing a Constitution for Europe was signed on 29 October 2004. I do not believe that a completely new constitutional legal order will emerge as a result of this Treaty simply because, even within its current legal framework, the EU is to a large extent a constitutional legal order. Nevertheless, it is a clear indication that European integration evolves and progresses dynamically. Hence, uniform

[8] For a more complete analysis of the problems arising from the parallel application of three systems of protection of fundamental rights see Skouris, 'Introducing a Binding Bill of Rights for the European Union: Can Three Parallel Systems of Protection of Fundamental Rights Coexist Harmoniously?' in *Verfassung im Diskurs der Welt, Liber Amicorum für Peter Häberle* (Mohr Siebeck, 2004) 261–73.

interpretation of EU law throughout the Union becomes even more essential. Achieving this uniformity is not an easy task especially in a European Union of 25 Member States, 25 national legal systems, 25 national legal traditions and much more than 50 national supreme courts.

In that respect, the preliminary reference procedure certainly provides a formidable statutory framework for institutional dialogue between national courts and the ECJ. However, tensions between the case-law of the ECJ and that of national supreme or constitutional courts can always arise and have actually arisen in the past both on minor and major issues. The question of Kompetenz-Kompetenz and the famous Solange and Maastricht judgments of the German Bundesverfassungsgericht are certainly pertinent in that respect.[9] Therefore, promoting and strengthening the cooperation between the ECJ and national supreme and constitutional courts even outside the confined boundaries of the preliminary reference procedure will be essential for the efficient functioning of the EU legal order and the furthering of European integration.

D. THE ECJ AND THE EFTA COURT: A PARADIGM FOR INTERNATIONAL COOPERATION BETWEEN JUDICIAL INSTITUTIONS?

The two examples presented above clearly illustrate the need for the cooperation of judicial institutions especially in Europe where a number of supranational structures and legal orders are required to coexist. It is also clear that the rapport between the ECJ and the EFTA Court and their cooperation over the last 10 years has been very successful. Could this model of cooperation be applied on a more general scale in Europe? Can the relationship between these two Courts be used as a paradigm for the cooperation of judicial institutions at an international level?

It could be argued quite convincingly that the context in which the ECJ and the EFTA Court have been operating has many particularities and therefore this model of cooperation cannot be applied on a larger scale. First of all, the rapport between the ECJ and the EFTA Court is essentially on a bilateral level. Second, both courts have similar areas of competence within their respective legal orders. Third, there are specific statutory provisions aimed at achieving the harmonisation of the case-law of the EFTA Court and the ECJ. Last, the seat of both courts is in the Grand Duchy of Luxembourg.

Notwithstanding those obvious specificities characterising the relationship between the ECJ and the EFTA Court, I would nevertheless suggest that the

[9] This debate on judicial *Kompetenz-Kompetenz* is encountered in its liveliest form in Schilling, 'The Autonomy of the Community Legal Order—An Analysis of Possible Foundations' (1996) 37 *Harvard Intl L J* 389 and JHH Weiler and U Haltern, 'Constitutional or International? The Foundations of the Community Legal Order and the Question of Judicial *Kompetenz-Kompetenz*' in A-M Slaughter, *et al* (eds), *The European Court and National Courts—Doctrine and Jurisprudence* (Oxford, Hart Publishing, 1998).

ECJ-EFTA Court model of cooperation can serve as a more general paradigm of institutional dialogue between judicial institutions. In my view, the reasons for the successful cooperation between the ECJ and the EFTA Court lie far beyond the similarity of their competences, the pertinent statutory provisions or the geographic proximity of their seat. The success of the ECJ-EFTA Court model of cooperation resulted primarily from the fact that these two institutions have managed, through consistent efforts, to attain a very high level of mutual understanding which allowed them not only to accomplish homogeneity and coherence in their case-law, but also to further develop their jurisprudence.

Achieving such a high level of mutual understanding of the position and case-law of each court involved is the key to the successful cooperation of judicial institutions. It is of course true that this task is much more complicated when cooperation is sought at a multilateral and international level. However, by its very nature, a paradigm has to be simple. In that sense, I believe that the cooperation of the ECJ and the EFTA Court over the last ten years and the results it produced constitute a true paradigm for international cooperation between judicial institutions.

PER TRESSELT

Thank you, Mr President, for your important statement. The organizers have not foreseen that there would be a grilling of the President after his statement, so I will go on to our next speaker, Justice Karl Arne Utgård, who has been a member of the Supreme Court of Norway since 1999. In addition to the required training phase as a deputy judge in a district court, he has had his pupilage as an Advocate in the Chambers of the Attorney General for Civil Affairs during the 10 years of the EFTA Court's second president Mr Bjørn Haug, who is with us also this afternoon. Mr Utgård was appointed a Justice of the Supreme Court directly from a distinguished practice at the bar. He will speak on the operation of the rules of civil procedure in relation to the goal of homogeneity for the substantive rules governing the single market.

Procedural Aspects of Homogeneity: International Coordination and Harmonisation in the Area of Civil Procedure, Particularly within the European Economic Area (EEA)

KARL ARNE UTGÅRD

A. INTRODUCTION

MAY I START by extending my thanks for the invitation to take part in the celebration of the 10th anniversary of the EFTA Court. There can be no doubt that this Court has made its presence felt through its quality and its strength. It has rendered key normative decisions on the understanding of the rules of the EEA, as well as on the fundamental relationship between the EEA rules and national law. The decade on which we are now looking back witnessed an unparalleled development in the use by Norway and the other EFTA States of international sources of law in their national legal orders. The EFTA Court has played a central role in this process.

It is no secret that the Norwegian people remain divided on the question of Norway's future ties to the European Union, and I am therefore not entirely certain as to whether I should give the EFTA Court my best wishes for the next ten years. It might perhaps be better to turn to a subject that is unquestionably of major common European interest, namely procedural aspects of homogeneity within the civil procedure law. I will confine my comments to issues of certain relevance to the European Economic Area, rather than considering the questions in a broader international perspective.

B. EXISTING NATIONAL CIVIL PROCEDURE LAWS

With the exception of matters regulated by the Brussels and Lugano Conventions and certain other strictly delimited areas of law, there is no uniform civil procedure within the European Economic Area. Civil procedure has grown out of the historical, social and political conditions in the individual state. The right to organise the courts and, accordingly, procedures conducted before these courts, has generally been viewed as part of national supremacy. True, in times past studies were made of the civil procedure of other countries, contributing to the development of domestic legislation. But it is unlikely that the legislators ever thought that it might be necessary to coordinate these rules, or to have fairly similar regulation. Nor has emphasis been placed on such harmonisation in case law.

Over the last decades, a number of new European civil procedure laws have been introduced. Of these, the legislation in England and Wales that came into force in 1999 has attracted particular interest. Although the legislation is based on common law, it is nevertheless remarkable that in such a recent reform little emphasis seems to have been placed on finding solutions that might contribute to the achievement of a common European legal situation.[1] In my own country a report has been published on a new statute in this area, but here again there seems to be little emphasis on international coordination.[2]

It is probably true to say that certain underlying goals were defined in advance of the revisions in the United Kingdom and the report in Norway, for example the requirement that cases should be effectuated quickly, the establishment of a separate track for small claims, and that proceedings should not spread beyond the area that the dispute provides specific grounds for a proportionality requirement. Obviously, in both cases every effort was made to safeguard commitments under international conventions, not least in relation to EU/EEA law and the European Convention on Human Rights.

C. DEVELOPMENTS IN LAW INTERNATIONALLY

1. Developments within the European Union

(a) The Development of Rules

Within the EU attempts have been made to achieve more or less full harmonisation in the area of civil procedure. In 1987, a working party was established—known as the Storme Group—comprising one legal expert on procedure from

[1] Access to Justice, Final Report by Lord Woolf, July 1996, http://www.dca.gov.uk/civil/final/index.html.

[2] Norwegian Official Report 2001: 32 vols A and B. The legislative committee was chaired by the then Supreme Court Justice—now Chief Justice, Tore Schei. The Report is also available on the Internet. Part IV is an English version of 'Draft statute' which can be found at http://odin.dep.no/jd/norsk/publ/utredninger/NOU/12,001–20,015/hov064–bn.html.

There is also an extensive summary in English, 'Brief Summary and Overview of the Report' at http://odin.dep.no/jd/norsk/publ/utredninger/NOU/12,001–20,015/hov065–bn.html.

each member state. The objective was to establish a 'European Judicial Code', and an extensive report was presented to the Commission at the end of 1993/beginning of 1994 in which the civil procedure systems of the EU states and the scope for harmonisation were discussed. However, the report brought to light the many differences between the legal cultures and procedural traditions within Europe. Neither the Commission nor the EU states themselves have taken steps to continue the work of the Storme Group or to develop the ideas and possibilities presented in the report. It was only with the conclusion of the Treaty of Amsterdam in 1997 that coordination of the rules of civil procedure became a goal for the European Union. This was followed up at a meeting organised by the European Council in Tampere in October 1999. The most recent document relating to this issue is a communication from the Commission to the Council and the European Parliament dated 2 June 2004.[3] One of the objectives defined in this document was to:

> 2.6 Establish a European judicial area respecting the legal traditions and systems of the Member States . . .

The document continues:

> The development of the European judicial area has neither the object nor the effect of challenging the legal and judicial traditions of the Member States. . . . The principle of mutual recognition has been placed at the heart of European integration in this field.
>
> However, mutual recognition requires a common basis of shared principles and minimum standards, in particular in order to strengthen mutual confidence.

Item 2.7 of the report then highlights certain specific areas of law in which legislative reforms might be appropriate.

In the longer term, it is of course of particular importance that the aim should be for the provisions of the European Convention on Human Rights and certain other fundamental provisions that may have procedural aspects to form part of the EU Charter of Rights.

(b) On the Brussels and Lugano Conventions in Particular

The Brussels and Lugano Conventions apply, firstly, to international choice of legal venue and, secondly, to the recognition and enforcement of foreign judgements. The Brussels Convention as it is known was concluded as long ago as in 1968. The parties to the Convention were the then Common Market states. An equivalent convention was concluded at Lugano in 1988 between the EC states and the EFTA states. In 1999, a working party was established by the EU to evaluate and reform the Brussels Convention, and on 1 March 2002 what was known as the Brussels I Regulation[4] came into force with effect for all EU states

[3] COM (2004) 401 final.

[4] Council Regulation (EC) No 44/2001 of 22 December 2000 on jurisdiction and the recognition and enforcement of judgments in civil and commercial matters, OJ 2001 L 12, p 1.

except Denmark, which for the present has opted to remain outside. A revision of the Lugano Convention is also pending, although this process has at present come to a halt.

(c) The European Court of Justice

Not surprisingly, the European Court of Justice plays a key role in procedural law, to a considerable extent developing procedural law, including law that extends beyond the proceedings before the Court itself.

(d) The EFTA Court

As time is limited, I have chosen neither to elaborate on the case law of the ECJ, nor the case law of the EFTA Court. However, it is worth noting that the EFTA Court has handled several cases involving matters of civil procedure. For instance, the question of legal interest was dealt with in *Scottish Salmon* (Case E–2/94), *The Norwegian Bankers' Association* (Case E–4/97) and *Technologien Bau- und Wirtschaftsberatung GmbH and Bellona Foundation* (Case E–2/02). For us, these are key decisions not only in relation to Community law, but also laying down national law generally.

(e) The European Convention on Human Rights

I do not intend to say much about the European Convention of Human Rights. It is worth noting that in particular Article 6 focuses on procedure in civil cases. Through a dynamic interpretation of the Article, a number of what may perhaps be termed minimum standards has been established. These include the right to be heard and the requirement that the court's reasoning must be based on the key submissions of the parties.

2. Arbitration

Arbitration generally involves commercial as well as transborder relations, as a result of which there has been considerable interest in establishing uniform rules for various states. The New York Convention on the recognition and enforcement of foreign arbitral awards of 1958 has been signed by approximately 125 states. The Convention regulates the situations in which states are bound to recognise foreign arbitral decisions as binding and to enforce them as domestic arbitral decisions.

Reference must also be made to 'UNCITRAL[5] Model Law on International Commercial Arbitration'. The Model Law provides a template for statutes on

[5] 'United Nations Commission on International Trade Law' formed in 1966. It is a UN agency tasked with the task of promoting the harmonisation of the trade law of the various states.

international arbitration that may be adopted wholly or in part into the national legislations of states. The law represents a major breakthrough in the efforts to achieve the greatest possible homogeneity of law in the area of international arbitration. Since 1985, 47 individual jurisdictions have adopted the Model Law more or less completely into their national legislations,[6] and in addition, a number of states have attached considerable emphasis to the Model Law when revising their own laws.

D. IS HOMOGENEITY WITHIN CIVIL PROCEDURE POSSIBLE AND DESIRABLE?

1. The Background to the Question

So far, I have spent some time outlining the situation of civil procedure within the EEA. I will now turn my attention to the question of whether it is possible and desirable to continue the work on homogeneity.

Before doing so, let me briefly remind you of the background to the question: The process of European integration, with the free movement of goods, services, people and capital. In part, this integration is of primary concern to interests involving transborder activity within the area of business and industry. But it is also reflects the fact that people move between countries, or perhaps have ties to several countries, with marriages, children and family values that may perhaps be linked to several states. Viewed in isolation, these interests might point in the direction of as great a degree of similarity between systems of procedure as possible.

It should also be remembered that there is interplay between substantive rules and procedural rules. Substantive rules have little value if they are not supported by procedural rules. Thus, the effects of the introduction of substantive rules will differ widely depending on the effectiveness of the procedural rules in place in the individual state.

Procedure has often been viewed as a purely technical issue, one that is apolitical and can best be left to the jurists. In my mind, however, there can be no doubt that procedure in its broadest sense, taking in, for example, institutions and competence is highly political and not particularly technical. One needs look no further than the judiciary's power to review statutes and administrative decisions, including decisions adopted by the other major organs of state.

[6] Thus Norway in the Act of 14 May 2004, No 25.

2. Confidence in the Systems

The Communication of 2 June 2004 to which I referred earlier places considerable emphasis on the need to create mutual confidence in the systems. It is worth remembering the very broad scope for choosing legal venue in a broad range of countries afforded by the Brussels and Lugano Conventions with the corresponding scope of enforcement. I have not researched what is happening to these conventions in connection with the expansion of the European Union, but it is easy to see that ensuring that the Conventions are fulfilled in ways that secures due process will provide extensive challenges for many years to come.

I agree with the Commission that work is required to ensure mutual confidence in the legal systems of the various states, both to ensure that existing arrangements function as intended and to ensure the future extension of common areas.

A number of measures in place within the European Union are aimed at achieving an increase in competence. One of these is the establishment of the European judicial training network,[7] the aim of which is largely to spread knowledge about European systems. This is of course a positive measure.

Nevertheless, it might also be appropriate to ask whether the aim also should be to improve knowledge about process in general, not least knowledge about national systems, purely with a view to irrigating the national systems. There are no easy answers to what should be the next step, but to me it is clear that it would be useful to achieve greater mutual insight into the national systems of procedure of the various states. Confidence in this context does not mean confidence in Community law, but confidence that all the convention states or union states have internal rules that ensure that due process can be achieved not only in one's home state, but in any state. As such, this confidence can be achieved either by the introduction of homogenous systems or by raising the standards of the systems of the individual nations.

What I am arguing for here is a major increase in investment in civil procedure studies within Europe. To some extent, this could be achieved in the individual country, for example by injecting earmarked resources into national courts and universities. However, more could also be invested in comparative civil procedure studies at certain European universities, with a view to developing common European principles and concepts.[8] In addition, this could provide a sound foundation for assisting other states to develop their legal systems. I am thinking here in part of former communist states, but also of providing assistance elsewhere in the world.

[7] CNS/2000/0829.

[8] See PH Lindblom, *Progressive Process* (Uppsala, 2000) 465; and Rosett, 'Unification, Harmonization, Codification and Reform' (1992) *American J Comparative L* 683 *et seq*.

3. National and Historical Values

As I touched upon earlier, homogeneity considerations are not stressed to a notable degree, not even in the more recent civil procedure reforms. This suggests that the states themselves have not viewed the achievement of homogeneity in this area as an area of priority.

In my view, one important reason for this is that civil procedure systems are deeply embedded in the history and thinking of the individual country. We see this clearly in the systems of common law and civil law. In addition, the organisation of the courts and the roles that the courts should play in society is based on underlying, fundamental principles, and they cannot readily be changed. The legal system represents a central pillar of the culture of a country.

In my own country, this is illustrated by the fact that the report on a new civil procedure code includes the history of our legal institutions extending as far back as their earliest days. By and large, this system has remained unchanged over the last two centuries, but in reality there has been a natural process of development for a great deal longer than this. I do not believe that my country is in any way different from other countries in this respect.

4. Common Law versus Civil Law

One fundamental question is whether it is possible to build a bridge between common law, as practised in the United Kingdom and Ireland, and civil law. Even with the changes that have now been introduced into British civil procedure there is no doubt considerable differences between these systems.

The report on a new Norwegian civil procedure code suggests that the present Norwegian—and Scandinavian—civil procedure law might be described as something between common law and civil law. As far as I know, many other European states have also in their own ways reached intermediate solutions of this nature.

It is unlikely that there are any quick and easy answers to the question of whether it is possible to build a bridge between common law and civil law. In areas in which there are thought to be major differences between the systems, it could perhaps be possible to find practical and agreed solutions when dealing with specific issues. And thoughts may be given to what might be transferred to the legal systems of other countries, both in our immediate locality and beyond.

As far as I can tell, differences in terms of principles will of themselves represent a barrier to the introduction of a common civil procedure for Europe. Nevertheless, the Brussels and Lugano Conventions have shown that it is possible to achieve procedural communality across the systems, although it could perhaps be objected that the Convention applies to issues beyond those of procedure and also addresses questions in which the differences between national legal systems are not particularly visible. All the same, it is clear that there are other points that could be addressed without over-emphasising differences in principle.

5. How Should a Uniform Civil Procedure be Formulated?

I have spent some time describing the situation today. This gives me an opportunity to reflect on what models might be used for formulating a Community law.

The work of the Storme Group shows very clearly the difficulties involved in reaching a common solution. I think I can say fairly confidently, that no credible description has ever been given of what such an arrangement should encompass.

The conventions of Brussels and Lugano show that it is possible to establish systems that are reasonably effective and that are agreed upon. Nevertheless, these are rules that do not intervene in the contents of civil procedure and nor do they change the institutions. International experience of arbitration has generally proved fruitful, because in this field it has proved possible to reach reasonably uniform rules, based on a model law. Even so, this is an area that is detached from the legal institutions of the individual state, largely focusing on commercial issues and where a more or less homogenous tradition has been established over a long period of time.

Clearly, it is not a practicable solution to apply different rules in national cases and international cases. Where conventions are drafted, for example in the areas of marriage and succession, it is unlikely to be possible to prevent the substantive rules from bringing with them certain procedural effects. Beyond this, it would not, in my view, be desirable for separate Community law on procedure to be established for such cases. Clearly, such rules would be problematical from the perspective of equality of treatment. Thus in my view it is without doubt appropriate and will remain the only option for the foreseeable future for a European judicial area to respect the legal traditions and systems of the Member States, as the Commission has stated.

6. Moving Forward by Degrees

The establishment of European courts has created a number of common generators of law, which at both national and international level determine what constitutes the law, including within the area of civil procedure. It is clear that much will happen in this area in the future. Courts such as the European Court of Justice, the EFTA Court and the European Court of Human Rights will to an increasing extent and with increasing speed outline not only principles of civil procedure, but also the details of procedure. The introduction of the EU Charter of Rights will provide a legal framework that in many cases will probably make it essential for the Court of Justice to develop law in this way.

In addition, it is clear that over time more legal instruments, conventions or EU directives will be adopted, regulating specific issues in the area of civil procedure. Together with instruments that although they focus on substantive questions, also have procedural aspects, this will result in extensive step-by-step regulation of civil procedure.

Let me add, that I am aware of the regulations within the European Union concerning service of documents in Europe (No 1348/2000) and the regulations of cross border taking of evidence in Europe (No 1206/2001). I could certainly also have mentioned other examples of what I consider to be small steps on the long way to establish common principles.

7. The Establishment of European Minimum Standards

The establishment of common rules will undoubtedly increase in a number of areas. However, I share the view that steps should be taken to establish a number of minimum standards for legislation. This will undoubtedly be a question both of drawing up rules for what should be included and of specifying principles for solutions.

I should perhaps be careful not to be too specific on the subject of universal minimum standards. Concrete requirements as to processing time, are clearly universally viewed as essential as regards maintaining confidence in the legal system. The right to be heard can be formulated in rules, and the same applies to the extent to which the grounds for judgments must be based on the submissions of the parties. The right to appeal and requirements as to the competence of the appellate court can provide the basis for the introduction of minimum requirements. The outcome of a dispute may also vary depending on the rules applicable to process management and the delimitation of process material.

To digress again: Efficient social institutions are essential in order for a state to be competitive across a broad base. This applies not only to businesses and persons already located in a country, but also to those considering possible relocation. This is a further point in favour of the introduction of general standards.

A cautionary note might perhaps be appropriate here. One objection against too broad a degree of international regulation of the requirements made of individual states is that the processes of change will then become excessively complex. Change will involve looking to a double set of rules: Both conventions or regulations and national legislation. This could retard procedure as a living instrument, and thereby the competitiveness of the courts and the state.

E. CONCLUSION

It is by no means easy to identify simple solutions for those seeking a common civil procedure in Europe. As a result of historical and political developments, most states have chosen to develop their own systems for regulating their courts and procedural arrangements. Although there might appear to be an increase in interest of harmonisation, this is probably confined to limited areas. It is undoubtedly the case that a development is occurring through international courts and conventions or regulations on specific areas of law. Nevertheless, the organisation of the courts and procedural law are so deeply embedded in the individual country that for the foreseeable future we must expect to have to live with countries maintaining their own civil procedure legislation.

F. DISCUSSIONS

PER TRESSELT

Thank you, Justice Utgård. Are there any questions, comments, declarations of dissent?

CARL BAUDENBACHER

Thank you very much, Justice Utgård, for this interesting presentation. You are, and I can see why, you are rather skeptical with regard to whether a homogeneous order of civil procedure will be achieved all over Europe, but you have also pointed to the differences between civil law and common law and in that context competition law has come to my mind. If we take the common law, not so much in the meaning of the English common law, but of the American common law, we see that in US competition law, we are having private enforcement to a much larger extent than in Europe, and since we have high representatives of the Commission present, I may take up this issue. Would it be feasible that in the near future we would have at least a partial harmonization of civil procedural law in the area of competition law, in order to facilitate private law suits, in order to improve private enforcement of EC and probably even EEA competition rules? In talking about American law, I would just mention incentives such as pre-trial discovery or treble damages or the contingency fee system. Now, under the modernized EC competition law which one day will probably be extended to the EFTA countries and I hope it is going to happen very soon, the national courts are supposed to directly apply Article 81 of the EC Treaty as a whole, including its paragraph 3. But at the same time, it remains unclear whether this will lead to sufficient private enforcement if no steps are taken with regard to a future harmonization. That question is directed to our speaker, but also probably to Mr Marenco.

PER TRESSELT

Thank you. Has this intervention engendered a strong desire to speak on the part of representatives of the Commission or the Surveillance Authority, or do I see John Temple Lang asking for the floor? I feel this is an inverted auction. Justice Utgård, would you care to respond?

KARL ARNE UTGÅRD

Well, it is easy to see, and I think I mentioned it, of course there will be certain areas where there will be uniform laws and then we will have laws concerning competition that also includes procedural aspects. But what I discussed was all sorts of court decisions, and my scope was the Brussels Convention, the Lugano Convention and what is necessary, what is possible to do to secure mutual confidence, that in the long term it is necessary to have these conventions work.

SVEN NORBERG

I don't intend directly to reply to the question put by Carl Baudenbacher, but I can make a few comments on that, because I also was struck when listening to the presentation by Justice Utgård that the revolutionary reform of modernization of the enforcement of competition law, that just entered into force on the 1 May this year is of interest here also. You know that this reform, which has been embodied in Regulation 1/2003, decentralizes the enforcement of Articles 81 and 82 to the national level to a great extent, not only with regard to competition authorities but also, in particular, with regard to national courts. Although this reform is not exactly regulating the procedure at national level, because we don't deal with that at all, it is expected that private enforcement of these provisions before national courts will take place to a much greater extent than before. We have therefore also introduced a new element in that Regulation, which in Article 15 extends a means for cooperation between the European Commission and the national courts. Thus the Commission will assist national courts by offering advice on both substantive issues, like facts and interpretation of relevant provisions of EC competition law. But there is also another element in this reform. The Commission is at present considering how to stimulate the procedures for private action at a national level. To this end the Commission published in the beginning of September this year on its website a consultancy study that has been made regarding the situation in all the Member States. It is quite clear that with regard to private action there is a very differing picture. In many countries there are very few examples of private actions being brought to judgment. The Commission has the intention to produce during next year a Green Paper on how to promote private actions. That Green Paper will hopefully create a lot of discussion and debate on these issues and on the basis thereof we will see how we can get further. It is clear that this is only one step, but in a very important area. Thank you.

PER TRESSELT

I thank Sven Norberg for giving us a very welcome update. Yes, a microphone appears to be on its way to Professor Pescatore.

PIERRE PESCATORE

Mr President, I do not exactly know where we stand. If I understand well, I would say that we are here to discuss questions relating to the relationship between the EFTA Court and the EC Court. This has been pertinently explained by President Skouris, when he said that the context in both systems is not the same. EFTA is based, I would say, on free trade simple, whereas the EEC is based on a combination of free trade inside with extreme commercial protectionism towards the outside. Personally, I am very much concerned by the fact that this sort of internationalist protective mood has also spread to the Court of Justice of the Communities. I give you two examples: The first is the example of the ignorance by the EC Court of the rules of GATT, which have not been admitted to have direct effect in the Community system. And a second example is the non-admission of the internationalist view of the exhaustion of intellectual property rights as it has been developed in the *Silhouette* case which, in my opinion, is a disgrace in the EC case law. So, what should the EFTA Court do, in view of this basic difference of principles and approach, if it finds itself either in the situation that it has to cope with a problem which is new and which has, so far, not be tackled by the EC Court, or, if it does not agree with the already existing case law of the EC Court, because it is defensive and protective in contradiction to the basic principles of EFTA? What would I do, if I had the privilege of being in President Baudenbacher's place? I would go to the extreme limit of EFTA's own mission by fostering free trade and try my best to dissuade the EC Court from indulging further in protectionist tendencies. Thank you.

PER TRESSELT

Thank you, Professor Pescatore, I think we always have benefit from your good advice. I would ask Justice Utgård whether he at this stage had any further comments. I think I will sum up by saying that the speaker said there were no easy answers, whereas too many unanswered questions.

For the next speaker, I am happy to say that Professor Stefán Már Stefánsson comes to this Symposium as one of the EFTA Court's own. He is one of our indispensable *ad hoc* judges. He graduated in law from the University of Iceland, and has absolved further studies in Germany, Norway and Denmark. He has published widely and deeply in his specialities: procedural law, company law and European law. He has been a City Court judge and a professor at the University of Iceland since 1979. He will take us through the intricacies of state liability in the European Community and in the EEA and he will make an attempt to show us how Power Point works in the Cercle Municipal.

State Liability in Community Law and EEA Law

STEFÁN MÁR STEFÁNSSON

A. THE ORIGIN OF STATE LIABILITY IN EC LAW

The EC Treaty is silent on the issue as to whether Member States may be liable in damages to injured parties for breach of Community law. Traditionally, it was accepted that the issue was governed by national law.[1] The principle of State liability was stated for the first time in the seminal judgment in *Francovich*,[2] which dealt with the non-implementation of a particular EC directive. As the said directive did not fulfil all the conditions necessary to achieve a direct effect, the claimant had to rely on theories of State liability. The Court found that three conditions had to be fulfilled for such liability to be established:

—the directive involved rights conferred on individuals;
—the content of the rights could be identified on the basis of the directive;
—a causal link between the State's failure and the damage sustained.

The main arguments in the *Francovich* case for State liability can be described as follows:

—Community law must ensure that it takes full effect and must protect the rights it confers on individuals;
—under Article 5(10) of the Treaty the Member States are required to take all appropriate measures, whether general or particular, to ensure the implementation of Community law;

[1] T Tridimas, *The General Principles of EC Law* (Oxford, OUP, 1999) 321.
[2] Joint Cases C–6/90 and C–9/90 *Francovich v Italy* [1991] ECR I–5357, paras 22 and 35.

—full effectiveness of Community rules would be impaired and the protection of the rights which they grant weakened if individuals were unable to obtain reparation when their rights are infringed.[3]

The underlying idea is that the Member States are under an obligation to nullify the unlawful consequences of breaches of Community law. Therefore, State liability is usually regarded as a necessary corollary of the principle of direct effect of a Community provision and the principle of conform interpretation ('indirect effect') in Community Law. Since *Francovich*, the ECJ has repeatedly ruled that a Member State can be held responsible for loss and damage caused to individuals for breaches of Community law. State liability is therefore a well-established theory in EU law.

In the joint *Brasserie/Factortame* case,[4] questions were raised about the application of the *Francovich* principle in cases where primary Treaty provisions were violated by virtue of domestic legislation rather than a failure to implement a directive. Treaty provisions as well as secondary legislation can have both direct effect as well as superiority over domestic legislation. The ECJ did not find this to be a material difference. The Court found 'that that principle [State liability] holds good for any case in which a Member State breaches Community law, [. . .].' However, new arguments were added to the theory of State liability and other things were clarified. They included:

—the principle of state liability is an additional device to enforce rights;
—general conditions for State liability were defined;
—reference to Articles 220 and 288(2) TEC.

[3] The ECJ in *Francovich*:

> 31 It should be borne in mind at the outset that the EEC Treaty has created its own legal system, which is integrated into the legal systems of the Member States and which their courts are bound to apply. The subjects of that legal system are not only the Member States but also their nationals. Just as it imposes burdens on individuals, Community law is also intended to give rise to rights which become part of their legal patrimony. Those rights arise not only where they are expressly granted by the Treaty but also by virtue of obligations which the Treaty imposes in a clearly defined manner both on individuals and on the Member States and the Community institutions (see the judgments in Case 26/62 *Van Gend en Loos* [1963] ECR 1 and Case 6/64 *Costa v ENEL* [1964] ECR 585).
>
> 32 Furthermore, it has been consistently held that the national courts whose task it is to apply the provisions of Community law in areas within their jurisdiction must ensure that those rules take full effect and must protect the rights which they confer on individuals (see in particular the judgments in Case 106/77 *Amministrazione delle Finanze dello Stato v Simmenthal* [1978] ECR 629 para 16 and Case C–213/89 *Factortame* [1990] ECR I–2433 para 19).
>
> 33 The full effectiveness of Community rules would be impaired and the protection of the rights which they grant would be weakened if individuals were unable to obtain redress when their rights are infringed by a breach of Community law for which a MS can be held responsible. . . .
>
> 36 A further basis for the obligation of Member States to make good such loss and damage is to be found in Art 5 of the Treaty . . .

[4] Joined Cases C–46/93 and C–48/93 *Brasserie du Pêcheur SA v Bundesrepublik Deutschland* and *The Queen v Secretary of State for Transport ex parte Factortame Ltd* [1996] ECR I–1029.

Furthermore, the Court answered the question whether the principle covers not only cases where a Member State breaches Community law but also where *its institutions* do so. According to the *Brasserie* case the answer is affirmative. It does neither matter which organ of the State is responsible for the breach nor whether the breach is a result of an act or omission. It follows that the state is responsible for all domestic acts and omissions whether they can be regarded as a legislative, executive or judicial breach of Community law.[5]

A question concerning the judiciary was raised in the course of an action for a declaration of liability brought by Mr Köbler against the Republic of Austria for an alleged breach of a provision of Community law in a judgment handed down by the Verwaltungsgerichtshof (Supreme Administrative Court) of Austria.[6] The ECJ stated:

> 36 Consequently, it follows from the requirements inherent in the protection of the rights of individuals relying on Community law that they must have the possibility of obtaining redress in the national courts for the damage caused by the infringement of those rights owing to a decision of a court adjudicating at last instance.

It appears therefore that State liability is a well-known principle in EU law. The principle can apply whenever Member States or their institutions are in breach of EU law by performance of EU's legislation and thereby causing loss or damage to individuals or economic operators.

B. THE CONDITIONS FOR STATE LIABILITY IN COMMUNITY LAW

The special conditions, which need to be met with regard to unimplemented EC directives, have already been discussed. In the *Brasserie* case, the ECJ raised three general conditions which must always be met.[7] They can mostly be seen as a further elaboration of the conditions set forth in the *Francovich* case. These conditions were:

—the rule of law infringed must be intended to confer rights on individuals;
—the breach must be sufficiently serious;
—a direct causal link must be established between the breach of the obligation resting on the State and the damage sustained by the injured parties.

[5] *Brasserie*, paras 32 and 35.

[6] Case C–224/01 *Gerhard Köbler v Republik Österreich* [2003] ECR I–10,239.

[7] At para 51. In the most recent judgment, these conditions are reiterated; see Case C–319/96 *Brinkmann Tabakfabriken GmbH v Skatteministeriet* [1998] ECR I–5255. Also *Dillenkofer*, paras 21 and 23 (referred to later) and *Denkavit International BV v Bundesamt für Finanzen*, para 48; Joint Cases C–283, C–291 and C–292/94 [1996] ECR I–5063. The same applies where a national court of last instance violates EC law in their ruling. See Case C–224/01 *Gerhard Köbler v Republik Österreich* [2003] ECR I–10,239, where the three conditions for State liability from the case in *Brasserie du Pêcheur* were reiterated. The Court continued and said: 'In any event, an infringement of Community law will be sufficiently serious where the decision concerned was made in manifest breach of the case-law of the Court in the matter.'

By comparison with the *Francovich* case it is evident that the requirement 'sufficiently serious' needs to be clarified. In *Brasserie*, the Court emphasized *inter alia* (the multiple test):[8]

—clarity and precision of the rule breached;
—the measure of discretion left by that rule to the national authorities;
—whether any error of law was excusable or inexcusable.

Consequently, *fault* as a precondition for State liability, is not a necessary condition provided that the breach is sufficiently serious in other respects. Given the lack of clarity of much EC law, and that Member States have no choice to act in breach of Community law, the crucial element in the 'multiple test' will often be the clarity and precision of the rule breached.[9] In *Francovich*, which dealt with an unimplemented directive, the question of 'sufficiently serious breach' was not mentioned. However, in *Dillenkofer*[10] the ECJ said: 'In substance, the conditions laid down in that group of judgments are the same, since the condition that there should be a sufficiently serious breach, although not expressly mentioned in *Francovich*, was nevertheless evident from the circumstances of that case.'

It is therefore likely that the non-implementation of directives (as in *Francovich*) were such an obvious breach that there was no need to mention the seriousness.[11] Non-implementation of EC rules will therefore normally result in State liability.

The Court did not rule on the *extent of reparation* in this case, but referred to the legal system of the Member State in question. However, such criteria must not be less favourable than that applying to similar claims in domestic

[8] The ECJ, para 56:

> The factors which the competent court may take into consideration include the clarity and precision of the rule breached, the measure of discretion left by that rule to the national or Community authorities, whether the infringement and the damage caused was intentional or involuntary, whether any error of law was excusable or inexcusable, the fact that the position taken by a Community institution may have contributed towards the omission, and the adoption or retention of national measures or practices contrary to Community law.
>
> 57 On any view, a breach of Community law will clearly be sufficiently serious if it has persisted despite a judgment finding the infringement in question to be established or a preliminary ruling or settled case law of the Court on the matter from which it is clear that the conduct in question constituted an infringement.

[9] See J Steiner and L Woods, *Textbook on EC Law*, 8th edn (Oxford, OUP, 2003) 115.

[10] Joined Cases C–178/94, C–179/94, C–188/94, C–189/94 and C–190/94 *Erich Dillenkofer, Christian Erdmann, Hans-Jürgen Schulte, Anke Heuer, Werne, Ursula and Trosten Knor v Bundesrepublik Deutschland* [1996] ECR I–4845.

[11] HA Jakobsen, 'Offentligrettslig erstattningsansvar ved brudd på EF– og EØS-retten' 39 *IUSEF* (Senter for Europarett, Universitetet i Oslo) 91. The same rule will normally apply to malimplementation; see Case C–319/96 *Brinkmann Tabakfabriken GmbH v Skatteministeriet* [1998] ECR I–5255.

law and there exist certain restrictions, including the total exclusion of loss of profit.[12]

One last question is if the direct effect of EC legislation as such (and its superiority over domestic legislation) excludes State liability. The ECJ seems to have answered this question negatively. As an argument for such a conclusion, the Court has *inter alia* pointed out that direct effect cannot secure in every case the benefit of the rights conferred upon individuals by Community law. The right of reparation is therefore seen as the necessary corollary rather than a substitute for direct effect.[13] The question remains however, whether an individual can make a state liable for damages in cases where he can achieve full redress by using the direct effect of an unimplemented directive. In such cases, it can be argued that the individual has not suffered any loss.

C. OTHER ASPECTS OF LIABILITY

To get a better overview and for the purpose of comparison it is useful to keep in mind some aspects related to State liability.

1. Community Liability

According to Article 288(2) EC, the Community shall, in the case of non-contractual liability, make good any damage caused by its institutions or by its servants in the performance of their duties in accordance with the general principles common to the laws of the Member States. It should be noted that there is in fact no common corpus of rules governing the non-contractual liability of public authorities in the national laws.[14] According to the case law of the ECJ three conditions must be fulfilled in order for the Community liability to incur. These are: a) an illegal act, b) damage must be sustained, and c) causal link between the unlawful conduct and the damage sustained.[15]

[12] The ECJ in *Brasserie*:

> 83 In the absence of relevant Community provisions, it is for the domestic legal system of each Member State to set the criteria for determining the extent of reparation. However, those criteria must not be less favourable than those applying to similar claims based on domestic law and must not be such as in practice to make it impossible or excessively difficult to obtain reparation. . . .
> 87 Total exclusion of loss of profit as a head of damage for which reparation may be awarded in the case of a breach of Community law cannot be accepted. Especially in the context of economic or commercial litigation, such a total exclusion of loss of profit would be such as to make reparation of damage practically impossible.

[13] *Brasserie*, para 22.

[14] T Tridimas, *The General Principles of EC Law* (Oxford, OUP, 1999) 314.

[15] *Ibid.*

2. State Liability under Article 41 of the ECHR

If the Court finds that there has been a violation of the Convention or the protocols hereto and if the internal law of the High Contracting Party concerned allows only partial reparation to be made, the Court shall, if necessary afford just satisfaction to the injured party. The Court[16] has explored many questions relating to the entitlement to compensation. As far as pecuniary loss is concerned practice seems to have demonstrated that compensation is obtainable provided that: a) the loss is sufficiently proved, b) the loss in question was actually caused by the breach of the Convention.[17] These conditions appear to be an impediment in many cases.

3. Private Liability

The question of private liability arises also under EC law. An example of this is the *Courage* case.[18] An owner of a pub (in Britain) had concluded an exclusive contract with a brewery. He was in breach of the contract because he began to buy beer supplies from another supplier for a better price. The brewery sued the pub owner for breach of contract whereas the pub owner alleged that the exclusive contract was in breach of EC rules, notably Article 81 EC and that he had the right to compensation for the price difference which he had to pay under the exclusive contract. Under English law, it is impossible to claim damages deriving from an illegal contract. The ECJ stated: 'a party to a contract liable to restrict or distort competition within the meaning of Article 85 of the Treaty can rely on the breach of that article to obtain relief from the other contracting party'.[19]

Article 85 of the Treaty precludes a rule of national law under which a party to a contract liable to restrict or distort competition within the meaning of that provision is barred from claiming damages for loss caused by performance of that contract on the sole ground that the claimant is a party to that contract.

Community law does not preclude a rule of national law barring a party to a contract liable to restrict or distort competition from relying on his own unlawful actions to obtain damages where it is established that that party bears significant responsibility for the distortion of competition.

Consequently, the Community law contains rules on private liability. Domestic law cannot for instance exclude liability on the sole ground that the

[16] Ie, the European Court of Human Rights.

[17] JG Merrills and AH Robertson, *Human Rights in Europe: A Study of the European Convention on Human Rights* (Manchester, MUP, 2001) 320.

[18] Case C–453/99 *Courage Ltd v Bernard Crehan* and *Bernard Crehan v Courage Ltd* [2001] ECR I–6297.

[19] At para 36.

claimant is a party to an agreement contravening Community law. On this point, the EEA Agreement is likely to contain similar rules.

4. Domestic Legislation

Rules are normally found in the Member States where individuals or firms can hold the state responsible for breaches of their obligations. Such responsibility can also cover breaches of international obligations. The conditions for such liability are governed by the domestic legislation of the state in question. An example of this is demonstrated under the heading 'Was the EEA rule on State liability really needed?' below.

D. DOES THE PRINCIPLE OF STATE LIABILITY APPLY TO EEA LAW?

When dealing with this question one has to keep in mind that public international law does not entail any rule that obliges states to accept private liability claims for damages due to faulty performance of a treaty.[20] Although some of the arguments underlying the principle of State liability in *Francovich* and *Brasserie* are reflected in the EEA Agreement other arguments are far less significantly reflected, such as:

—no direct effect of EEA rules (directives);[21]
—different rules on priority of legislation (a twin to direct effect);[22]
—the reference to EC Article 215(2) (now Article 288(2)) (general principles in the Member States on non-contractual liability);
—the reference to EC Article 164 (now Article 220) on the role of the ECJ;
—different aims of integration;
—different power of institutions.

It is true to say that the EEA Agreement strives for homogeneity and imposes a duty on the Contracting parties to implement EEA legislation in accordance with Article 7 of the Agreement under the principle of solidarity. Furthermore,

[20] M Eyjólfsson [2000] 1 *Common Market L Rev* 191–211.

[21] This can clearly be seen from the EFTA Court judgment in Case E–4/01 *Karl K Karlsson hf v The Icelandic State* [2002] EFTA Ct Rep 242: '28 It follows from Article 7 EEA and Protocol 35 of the EEA Agreement that EEA law does not entail a transfer of legislative powers. Therefore, EEA law does not require that individuals and economic operators can rely directly on non-implemented EEA rules before the national courts.' See also the judgment of the Supreme Court of Norway in the *Finanger* case, Rt 2000 s 1811 at 1831–32.

[22] A ruling to this effect is found in the Icelandic Supreme Court judgment in Case 236/1999 *The Icelandic State v Erla María Sveinsbjörnsdóttir,* Court Rt p 4921. The Court said: '. . . According to that protocol [protocol 35] the Contracting Parties were not required to transfer legislative power to any institution of the European Economic Area, and the aims of the Agreement were consequently to be achieved through national procedures'.

references can be found as to the equal treatment and equal opportunities of individuals and economic operators.

However, the differences between the two legal systems, EU law on one hand and EEA law on the other, are substantial.

From the outset, it was therefore quite unclear whether EEA law really contained the EC principle on State liability in spite of the general requirement of homogeneity of the EEA Agreement, which is *inter alia* envisaged in Article 6 EEA and Article 3 SCA.[23]

E. THE CASE OF *ERLA MARÍA SVEINBJÖRNSDÓTTIR* (CASE E–9/97)

In the well-known case of *Erla María Sveinbjörnsdóttir*, the EFTA Court answered the question whether, and under which conditions, the principle of State liability would apply to EEA law in the case of incorrect implementation of a directive. The EFTA Court accepted State liability. The main arguments for the Court's ruling were:

—That the EEA Agreement is an international treaty sui generis which contains a distinct legal order of its own, including an enhanced free trade area;
—that homogeneity is an objective of the EEA Agreement;
—that an objective of the EEA Agreement is to establish the rights of individuals and economic operators to equal treatment and equal opportunities within the EEA.

From this ruling of the EFTA Court it can be seen that the special nature of the EEA Agreement, its objectives of homogeneity and of granting individuals and economic operators equal treatment and opportunity, was used as an argument to overcome the discrepancies between the EC Treaty and the EEA Agreement. It is noteworthy that the EFTA Court did not refer to Article 6 or Article 3 SCA in this connection, nor did it cite earlier case law of the ECJ. The logical reason for this appears to be that 'no provisions are here identical in substance'.

The Court's finding should not be regarded as a surprise. The homogeneity principle is strongly emphasized in the EEA Agreement. The principle of State liability is an important device to uphold EC/EEA legislation. Any non-acceptance of the principle could easily have lead to a decline of the EEA Agreement. Consequently, the EFTA Court had good and logical reason not to deviate from that principle in this case.

It is a separate question whether or not the said discrepancies between EC/EEA laws could lead to a different interpretation of the conditions for State liability. In this connection, it is useful to know what the Court said about the conditions for applying the rule of State liability.

[23] An abbreviation for the Agreement between the EFTA States on the Establishment of a Surveillance Authority and a Court of Justice (ESA/Court Agreement).

In *Erla María Sveinbjörnsdóttir*, the EFTA Court, in paragraph 66, referred to the same conditions as enumerated in *Brasserie*[24] and then later in paragraph 67 it cited the *Francovich* judgment.[25] The EFTA Court found that these conditions had been fulfilled. When evaluating whether the breach of an obligation under the EEA Agreement was sufficiently serious, the EFTA Court followed pretty much the same line as the ECJ previously, and referred to such factors as the clarity and precision of the rule breached as well as other factors.[26]

In the light of the above, there is reason to believe that the EFTA Court will stay in line with the case law of the ECJ although the Court has clearly reserved its right to deviate from the case law as demonstrated both in *Erla María Sveinbjörnsdóttir* and in the *Karlsson* case. This possible deviation will be further dealt with under the heading 'Are the rules on State liability the same in EEA and EC law?' below. It is also clear from the *Karlsson* case that the EFTA Court is of the opinion that the extent of reparation shall be based on national liability law with similar restrictions as those under EC law.[27]

F. THE ECJ AND THE PRINCIPLE OF STATE LIABILITY IN THE EEA AGREEMENT

The *Erla María Sveinbjörnsdóttir* case dealt with the question whether or not homogeneity could be achieved between EEA law and EU law in an EFTA context. The EEA Agreement is a part of the Community rules. Consequently, there is no less need for homogeneity between EEA rules as interpreted and applied in the EFTA countries on the one hand and EU countries on the other. In other words, as the EEA Agreement aims to bring about the same rules and their interpretation within the whole EEA area, the question arises whether the ECJ has handed down any ruling on the same question, as did the EFTA Court in the *Erla María Sveinbjörnsdóttir* case.

[24] Ie, that the rule confers rights upon individuals, the breach sufficiently serious and a direct causal link between the obligation and damage sustained.

[25] The Court said:

> With regard to the present case, the Court notes that the purpose of Council Directive 80/987/EEC, as amended, is to grant to employees a right to a guarantee of payment of their unpaid wage claims. For similar reasons as in the case law of the ECJ, the scope and content of that right can be identified on the basis of the provisions of the Directive, see for comparison the judgment in Joined Cases C–6/90 and C–9/90 *Francovich* [1991] ECR I–5357, paras 10 *et seq*. Thus, it appears that the first condition is fulfilled.

[26] *Erla María Sveinbjörnsdóttir* case para 69:

> The factors which the competent court may take into consideration include the clarity and precision of the rule breached, the measure of discretion left by that rule to the national authorities, whether the infringement and the damage caused was intentional or involuntary, whether any error of law was excusable or inexcusable, the fact that the position taken by an EEA or Community institution may have contributed towards the omission, and the adoption or retention of national measures or practices contrary to the EEA Agreement.

[27] *Karlsson*, para 33.

In the *Andersson* case,[28] the ECJ dealt with the question whether the failure by the Swedish authorities, to correctly implement a directive would result in a State liability. The case was dismissed on formal grounds. However, it is interesting to note that the Advocate General stated that the EEA Agreement did not allow such a conclusion.

In the *Rechberger* case,[29] a similar problem was referred to the ECJ. The subject matter of this case related to the period when Austria was a party of the EEA Agreement. The case was also dismissed on formal grounds. However, the ECJ noted as follows:

> 39 (. . .) in view of the objective of uniform interpretation and application which informs the EEA Agreement, it should be pointed out that the principles governing the liability of an EFTA State for infringement of a directive referred to in the EEA Agreement were the subject of the EFTA Court's judgment of 10 December 1998 in *Sveinbjörnsdóttir* (E–9/97, not yet published in the EFTA Court Reports).[30]

This premise is clearly just a note with a view to any rulings of the Court. The ECJ said absolutely nothing of its own about the principle of the State liability resulting from the EEA Agreement. Consequently, there is no reason to draw any conclusion from this note. It must therefore be concluded that the ECJ has not yet handed down any rulings on the principle of State liability within the EEA.

G. ARE THE RULES OF STATE LIABILITY THE SAME IN EEA AND EC LAW?

In *Erla María Sveinbjörnsdóttir,* the EFTA Court did not make any reference to the ECJ case law regarding the principle of State liability. It merely said that the Contracting Parties are 'obliged to provide for compensation for loss and damage caused to individuals by breaches of the obligations' under the EEA Agreement.

As a further elaboration of this, the EFTA Court stated in the *Karlsson* case: 'The finding that the principle of State liability is an integral part of the EEA Agreement differs, as it must, from the development in the case law of the ECJ of the principle of State liability under EC law. Therefore, the application of the principles may not necessarily be in all respect coextensive.'[31]

[28] Case C–321/97 *Ulla-Birth Andersson and Susanne Wåkerås-Andersson v Swedish State* [1999] ECR I–3551.

[29] Case C–140/97 *Walter Rechberger v Rebublic Austria* [1999] ECR I–3499.

[30] Here, as in *Andersson*, the ECJ came to the conclusion that it had no jurisdiction on the State liability question. Thus the ECJ, at para 40 'Accordingly, the Court only has jurisdiction to rule on the question whether a Member State which acceded to the European Union on 1 January 1995 has properly transposed Art 7 of the Directive if it has adopted legislation which protects travellers who booked package travel after 1 January 1995 but limits that protection to trips with a departure date of 1 May 1995 or later.'

[31] Para 30.

The EFTA Court is here obviously reserving itself the right to develop the principle of State liability within the framework of the EEA Agreement and independently from the future development of Community law.

As previously mentioned the EFTA Court's findings in *Erla María Sveinbjörnsdóttir* were limited to the 'incorrect implementation of directives'. In the *Karlsson* case, the question was raised whether the *Erla María Sveinbjörnsdóttir* case could also be used as a basis for State liability for infringement of the main part of the EEA Agreement. The EFTA Court found that an EEA State could be held responsible in such cases if the general conditions for liability were met, thereby reiterating the conditions required in *Erla María Sveinbjörnsdóttir*.[32] Consequently, an EEA state may, in principle, be held liable for breaches of obligations under both 'secondary acts' of EEA legislation as well as the main part of the EEA Agreement.

But to what extent are the EEA rules on State liability the same or unlike those in Community law? The EEA Agreement differs from the EU Treaty, both with regard to its objectives and the power of institutions, as well as important principles and legislation, although there is a stringent requirement for homogeneity. Differences of this kind are likely to lead to different conclusions. Hence, it is important to look at briefly two aspects in this context:

Firstly, the *scope of application* of State liability in the EEA would be both narrower and wider than that of the EU. It is narrower because the EEA Agreement does not cover all areas covered by the EU. It is wider with regard to non-implementation of directives with direct effect. In EU such situations would release the direct effect whereas in the EEA one would in the EFTA member states have to rely on the principle of State liability. The same seems to apply to EU regulations.

Secondly, *the conditions* for State liability can prove to be slightly different. If, for example, a court in an EFTA State would not follow an advisory opinion of the EFTA Court that court would not be violating any EEA rule because the opinion was only advisory and hence not binding.[33] By comparison, a court of last instance in the EU would be bound by the findings of the ECJ in a preliminary ruling. Differences of this kind can lead to different conclusions when dealing with State liability. Another related example is the duty of a court of last instance in an EU Member State to refer questions to the ECJ for preliminary ruling. Such a duty exists in the EC but does not ever exist under the EEA system. A mistake regarding the interpretation or application of EC/EEA legislation which can be traced to such a 'non-reference' would therefore probably have to be evaluated differently in the two legal systems.

[32] *Karlsson*, para 32, 'An EEA state can be held responsible for breaches of its obligations under EEA law . . .'.

[33] This does not mean that the courts in the EFTA States are totally free to deviate from an advisory opinion of the EFTA Court. It follows from the principle of loyalty under Art 3 of the EEA Agreement that they are under the duty to consider such an opinion and to use the principle of presumption where possible.

H. IS THE EEA PRINCIPLE OF STATE LIABILITY A PART OF ICELANDIC LAW?

The EEA Agreement is an international agreement, which shall be interpreted in the light of its wording and objectives. In the *Erla María Sveinbjörnsdóttir* case, the EFTA Court made the following ruling:

It follows from Article 7 EEA and Protocol 35 to the EEA Agreement that the EEA Agreement does not entail a transfer of legislative power. However, the principle of State liability must be seen as an integral part of the EEA Agreement as such. Therefore, it is natural to interpret national legislation implementing the main part of the Agreement as also comprising the principle for State liability.

Here the EFTA Court is suggesting what would be the natural interpretation of *Icelandic law*. According to Article 34 of the SCA the EFTA Court is limited to give advisory opinions on the interpretation of the *EEA Agreement as such*. A suggestion like this has therefore a limited legal weight.

On 5 November 1997, the District Court of Reykjavík requested an advisory opinion of the EFTA Court in the *Erla María Sveinbjörnsdóttir* case. In continuation of the advisory opinion of the EFTA Court, the District Court came to the conclusion that the state should be held liable for the loss of the claimant. That decision was appealed to the Icelandic Supreme Court,[34] which came to the following conclusion:

—that the EEA Agreement did not entail a transfer of legislative power;
—that it was within the power of the Icelandic courts to rule whether State liability had adequate support in Icelandic law;
—that the Icelandic courts were under the duty to consider the advisory opinion of the EFTA Court if nothing is brought forth to the effect that this should be disregarded;
—that Iceland was under the duty to implement the respective directive and to accord individuals their rights leading from it;
—that the respective directive had been incorrectly implemented with the result that the discrepancy between the directive and Icelandic law was substantial;
—that as the main part of the EEA Agreement had been enacted in Icelandic law (law No 2/1993) it was reasonable to interpret it in conformity with the principles of the EEA Agreement, providing that individuals are legally entitled to conformity between Icelandic law and the EEA rules;
—if conformity could not be brought about Iceland should be liable according to Icelandic law in the event of failure in this respect.

To summarise, it can be said that the Icelandic Supreme Court followed the advisory opinion of the EFTA Court by saying that the individuals (and economic

[34] Case 236/1999 *The Icelandic State v Erla María Sveinbjörnsdóttir* (16 December 1999, Icelandic Supreme Court).

operators) had the right to conformity of EEA Agreement and Icelandic law and that a failure of this could result in State liability according to Icelandic law. However, the Icelandic Supreme Court also came to the conclusion that such liability should be *governed by the general Icelandic rules on State liability*.

Therefore, it is useful to reiterate the main features of the Icelandic rules on State liability to determine whether they do in fact differ from the EU/EEA rules on State liability. The main features are as follows:

—a necessary base for the liability, ie, usually the culpa rule, the rules on objective liability or any other rule which may lie there in between;
—a causal link must be found between the act and the damage sustained;
—economical damage or loss must be suffered.

Taken as a whole these rules do not differ much from the conditions of State liability which lead from the judgment in *Brasserie*. The Supreme Court did not comment on whether or not the directive concerned was intended to confer rights on the claimant. The reason for this is supposedly that such a right was obvious in the case. As to whether the failure was sufficiently serious, the Court said that it was 'material' thereby using similar factors as in the *Brasserie* case.

In view of the fact that the Icelandic legislator was bona fide when interpreting and legislating the rather unclear wording of Council Directive 80/987/EEC (of 20 October 1980 on the approximation of the laws of the Member States relating to the protection of employees in the event of the insolvency of their employer) which gave rise to the proceedings in the *Erla María Sveinbjörnsdóttir* case, it is fair to say that a bona fide intent of the legislator may not suffice to avoid liability. There must be, in addition, sufficient objective grounds at hand which justify the breach.

It seems to follow that the EEA principle on State liability is a part of Icelandic law. It is likely that the Icelandic courts will not deviate radically from the ruling of the EFTA Court when dealing with the principle of State liability, even when solely using the Icelandic rules on State liability.

I. WAS THE EEA RULE ON STATE LIABILITY REALLY NEEDED?

In January 1995, an invitation to submit tenders for the award of a public contract for construction work for the school Borgarholtsskóli was sent out in the EEA. The contracting authorities were the Government of Iceland, the City of Reykjavík and the Municipality of Mosfellsbær (the defendant). One of the contractors, Fagtún ehf, (the appellant) instituted proceedings against the authorities claiming damages for an alleged breach of EEA law.

The Icelandic Supreme Court[35] sought an advisory opinion from the EFTA Court asking *inter alia* whether Article 11 of the EEA Agreement prohibits the

[35] Case 169/1998 *Fagtún ehf v Icelandic State* [1999] Supreme Ct Rep 4429 (18 November 1999).

inclusion in a works contract of a provision to the effect that roof elements are to be produced in Iceland.

The EFTA Court concluded in Case E–5/98 that a provision in a works contract requiring that roof elements be produced in Iceland was contrary to Article 11 EEA Agreement. The Court stated that by including the clause: 'The contractor's main tender is the basis for the contract and it is agreed that roof elements will be produced in the country', the defendants excluded all products made abroad. The Court found that this amounted to clear discrimination in favour of national production.[36]

The Icelandic Supreme Court based its findings on this opinion of the EFTA Court regarding the breach of EEA law. It came to the conclusion that the appellant had lost the contract because of the attitude of the defendant which was considered both illegal and faulty. Consequently, the defendant was found obliged to refund the appellant all damages caused to him by the defendant's behaviour.

It is noteworthy that the Icelandic Supreme Court was here using Icelandic law on State liability but not EEA State liability rules. Therefore, it is good reason to ask whether the rule in the case of *Erla María Sveinbjörnsdóttir* on State liability has changed the legal situation in the EFTA States as radically as has been previously thought.

J. DOES THE PRINCIPLE OF STATE LIABILITY INVOLVE A TRANSFER OF LEGISLATIVE POWERS?

The aims of the principles of direct effect (and indirect effect) as well as State liability are to ensure the correct interpretation and application of EC law. As previously mentioned, the ECJ has furthermore said[37] that the right to reparation is a necessary corollary of the direct effect.

Both the EFTA Court and the Icelandic Supreme Court have ruled in the *Erla María Sveinbjörnsdóttir* cases that the EEA Agreement does not entail any transfer of legislative power. Is this correct, with regard to the power that legislator is accorded by the Icelandic Constitution? Is it possible to argue that the effect of the infringement of EEA law (ie, the State liability) is tantamount to a transfer of legislative power? If the legislator in an EFTA State would for instance intentionally implement an EU directive in a certain way, thereby breaching the directive, such an act would in most cases constitute State liability. The same would probably apply to other acts such as EU regulations introduced in the EEA.

As described earlier, *private persons and economic operators* can often effectively hold the state (including the legislator) responsible for acts which are in

[36] Case 5/98 *Fagtún ehf* [1999] EFTA Ct Rep 53, para 32.
[37] *Francovich*, para 35.

breach of EU/EEA rules. It follows that the freedom of the legislator to act freely is drastically limited in such situations because it cannot act freely without being held liable by *individuals or firms*. Therefore, there are good reasons to ask whether this arrangement binds the legislator in such a way that it can be equalled to direct effect of a Community directive or any other secondary legislation.

However, the difference still persists that individuals (and firms) can under EEA law only rely on the law made by the national legislator. In principle, an individual or a firm cannot invoke the rights granted to them in an unimplemented secondary legislation the right is limited to financial. A national law can never be overruled in an EFTA State by an unimplemented EEA law except indirectly, ie, either through the principle of friendly interpretation or the principle of State liability.

Perhaps the EEA/EFTA states have reached the possible limit how far a state can operate without transferring its legislative power.

K. DISCUSSIONS

PER TRESSELT

Thank you very much. First of all, we have some time for questions, comments and challenges, after Professor Stefánsson's introduction and I call for commentators.

HANS PETTER GRAVER

Thank you very much for this very enlightening and interesting presentation on State liability and also on the reports on the reception of this by the Icelandic Supreme Court. I noted with interest, that you stressed in the acceptance by the Supreme Court in the '*Erla María*' case, that the Icelandic Supreme Court resolved this on the bases of Icelandic law, not on the bases of the EEA Agreement, as such. I think that is a more general trait that can be seen in the quotes of the EFTA States, because in my view it is exactly the same approach that the Norwegian Supreme Court took to the question of direct effect and interpretation obligations in the *Finanger* case, where the Norwegian Supreme Court went into the obligation of interpretation of national law and Community law and left the question open whether this was also an obligation under the EEA Agreement and resolved this by the Norwegian principle of presumption when interpreting national law under international obligations and stating explicitly that this Norwegian principle was not less far-reaching than an obligation under Community law. I think that what we see is on the one side that the Courts of the EFTA States reserve themselves on applying the more supranational principles of Community law in the EEA Agreement, but on the other side, they fulfil their obligations by finding similar solutions or by finding solutions in national law, which leads to the same results. I think this is a very interesting element of the relations between national laws and the EEA Agreement. I would also like to comment on the last slide you have here. If the principle of State liability in fact involves a transfer of legislative power in the EEA/EFTA countries, it may not be so interesting in a purely legal context, but I think it is important to stress that the most important part of transfer of legislative power is not entailed in the EEA Agreement. There is no EEA legislator and on the basis of being obligated or not, it is decisions in the EEA Committee, where of course the EFTA countries are under no legal obligation to adapt EC legislation into the EEA Agreement. I think this is an important difference, and of course, if we look at regulations, this is the legislative power of the Community or of the EU; there is no such equivalent legislative power within the EEA Agreement. So, it is easy to overlook this, because this is a simple legal issue, but I think it is of great importance. What we are discussing are the marginal issues. Thank you!

STEFÁN MÁR STEFÁNSSON

Yes, I am more or less of the same opinion as you are. Now, as I said earlier, our Supreme Court came to the conclusion that the conditions for the State liability came under Icelandic law. Maybe I do not understand this fully, but for me it is a little bit confusing because of the State liability. Are they then just accepting the principle as such? Because conditions is all what matters. This is one point I would like to raise.

The second point, we should have also. We can agree upon that our legislator has the formal right to legislate. That is true. If there are so many elements around, that the formal right is really nothing, then you can question: What have you really done? Have you really transferred the power? That was my point.

PER TRESSELT

Any further comments at this stage? Professor Pescatore.

PIERRE PESCATORE

I apologize for speaking again, but as you were so kind to invite me, I try to be as useful as I can in this discussion. Therefore, I would enlarge on the remarks that have just been made by Professor Graver, by drawing, as an international lawyer, your attention to the fact, that in the meantime the rules on State liability have been codified by the International Law Commission. There is now a text of over 50 articles which have been passed by the General Assembly of the United Nations. Nobody knows whether there will be an international Conference on this matter, but the codification is there in substance. My opinion is therefore that whenever we speak about State liability, we should first look at what the ILC which has induced a text, convergence between the Common law and the Roman law perceptions of liability. In my opinion, apart from the horizontal effect which these articles will have in the State-to-State relations, I think that there is also a vertical effect that these articles have unified the whole terminology in the matter. By this process we shall gain a unification and harmonisation at a universal level, because these articles are a rule for all States in this world.

PER TRESSELT

Thank you, Professor Pescatore, I think it is very appropriate to point out that we now have a set of written rules relating to State responsibility, and I would certainly not exclude that these principles will have repercussions within a Union of 25. Thank you.

The final speaker is Judge Allan Rosas, Professor, and Dr of Law from the University of Turku, at which University he has taught, as well as at Åbo Akademi, the Swedish language University in Turku. His first interest was Human Rights Law and he was Director of the Åbo Akademi, Institute for Human Rights for 10 years from 1985. Now, it is my experience that Human Rights lawyers tend to develop sympathy for the underdog. And that is, as a manner of speaking, looking at the law from the bottom up. Allan Rosas then came to the Legal Service of the European Commission. That requires looking at the law from the centre onto the periphery, advising and guiding, inspiring and cautioning the exercise of power and the planning of policy. When he became a Judge at the European Court of Justice in 2002, we could perhaps say that he had ascended to a more Olympic level. No one will speak with more authority about fundamental rights in the Courts of Luxembourg and Strasbourg.

Fundamental Rights in the Luxembourg and Strasbourg Courts

ALLAN ROSAS

A. INTRODUCTION

ONCE UPON A time—or sixty years ago, to be more exact—Europe was in ruins. The primordial task of building a sustainable peace required new structures, institutions and principles at the European level. One strand consisted of the focus on democracy, human rights, and the rule of law, with the Council of Europe (1949) and the European Convention on Human Rights (ECHR, 1950) as one of its main ingredients. Another strand consisted of deep economic integration, starting with the European Coal and Steel Community (1952) and later the European Economic Community (1957) and the European Atomic Energy Community (1957).

The institutional framework of the first strand, the Council of Europe, was entrusted with a broad agenda but with a rather modest level of integration. With the introduction of the ECHR, including in particular its Commission and Court of Human Rights, the intergovernmental framework of the Council of Europe obtained a more integrationist dimension. This facet of the Strasbourg system has been strengthened by subsequent institutional[1] and jurisprudential developments and one can today speak of the 'quasi-constitutional role' of the European Court of Human Rights.[2] In this context, the strengthening of the control system of the European Social Charter (1961), including a system of collective complaints, which can be submitted to the European Committee of Social Rights, also deserves to be mentioned.[3]

[1] Such as the coming into force, on 1 November 1998, of Optional Protocol 11, which provides for an obligatory system of individual complaints and the jurisdiction of the European Court of Human Rights.

[2] L Wildhaber, 'Foreword' in R Blackburn and J Polakiewicz, (eds), *Fundamental Rights in Europe: The European Convention on Human Rights and its Member States, 1950–2000* (Oxford, OUP, 2001) xiv.

[3] The Additional Protocol to the European Social Charter Providing for a System of Collective Complaints of 1995 entered into force on 1 July 1998. At the time of writing (October 2004), it binds

The story of the birth and development of the European Communities and the European Union (EU) is quite different: The process started as deep integration, with supra-national features, including, of course, the establishment of the Court of Justice already in 1952, but with an integration agenda of relatively limited scope. And so it is perhaps not surprising that in the early days, the Court of Justice held that it lacked competence to examine whether a European Coal and Steel Community decision constituted an infringement of fundamental rights as recognised in the constitution of a Member State.[4]

B. FUNDAMENTAL RIGHTS IN COMMUNITY LAW SINCE *STAUDER* (1969)

Given the supra-national nature of Community integration and Community law, coupled with its inherent tendency to broaden its own scope, fundamental rights were bound to enter into the picture. There is no need here to explain in detail the developments since 1969 and the judgment in *Stauder*.[5] Let me only recall that the case-law of the Court of Justice, declaring fundamental rights to form part of the general principles of Community law the observance of which the Court ensures, has been followed and accompanied by, first, political declarations relating to fundamental rights adopted by the Community institutions, then Treaty changes such as Article 6 of the Treaty on European Union (TEU) as well as human rights clauses in secondary Community law (regulations and international agreements).[6]

This development culminated in the proclamation, on 7 December 2000, by the three main political institutions, of the Charter of Fundamental Rights of the EU.[7] While the Charter is not formally binding *per se*, it has started to play a certain role in adjudication as a 'soft law' instrument, and has been cited, *inter alia*, by the Court of First Instance and the Advocates General of the European

only 11 Member States of the Council of Europe, however. See, eg, RR Churchill and U Khaliq, 'The Collective Complaints System of the European Social Charter: An Effective Mechanism for Ensuring Compliance with Economic and Social Rights?' (2004) 15 *European J Intl L* 417–56.

[4] Case 1/58 *Stork v High Authority* [1959] ECR 43. See also Joined Cases 36–38/59 *Geitling v High Authority* [1960] ECR 423; Case 40/64 *Sgarlata v Commission* [1965] ECR 280. See also G Tesauro, 'The Role of the Court of Justice in the Protection of Fundamental Rights' in N Colneric, *et al*, (eds), *Une communauté de droit. Festschrift für Gil Carlos Rodríguez Iglesias* (Berlin, Berliner Wissenschafts-Verlag, 2003) 103, 104.

[5] Case 29/69 *Stauder v City of Ulm* [1969] ECR 419. See also Case 11/70 *Internationale Handelsgesellschaft* [1970] ECR 1125; Case 4/73 *Nold* [1974] ECR 491.

[6] For an overview of the different sources of EU fundamental rights see, eg, A Rosas, 'The Legal Sources of EU Fundamental Rights' in N Colneric, *et al*, (eds), *Une communauté de droit. Festschrift für Gil Carlos Rodríguez Iglesias* (Berlin, Berliner Wissenschafts-Verlag, 2003) 87–102.

[7] OJ C 364, 18 December 2000, p 1.

Court of Justice[8] as well as by the European Court of Human Rights.[9] The entry into force of the Treaty establishing a Constitution for Europe, signed in Rome on 29 October 2004, would clearly strengthen the legal status of the Charter, which, with minor modifications, has been integrated into the new Treaty. The Rome Treaty would also settle a controversy of some historical standing, containing as it does a clause envisaging the accession of the EU to the ECHR.[10]

While the wider EU integration agenda has brought in its wake certain forms of co-operation falling short of supra-national integration, notably Title V TEU on a Common Foreign and Security Policy (the 'Second Pillar'), the increased focus on fundamental rights has, on the contrary, arguably strengthened a Community approach:

The objective of protecting fundamental rights tends to further the idea of jurisdictional control of the activities of the EU political institutions, as can be seen from the provisions on the—albeit limited—jurisdiction of the Court of Justice included in the 'Third Pillar' (Title VI on Police and Judicial Cooperation in Criminal Matters) and the proposed integration of this Pillar into a Community framework in the Treaty establishing a Constitution for Europe.[11] The need for judicial control also extends to the EU Member States when they apply and implement Community law. The Court of Justice has held that EU fundamental rights bind the Member States in situations falling within the scope of Community law.[12]

[8] As to the opinions of the Court's Advocate Generals, the first reference seems to have been in the Opinion of Advocate General Alber of 1 February 2001 in Case C–340/99 *Traco* (para 94). The first discussion on the legal relevance of the Charter is to be found in the Opinion of Advocate General Tizzano of 8 February 2001 in Case C–173/99 *BECTU*, where it is held that in proceedings concerned with the nature and scope of a fundamental right, 'the relevant statements of the Charter cannot be ignored' and that, where its provisions so allow, it should 'serve as a substantive point of reference for all those involved' (para 28). For a recent citation, with references to other opinions, see the Opinion of Advocate General Kokott of 14 October 2004 in Joined Cases C–387/02, C–391/02 and C–403/02 *Silvio Berlusconi*, para 109, n 83. As to the Court of First Instance, see cases T–112/98 *Mannesmannröhren-Werke* [2001] II–729, para 76; T–52/01 R *Schäfer*, Order of the President of the Court of First Instance of 21 May 2001 [2001] ECR III–543, para 44; T–54/99 *Max.Mobil* [2002] ECR II–313, para 48; T–198/01 R *Technische Glaswerke*, Order of the President of the Court of First Instance of 4 April 2002, paras 85–86; T–177/01 *Jégo-Quéré* [2002] ECR II–2365, para 42; Joined Cases T–116/01 and T–118/01 *P & O European Ferries* [2003] ECR II–2957, paras 207–9; T–67/01 *JCB Service*, (13 January 2004), para 36; Joined Cases T–67/00, T–68/00, T–71/00 and T–78/00 *JFE Engineering Corp*, (8 July 2004).

[9] Case of *Goodwin v United Kingdom*, (11 July 2002), Reports of Judgments and Decisions 2002–VI, paras 58 and 100, see also n 36 below.

[10] The definitive text is to be found in the document drawn up by the Conference of the Representatives of the Governments of the Member States, Treaty establishing a Constitution for Europe, Brussels, 6 August 2004, CIG 87/04.

[11] See, eg, Art I–1, according to which the Union shall exercise its competences 'on a Community basis', and Arts III–376 and III–377. With respect to judicial cooperation in criminal matters and police cooperation, Art III–377 does contain certain limitations on the jurisdiction of the Court of Justice, but these limitations are less severe than those contained in Art 35 TEU.

[12] See, eg, Case 5/88 *Wachauf* [1989] ECR 2609, para 19; Case C–260/90 *ERT* [1991] ECR I–2925, para 42; Case C–159/90 *Grogan* [1991] ECR I–4685, para 31; Case C–299/95 *Kremzow* [1997] ECR I–2405, para 15.

C. LUXEMBOURG CASE-LAW IN THE AREA OF FUNDAMENTAL RIGHTS

Today, the extensive case-law of the European Court of Justice and the Court of First Instance relating to fundamental rights covers a wide array of Community law areas.[13] The case-law of the EFTA Court, whose ten year anniversary we are celebrating, should also be mentioned in this context, as the Court has held that the provisions of the EEA Agreement and the procedural provisions of the Surveillance and Court Agreement 'are to be interpreted in the light of fundamental rights'.[14]

As for the fundamental rights upheld by Luxembourg case-law, they have included civil rights (such as the right to fair trial, the prohibition of retroactive penal legislation and the right to privacy), political freedoms (such as freedom of expression and freedom of assembly) and social rights (such as the right of men and women to equal pay, which has been described by the Court of Justice as a fundamental right[15]).

The list of fundamental rights does not seem to be closed: The Court has stated that it draws inspiration 'from the constitutional traditions common to the Member States and from the guidelines supplied by international treaties for the protection of human rights on which the Member States have collaborated or of which they are signatories'.[16] While the ECHR has been described as having 'special significance' (see below), the Court or its Advocates General have sometimes referred expressly to the two International Covenants of 1966, the European Social Charter or certain International Labour Organisation conventions.[17]

It is, in this context, also significant that the Charter of Fundamental Rights, whatever its precise legal status, lists a broad range of rights as EU fundamental rights and states in its preamble that it reaffirms rights

> as they result, in particular, from the constitutional traditions and international obligations common to the Member States, . . . the European [Convention on Human

[13] See, eg, N Neuwahl and A Rosas, (eds), *The European Union and Human Rights* (The Hague, Martinus Nijhoff, 1995); E Gould and G Lesieur, *The European Court of Justice on the European Convention on Human Rights: Who Said What, When?* (London, Kluwer Law International, 1998); P Alston, (ed), *The EU and Human Rights* (Oxford, OUP, 1999).

[14] Case E–2/03 *Ákæruvaldid (The Public Prosecutor) v Ásgeir Logi Ásgeirsson, Axel Pétur Ásgeirsson and Helgi Már Reynisson* [2003] EFTA Ct Rep 187, para 23. See also Case E–8/97 TV 1000 *Sverige v Norway* [1998] EFTA Ct Rep 68, para 26; Case E–2/02 *Technologien Bau—und Wirtschaftsberatung und Bellona v EFTA Surveillance Authority* [2003] EFTA Ct Rep 54, para 37.

[15] See, eg, Case C–13/94 *P v S and Cornwall County Council* [1996] ECR I–2143; Joined Cases C–270/97 and C–271/97 *Deutsche Post* [2000] ECR I–929, para 57.

[16] See, eg, Opinion 2/94 *European Convention on Human Rights* [1996] ECR I–1759, para 33.

[17] A Rosas, 'The European Union and International Human Rights Instruments' in V Kronenberger, (ed), *The European Union and the International Legal Order: Discord or Harmony?* (The Hague, TMC Asser Press, 2001) 53, 57–58.

Rights], the Social Charters adopted by the Community[18] and by the Council of Europe and the case-law of the Court of Justice of the European Communities and of the European Court of Human Rights.

The Charter also contains a provision (Article 53), according to which nothing in the Charter shall be interpreted as restricting or adversely affecting human rights as recognised, *inter alia*, by 'international law and by international agreements to which the Union, the Community or all the Member States are party'.

Do these developments imply that the Luxembourg Courts have become human rights courts in a way comparable to the Strasbourg Court? No, I do not think so. The Luxembourg Courts are general courts, with jurisdiction over the entire—and today extremely wide—range of Community law matters (or, in the case of the EFTA Court, the EEA Agreement). Like national courts, they are called upon to apply and interpret fundamental rights as an integral part of their day-to-day activities. There is no specific human rights/fundamental rights jurisdictional remedy open to the citizen, nor are there any internal organisational mechanisms devised specifically for dealing with fundamental rights cases. Fundamental rights are raised in the context of the normal procedures before the Courts, such as actions for annulment (Article 230 EC) and preliminary ruling requests from national courts (Article 234 EC). While fundamental rights figure in perhaps 20 or so judgments per year, which is not a very significant number compared to the overall number of judgments given each year by the Luxembourg Courts.[19]

D. FUNDAMENTAL RIGHTS v ECONOMIC FREEDOMS

In legal literature, it is sometimes argued that the Luxembourg Courts, in fact, give priority to the classic economic freedoms of the EC Treaty, at the expense of fundamental rights considerations.[20] Such a situation is conceivable particularly in a case where the protection of an economic freedom and that of a fundamental right point in different directions,[21] in other words when fundamental

[18] This refers to the 1989 Community Charter of the Fundamental Rights of Workers, originally adopted in September 1989 by 11 out of 12 Member States, and subsequently mentioned in Art 136 EC.

[19] For the period 2001–March 2003, I have found 37 judgments of the Court of Justice, 37 opinions of Advocate-Generals, and 22 judgments of the Court of First Instance, where explicit reference is made to fundamental rights as general principles of Community law. The EFTA Court, for its part, seems to have referred to fundamental rights in altogether three cases (see n 14 above).

[20] See, eg, M Poiares Maduro, 'Striking the Elusive Balance between Economic Freedom and Social Rights in the EU' in P Alston, (ed), *The EU and Human Rights* (Oxford, OUP, 1999) 449–72; J Heliskoski, 'Fundamental Rights versus Economic Freedoms in the European Union: Which Paradigm?' in J Klabbers and J Petman, (eds), *Nordic Cosmopolitanism: Essays in International Law for Martti Koskenniemi* (Leiden, Martinus Nijhoff, 2003) 417–43, with references.

[21] Heliskoski, see n 20 above, pp 430–39, discusses such a situation on the basis of cases C–353/89 *Commission v Netherlands* [1991] ECR I–4069; C–368/95 *Familiapress* [1997] ECR I–3689; and C–112/00 *Schmidberger* (still pending at the time of the writing of Heliskoski's article).

rights are invoked as a ground for derogating from an economic freedom, such as was the case in *Schmidberger*.[22]

It is true, that in this case the Court of Justice began by holding that the failure by Austria to ban a demonstration which resulted in the complete closure of a major transit route such as the Brenner motorway for almost 30 hours was to be regarded as constituting a measure of equivalent effect to a quantitative restriction and thus, in principle, incompatible with the EC Treaty unless that failure could be objectively justified. On the other hand, the Court noted that

> since both the Community and its Member States are required to respect fundamental rights, the protection of those rights is a legitimate interest which, in principle, justifies a restriction of the obligations imposed by Community law, even under a fundamental freedom guaranteed by the Treaty such as the free movement of goods.

In an effort to 'reconcile' the free movement of goods with the freedoms of expression and assembly, account should, according to the Court, be taken of the fact that the latter freedoms are, unlike certain absolute rights such as the right to life and freedom from torture, expressly subject to limitations justified by objectives in the public interest. In such a situation, the interests involved had to be weighed 'having regard to all the circumstances of the case in order to determine whether a fair balance was struck between those interests'.[23]

My reading of *Schmidberger* is not that the Court established a hierarchical relationship between a Treaty-based economic freedom and a fundamental right but rather saw these two rights as complementary. The reason why the Court took an alleged violation of the free movement of goods as its point of departure is simply that that was the question submitted to it by the national court. Moreover, if the fundamental right in question had been of a more absolute nature (such as the prohibition of torture), there would arguably not have been a need to justify the measure by reference to a proportionality test.[24]

E. THE ECHR IN LUXEMBOURG CASE-LAW

The relationship between the Luxembourg and Strasbourg systems has been one of gradual *rapprochement*. In its first judgments citing fundamental rights, the Court of Justice did not refer expressly to the ECHR. The first reference to the ECHR came in *Nold*, just after France as the (then) last Member State had

[22] Case C–112/00 *Schmidberger* [2003] ECR I–5659.

[23] See paras 64–81 of the judgment (n 22 above).

[24] The Court, in fact, observed that 'unlike other fundamental rights enshrined in that Convention, such as the right to life or the prohibition of torture and inhuman or degrading treatment or punishment, which admit of no restriction, neither the freedom of expression nor the freedom of assembly guaranteed by the ECHR appears to be absolute but must be viewed in relation to its social purpose' (para 80).

ratified the Convention.[25] As has already been mentioned, the Court subsequently characterised the ECHR as an instrument having 'special significance'.[26] In this context, it is telling that the ECHR is the only international human rights convention mentioned in Article 6, paragraph 2, TEU (which was introduced by the Treaty of Maastricht).[27] And more recently, the Luxembourg Courts have begun to refer to individual judgments of the European Court of Human Rights.[28]

One can thus note the following 'stages' in the case-law of the Court of Justice:

—fundamental rights outside the competence of the Court
—fundamental rights as part of the general principles of Community law (since 1969)
—explicit reference to the ECHR (since 1974–75)
—characterisation of the ECHR as having 'special significance'(since 1989)
—reference to individual judgments of the Court of Human Rights (since the 1990s).

Given that the Court of Justice has started to refer to individual judgments of the Court of Human Rights, it is not surprising that it has also indicated a willingness to adjust its own case-law in the light of developments in Strasbourg case-law. Thus in *Limburgse Vinyl Maatschappij*, the Court of Justice noted that there had been, since its *Orkem* judgment,[29] further developments in

[25] Case 4/73 *Nold* [1974] ECR 491, para 12. This reference, it is true, figures in a paragraph citing the assertions of one of the parties. For a reference to be found in the reasoning of the Court itself, see Case 36/75 *Rutili* [1975] ECR 1219, para 32. In the latter case, the Court noted that the ECHR had been 'ratified by all the Member States'.

[26] The first such statement seems to have been in Joined Cases 46/87 and 222/88 *Hoechst* [1989] ECR 2859, para 13. See also Case C–260/89 *ERT* [1991] ECR I–2925, para 41. These judgments refer in this respect to Case 222/84 *Johnston* [1986] ECR 1651, para 18, where, however, following a reference to the Joint Declaration adopted by the European Parliament, Council and Commission on 5 April 1977 (JO C 103, p 1) and the case-law of the Court itself, the Court simply stated that 'the principles on which that Convention is based must be taken into consideration in Community law'.

[27] The Treaty of Amsterdam (1997) included this provision among those falling under the jurisdiction of the Court of Justice, albeit with the limitation that only the actions of the EU institutions are concerned, and insofar as the Court of Justice has jurisdiction under the ECT and the TEU itself (Art L of the TEU as amended by the Treaty of Amsterdam, currently Art 47 TEU).

[28] Already in Case 374/87 *Orkem* [1989] ECR 3283, para 30; Joined Cases 46/87 and 227/88 *Hoechst* [1989] ECR 2859, para 18; Case 85/87 *Dow Benelux* [1989] ECR 3137, para 29; and Joined Cases 97– 99/87 *Dow Chemical Ibérica* [1989] ECR 3165, para 15, the Court noted the absence of relevant case-law of the European Court of Human Rights. And in Case C–13/94 *P v S* [1996] ECR I–2143, para 16, the Court referred expressly to a given judgment of the Court of Human Rights. See also K Lenaerts and P Van Nuffel, *Constitutional Law of the European Union* (London, Sweet & Maxwell, 1999) 541 (n 89). For recent citations of Strasbourg case-law, see, eg, Case C–60/00 *Carpenter* [2002] ECR I–6279, para 42; the *Limburgse Vinyl Maatschappij* cases mentioned in n 30 below; the *Roquette Frères* case mentioned in n 31, below, paras 29 and 52 of the judgment; Case C–112/00 *Schmidberger* (n 22 above), para 79; Joined Cases C–465/00, C–138/01 and C–139/01 *Rechnungshof v Österreichischer Rundfunk* [2003] ECR I–4948, paras 77 and 83; Case C–117/01 *KB*, (7 January 2004), para 33; Case C–71/02 *Karner*, (25 March 2004), para 51.

[29] Case 374/87 *Orkem v Commission* [1989] ECR 3283.

Strasbourg case-law that the Community judiciary should take into account in interpreting fundamental rights.[30] And in *Roquette Frères*, the Court of Justice referred expressly to the development of ECHR case-law relating to the right to privacy of commercial enterprises, in order to explain why, despite having suggested the opposite in its earlier judgment in *Hoechst*, such enterprises can, in principle, benefit from Article 8 of the ECHR:

> 29. For the purposes of determining the scope of that principle in relation to the protection of business premises, regard must be had to the case-law of the European Court of Human Rights subsequent to the judgment in *Hoechst*. According to that case-law, the protection of the home provided for in Article 8 of the ECHR may in certain circumstances be extended to cover such premises (see, in particular, the judgment of 16 April 2002 in *Colas Est and Others v France, not yet published in the Reports of Judgments and Decisions*, § 41) and second, the right of interference established by Article 8(2) of the ECHR might well be more far-reaching where professional or business activities or premises were involved than would otherwise be the case.[31]

In the light of this judgment, as well as the recent case-law of the Luxembourg Courts in general, I find the thesis, often put forward in legal literature,[32] that there is tension or even conflict between Luxembourg and Strasbourg case-law, somewhat exaggerated, to put it mildly. Harmony, rather than conflict, is a much more likely scenario. In this context, it should also be pointed out that according to Article 6, paragraph 2, TEU, the EU 'shall respect fundamental rights, as guaranteed by the [European Convention on Human Rights] . . . as general principles of Community law'.

As the EU (or the EC) is not a Contracting Party to the ECHR, the Convention is not, in itself, part of Community law but plays its role rather as an authoritative guideline for determining the general principles of Community law which the Court applies. While the ECHR and the Strasbourg case-law thus do not have the same legal force for the EU and its institutions as for the Contracting Parties to the ECHR,[33] there seems to be, in the light of Article 6, paragraph 2, and as reaffirmed in Article 52, paragraph 3, of the Charter of

[30] Joined Cases C–238/99 P, *et al*, *Limburgse Vinyl Maatschappij* [2002] ECR I–8375, para 274.

[31] Case C–94/00 *Roquette Frères* [2002] ECR I–9011, para 29. *Cf* Cases 46/87 and 222/98 *Hoechst* [1989] ECR 2859, para 18. In Joined Cases T–305/94 *et al*, *Limburgse Vinyl Maatschappij*, the Court of First Instance ruled that the development of the case-law of the European Court of Human Rights had no direct impact on the merits of the solution adopted in *Hoechst* (para 420 of the judgment). On appeal, the Court of Justice in case C–238/99 P, *et al* (see n 30 above), rejected the complaint relating to Art 8 of the ECHR without considering it necessary to rule on the merits of the position of the Court of First Instance (para 251 of the judgment). See also J Mischo, *Hoechst, Colas, Roquette*: illustration d'une convergence' in N Colneric, *et al*, (eds), *Une communauté de droit. Festschrift für Gil Carlos Rodríguez Iglesias* (Berlin, Berliner Wissenschafts-Verlag, 2003) 137–45.

[32] See, eg, C Turner, 'Human Rights Protection in the European Community: Resolving Conflict and Overlap between the European Court of Justice and the European Court of Human Rights' (1999) 5 *European Public L* 453, 457–63, with references.

[33] On the legal effects of the ECHR Strasbourg case-law in the legal orders of the Contracting Parties, see, eg, Order of the German Constitutional Court, 2 BvR 1481/04 (14 October 2004), http://www.bundesverfassungsgericht.de/entscheidungen/rs20,041,014_2bvr148,104.

Fundamental Rights, a need to take the Strasbourg case-law fully into account in Luxembourg as well as in Brussels.[34]

F. COMMUNITY LAW IN STRASBOURG CASE-LAW

Of course, this is not a one-way street. The European Court of Human Rights also refers, in its judgments, to Community law and Luxembourg case-law. It seems, in fact, useful to distinguish between the different ways in which Community law or Luxembourg case-law may be relevant for the Court of Human Rights.

First of all, the Court may rely on Community law solutions and Luxembourg case-law in indirect support of a certain interpretation of a provision of the ECHR. Such a situation arose, for instance, in the *Kress* case (2001), where the Court, in holding that the participation of the Government Commissioner in the deliberations of the French *Conseil d'État* constituted a violation of Article 6 ECHR, noted that it was 'confirmed in this approach' by the fact that at the Court of Justice of the European Communities, the Advocate General does not attend deliberations.[35] In *Goodwin* (2002), the Court referred to the wording of Article 9 of the EU Charter of Fundamental Rights (right to marry) to back up its decision that the refusal to recognise a change of sex for the purposes of marriage constituted a violation of Article 12 of the ECHR.[36]

[34] In Case T–112/98 *Mannesmannröhren-Werke* [2001] ECR II–729, the Court of First Instance held that, while it had no jurisdiction to 'apply' the Convention when reviewing an investigation under competition law, as the ECHR as such is not part of Community law (para 59), the Community law principles of the rights of defence and the right to fair legal process 'offer, in the specific field of competition law, at issue in the present case, protection equivalent to that guaranteed by Article 6 of the [ECHR]' (para 77). *Cf* Case T–347/94 *Mayr-Melnhof* [1998] ECR II–1751, para 311.

[35] *Kress v France*, (7 June 2001), Reports of Judgments and Decisions 2001–VI, para 86.

[36] *Goodwin v United Kingdom*, n 9 above, paras 58 and 100. In *Pellegrin v France*, (8 December 1999), Reports of Judgments and Decisions 1999–VIII, the Court of Human Rights announced that it will have regard, for guidance, to a Communication by the European Commission (EU) on the scope of the notion of 'employment in the public service' (relating to Art 39 EC on free movement of workers) for the interpretation of the scope of Art 6 ECHR with regard to civil servants. In *Meftah v France*, (26 July 2002), Reports of Judgments and Decisions 2002–VII, paras 32 and 45, the Court, in holding that national courts may under certain circumstances override a defendant's choice of legal counsel, observed that according to Directive 98/5/EC of the European Parliament and of the Council of 16 February 1998 to facilitate practice of the profession of lawyer on a permanent basis in a Member States other than that in which the qualification was obtained as well as the case-law of the Court of Justice (Case C–168/98 *Luxembourg v European Parliament and Council* [2000] ECR I–9131), EU Member States may lay down specific rules for access to their supreme courts, such as the use of specialised lawyers. In *Posti and Rahko v Finland*, (24 September 2002), Reports of Judgments and Decisions 2002–VII, para 54, the Court noted that its position on the scope of the right of access to a court 'resembles that adopted in the law of the European Community', where according to Art 230 EC and the case-law of the Court of Justice (the Court referred to Case C–358/89 *Extramet* [1991] ECR I–2501), a general measure such as a regulation may, in certain circumstances, be of individual concern so as to be open to an action for annulment. *Cf* the case of *Société Colas Est v France*, (16 April 2002), Reports of Judgments and Decisions 2002–III, paras 26–27, in which the Court of Human Rights mentioned the *Hoechst* case-law mentioned above, n 31, without following itself that (more restrictive) interpretation of Art 8.

Secondly, the Court may be confronted with certain peculiarities of the EU system and the possible implications thereof for Strasbourg procedures. For instance, the Court has held that the length of proceedings before the Court of Justice in preliminary ruling cases cannot be taken into account in considering whether the requirement that proceedings be conducted within a reasonable time has been respected.[37]

Thirdly, the existence of a violation of Community law may constitute a factor in determining whether there has also been a violation of the ECHR. Such a situation arose in the *Dangeville* case (2002), where the Court referred extensively to Luxembourg case-law on the supremacy of Community law, the legal effects of Directives and the temporal application and effects of certain VAT Directives (in relation to this last question, the Court referred to Case 70/83 *Kloppenburg* [1984] ECR 1075). In determining that an interference with the right to the peaceful enjoyment of possessions was not required in the general interest, the Court took account of the fact that French legislation and case-law was incompatible with Community law.[38]

Fourthly, the Strasbourg Court may be faced with the delicate question of whether, and to what extent, the EU Member States may be responsible for acts or omissions with a Community dimension, given that the Member States have transferred some of their powers to the EU, without accepting that the latter become a Contracting Party to the ECHR.

G. EU MEMBER STATES' RESPONSIBILITY UNDER THE ECHR FOR EU ACTIVITIES?

The last question deserves some further comment. The European Commission of Human Rights (which ceased to exist in 1999) held that, while the Contracting Parties remain, in principle, responsible for acts of their domestic organs allegedly violating the ECHR even if the act is a consequence of the requirement to comply with an international obligation, the transfer of powers to an international organisation such as the EU is not incompatible with the ECHR 'provided that within that organisation fundamental rights will receive equivalent protection'. As, according to the Commission of Human Rights, the EU fulfilled this condition, a Member State was held not to be responsible for the execution of a judgment of the European Court of Justice.[39]

[37] Case *Pafitis v Greece* (26 February 1998) Reports 1998–I, para 95, and *Koua Poirrez v France Koua*, (30 September 2003), para 61. On the other hand, in the case of *Dufuy v The European Communities and its Member States* (Application No 13,539/88), the European Commission of Human Rights held in 1989 that the legal remedies of Community law may constitute remedies which, under the ECHR, have to be exhausted before a case can be brought before the Strasbourg organs.

[38] Case of *SA Dangeville v France*, (16 April 2002), Reports of Judgments and Decisions 2002–III, paras 31–37, 53–58.

[39] Application No 13,258/87, *M & Co v Germany,* 64 Decisions & Reports, p 138. See also Application No 21,090/92, *Heinz* (concerning the European Patent Convention).

The European Court of Human Rights, for its part, has, on occasion, concluded that an EU Member State has violated the ECHR in an area at least partly covered by Community law, but in these cases the Member State concerned has enjoyed a certain discretion in implementing Community law[40] or has, as was the situation in *Matthews*, itself participated in the creation of a Community law rule which cannot be challenged before the European Court of Justice.[41]

In this context, the Court of Human Rights has stated that, while the ECHR does not preclude the transfer of powers to international organisations, this is on the condition that Convention rights continue to be guaranteed. The Court has added that Member States' responsibility subsists even after such a transfer[42] and that it would be incompatible with the purpose and object of the Convention if an attribution of tasks to international organisations or in the context of international agreements could absolve the Contracting Parties of their obligations under the ECHR.[43]

The question as to whether these general *dicta* imply that EU Member States could also be responsible for acts or omissions of the EU institutions themselves (such as Commission decisions or Court judgments), was raised in the *Senator Lines* case, which however, was subsequently declared inadmissible on the basis that the applicant could no longer claim to be the victim of a violation.[44] Given

[40] In the case of *Cantoni v France*, (22 October 1996), Reports of Judgments and Decisions 1996–V, (in which the Court, at paras 13–17, referred extensively to European Court of Justice case-law concerning the definition of medicinal products), the Court considered French legislation and national case-law concerning the definition of medicinal products in order to determine whether a criminal offence had been sufficiently clearly defined in law in view of Art 7 of the ECHR. While the Court noted that the fact that the French provision in question was based almost word for word on a Community directive (Directive 65/65/EEC of 26 January 1965, OJ L 369, 9.2.1965), this did 'not remove it from the ambit of Article 7 of the Convention' (para 30). In this case, it was clear that the definition of the criminal offence was a matter primarily for French law, and that not only the French legislation but also national case-law was at issue.

[41] *Matthews v United Kingdom*, (18 February 1999), Reports of Judgments and Decisions 1999–I. The Court, in finding that the UK had violated Art 3 of Protocol 1 of the ECHR by denying the applicant, a resident of Gibraltar, the right to vote in the elections for the European Parliament, held that the violation flowed from intergovernmental treaties (Maastricht, 1976) which had been freely entered into by the UK and which could not be challenged before the European Court of Justice (para 33). See also the case of *TI v United Kingdom,* (7 March 2000), Reports of Judgments and Decisions 2000–III, where the Court held that the UK could not escape responsibility for removing an asylum-seeker to Germany by relying on the Dublin Convention determining the State responsible for examining applications for asylum lodged in one of the Community Member States of 15 June 1990.

[42] The *Matthews* case (note 41, above), para 32.

[43] Cases of *Waite and Kennedy v Germany*, (18 February 1999), Reports of Judgments and Decisions 1999–I, para 67; *Beer and Regan v Germany*, (18 February 1999), *ibid*, para 57; *TI v United Kingdom*, n 41 above.

[44] Case of *Senator Lines*, (10 March 2004). The Commission decisions in the field of competition law triggered different cases and procedural phases before the Luxembourg Courts, see Case T–395/94 R *Atlantic Container Line v Commission,* Order of the President of the Court of First Instance of 10 March 1995 [1995] ECR II–595; Case C–149/95 P (R) *Commission v Atlantic Container Line,* Order of the President of the Court of Justice of 19 July 1995 [1995] ECR I–2165; Case T–395/94 *Atlantic Container Line and Others v Commission* [2002] ECR II–875; Case T–191/98 R *DSR Senator Lines*, on appeal Case C–364/99 P (R), Order of the President of the Court of Justice of 14 December 1999, [1999] ECR I–8733; Joined Cases T–191/98 and T–212/98 to T–214/98 *Atlantic Container Line v Commission*, judgment of the Court of First Instance of 30 September 2003.

that this case concerned decisions of the European Commission and the Luxembourg Courts, the Commission requested, and was granted, the right to intervene as a third party.[45] At least two other cases of a similar nature (alleged responsibility of EU Member States for acts or omissions of EU institutions) are pending before the Court of Human Rights.[46]

These cases raise complex and delicate questions of responsibility under the ECHR. If the EU Member States were to be held responsible for acts of the EU institutions, the ensuing consequences could take one of two directions: *Either* the Member States would be held responsible for activities in which, under Community law, they are not supposed to intervene (notably Commission decision-making and cases before the Luxembourg Courts) *or*, they would, in order to avoid such a result, be required to intervene, probably in violation of Community law. Such cases brought against EU Member States also raise the prospect of litigation against a party (the Member State) which did not take the decision in question, without the full participation in the proceedings of the party which is directly responsible for the said act (the EU and its institutions). In addition, one may wonder whether litigation before the Court of Human Rights on matters falling within the scope of Community law would always fully address all relevant aspects thereof.[47]

H. TOWARDS EU ACCESSION TO THE ECHR?

It is submitted that the best solution to these and similar problems would be to implement the approach taken in the new Treaty establishing a Constitution for Europe, in other words EU accession to the ECHR. The Opinion of the European Court of Justice, given in 1996, according to which the EC lacked competence to accede to the ECHR[48] was, of course, a ruling *de lege lata* and should not be seen as a negative stance on the appropriateness of accession.

In my view, the existence of an EU Charter of Fundamental Rights does not in any way make EU accession to the ECHR less important or desirable. The Charter is an internal constitutional instrument, while ECHR accession would

[45] A Clapham, 'The European Union before the European Court of Human Rights' in L Boisson de Chazournes, C Romano and R Mackenzie, (eds), *International Organizations and International Dispute Settlement: Trends and Prospects* (New York, Transnational Publishers, 2002) 73–88; A Rosas, 'International Dispute Settlement: EU Practices and Procedures' 46 *German Ybk Intl L 2003* (Berlin, Duncker & Humblot, 2004) 284, 314–15.

[46] *Bosphorus Airways v Ireland*, application No 45,036/98 (oral hearing on 19 September 2004); and *Emesa Sugar v Netherlands*, application No 62,023/00. In the former case, the European Commission has been authorised to intervene as a third party.

[47] In the *Matthews* case (see n 41, above), the Court of Human Rights does not appear to have discussed the question of whether the right to vote in European elections can be granted to persons (in the case at hand, some of the residents of Gibraltar) who are not, under Art 17 TEU, citizens of the EU The latter aspect has been raised in a case pending before the European Court of Justice, C–145/04 *Spain v United Kingdom*.

[48] See n 16, above.

subject the EU as a body to the same kind of external control that has, since the 1950s, been exercised over its Member States. Why should the powers of these Member States, if transferred to the EU, escape such external control? The implementation of Article I–9, paragraph 2, of the Treaty establishing a Constitution for Europe, according to which the EU 'shall accede' to the ECHR, would remove what I consider to be an outdated anomaly in today's European human rights system.

EU accession to the ECHR would obviously require some specific mechanisms, such as arrangements for EU participation in the surveillance bodies of the ECHR.[49] On the other hand, accession would not require any particular rules on the relationship between the ECHR and EU law, and between the Strasbourg Court and the Luxembourg Courts, rules which would be principally different from those concerning the relationship between the ECHR and its current Contracting Parties. The Court of Justice would simply find itself in a position similar to that of national constitutional and/or supreme courts under the current ECHR system.

Formal entry into force of the Charter of Fundamental Rights, and EU accession to the ECHR, would crown a development which, since 1969, has steadily built remarkable changes into the role of fundamental rights in Community and EU law. We have come far from the days when European integration was limited to the management of coal and steel. Indeed, the Coal and Steel Community is no longer in our midst.

[49] See Protocol No 32 relating to Art I–9(2) of the Constitution on the Accession of the Union to the European Convention on the Protection of Human Rights and Fundamental Freedoms, annexed to the Treaty establishing a Constitution for Europe.

I. DISCUSSIONS

PER TRESSELT

We come to a questions and comments section. The light in this hall is such that it is difficult to see people at the back of the hall, when you want to ask questions at the back of the hall, wave your place card prominently. Would anyone wish to comment on the issue of Human Rights? President Wildhaber?

LUZIUS WILDHABER

Thank you very much. Yes, I think I should respond and thank Judge Rosas, and before him President Skouris, very much for their contributions. We often speak of dialogue between courts and judges. There has been a very successful one, according to my conviction in the field of Human Rights between the Court of Justice and the EFTA Court and our Court, and I think that is how it should have been. As you put it, 'harmony' rather than 'conflict' should be the solution. There should be harmonisation of the case law, as far as possible. This is not the field for forum shopping where one should go around from one court to the other, to see what solution might be the better one, but we should try to consolidate the conclusions.

You spoke about the four situations that you had, and I wish to add a little bit procedurally. We may also have cases where strangely no one seems to care that there might be an EU Law before us. In the case of *Cantoni* vs *France*, a French Directive had a wording that was very similar to the one of the EU Directive. Somehow, no one seemed to care. The French Government did not; it pleaded the matter as an issue of French law. The Applicants did not, and we ultimately were very early on in the work of the new Court and also did not insist. Then we have the '*Senator Line's* situation where applicants go individually against all Member States. In the case *Senator Lines* it was 15, so it would have to be 25 Member States in the future. Whatever procedural solutions are conceivable, that does not seem to be the good one. The good one would be, as you also said, Judge Rosas, accession of the EU to the European Convention on Human Rights. The *Bosphorus Airways* case is a case where the Irish Government was brought before our Court for their application of EU Law. The EU Law was indeed maybe not clear at first sight. It is pending, I cannot say very much, you will understand that, and we will have to look very carefully at these problems. We have more and more of such problems. So, also from that perspective, accession would be very desirable.

But overall, just my sincere thanks for the organisers of today, and also to your Court for the good cooperation and the actually working cooperation.

PER TRESSELT

Thank you, President Wildhaber. Do I see further calls for the floor? Sven Norberg, please.

SVEN NORBERG

Yes, thank you very much. First of all, I think this was an excellent presentation; it was fascinating to listen to it. I have a question to your final concluding remark, Judge Rosas, where you said, that one should implement Article I–9, paragraph 2 of the Constitutional Treaty, which is to be signed next week, and thus arrange for the accession of the European Union to the Convention on Human Rights. I would like to know whether you would foresee, that this would take place in the way as the EU accedes to any other international agreements. Because my question is then, whether you have thought of the consequences for the ECJ, in particular, but also for the Court of Human Rights, that would follow from the competence of the ECJ to give preliminary rulings on the interpretation of every legal act that is part of Community law, including international agreements that have been acceded to by the European Union. You will realize that it, of course, could be tempting for a national judge interpreting a provision of the Convention on Human Rights but not having an opportunity to get assistance from the Court of Human Rights, instead to make a reference to the ECJ under Article 234 EC. Thank you.

ALLAN ROSAS

Yes, first of all it is obvious that EU accession to the European Convention on Human Rights would require working out quite a lot of detailed arrangements. Should there be a specific EU Judge and exactly how should that be done? There are of course already some preliminary ideas on that, which, in fact, have been discussed already since the 1970s.

On your more specific question, it is obvious that the European Convention with accession would, as any other international agreement, become part of Community law, as it is now, in most contracting parties to the Strasbourg system. Of course, there would be the possibility for national courts and parties before national courts to envisage asking for preliminary rulings. My comment would simply be that that would not dramatically change anything. First of all, that could obviously take place only within the framework of Community law. It would have to be a question of Community law, whereas Human Rights questions which fall completely outside Community law would still have to be addressed directly from the Member State concerned to Strasbourg. Secondly, as I tried to indicate, there is already today, a very intense regard from

Luxembourg to Strasbourg, including not only individual provisions of the European Convention on Human Rights, but also the interpretation of those provisions in the Court of Human Rights. I am not saying nothing would change, but I don't think that the change on that point would be in any way dramatic as compared to the situation as we already have it today.

PER TRESSELT

Thank you. Are there more requests for the floor? Yes, Dr Buschle.

DIRK BUSCHLE

I have one question regarding recent case law of the Court of Justice of the European Communities. One notices in some of the recent judgments that when referring to the judgments given by the European Court of Human Rights, the ECJ quite often also refers to the concept of 'margin of appreciation' of Member States as developed under the Human Rights Convention. This happened both in the area of fundamental freedoms and in the area of harmonized law. Do you see a conflict between the application of this concept in EC law and the doctrine of supremacy?

JUDGE ALLAN ROSAS

Not as a question of principle. Supremacy is one thing and content of that supreme law is another. If the content of that supreme law contains within it a margin of appreciation, that is then the case. Another question is of course the determination of what kind of margin of appreciation exists in a certain situation, if we are talking about Human Rights and the European Convention. On that point, there might be different views. If the EU becomes a party to the Convention on Human Rights, then, the last word in a certain sense, as to the interpretation on the Convention on Human Rights would be delivered by the Strasbourg Court. But that is exactly the same situation as you have today with the regard to the States that are Contracting Parties to the Strasbourg system.

PER TRESSELT

Thank you. If there are no further comments, it is for me only to thank our speakers this afternoon warmly to have engaged the audience and the audience for having responded. President Baudenbacher will present his concluding remarks.

Closing Remarks

CARL BAUDENBACHER

Ladies and gentlemen,

WE ARE AT the end of the symposium that marks the EFTA Court's Tenth Anniversary. This symposium has dealt with a variety of subjects, but I have the feeling that the speeches have mainly circled around a limited number of issues, probably not by coincidence. I would like to mention four in particular.

First of all, by the nature of the situation, homogeneity has been a core issue of this conference. I would like to quote President Skouris here, who called homogeneity the principal objective of the EEA Agreement. In fact, homogeneity seems to be more than just a statutory principle, or a principle based on a statute. It has evolved into a general principle. I may remind you, that in its very first judgment in the *Restamark* case, the EFTA Court held that the case law of the ECJ may also be relevant when interpreting procedural rules, although there is no statutory provision to that effect. That case was, *inter alia*, about the jurisprudence of the ECJ concerning the concept of a court or tribunal entitled to make a preliminary reference. I may add that the EFTA Court nevertheless took a more liberal approach than its 'big sister court' in this case. The Court of Justice of the European Communities appears to see the homogeneity principle essentially in the same way. I would refer here, for instance, to the well-reasoned judgment in the *Bellio Fratelli* case, in which Allan Rosas acted as a Judge Rapporteur, and in which homogeneity is defined in a very broad way, but also to the *Ospelt* judgment referred to by the President of the European Court of Justice.

I fully agree with you, Mr President, that the relationship between the Court of Justice of the European Communities and the EFTA Court could be used as a model for other inter-court relations. A line came to my mind, a comparison that was made by the former President of the European Court of Justice, Gil Carlos Rodríguez-Iglesias, who said in the light of what happened in the ECJ's Opinion 1/91, when the idea of establishing an EEA Court was struck down, 'we have to be close to each other, but still separated'. He said in Spanish: *Juntos, pero no revueltos*, which is probably best translated into English as 'joined, but not scrambled'.

Justice Utgård made it clear that homogeneity is also a core principle of the Lugano and Brussels Conventions, and I may add here, that a similar model has been implemented in the bilateral Agreement between the European Union and Switzerland on the free movement of persons. Always talking about homogeneity, Professor Graver has presented a very interesting theory, namely that when it comes to complying with EFTA Court rulings, EFTA States' national courts find solutions in their national law that lead to the same result as the one given by the EFTA Court. They are thereby fulfilling an 'obligation de résultat' without throwing overboard their own legal traditions. Professor Graver has also pointed to the fact that according to the Norwegian Supreme Court, judges in Norway are directly addressed by Article 3 of the EEA Agreement, and I cannot see that Professor Stefán Már Stefánsson has contradicted that; quite the opposite. He has made it clear that Icelandic courts, although formally sticking to dualism, have faithfully implemented the EFTA Court's rulings, and not only in the area of State liability.

The second issue I would like to mention is related to the statement made by Hans-Petter Graver that the EEA may serve as a yardstick for integration in general. So that the dividing lines would to a lesser extent be found between EU States on the one hand and EFTA States on the other, but more so between small states and big states, no matter whether in the European Union or in EFTA, or by more free trade oriented states and less free trade oriented states or between Nordic countries and non-Nordic countries. This is, to a certain extent, echoing the discussion on cultural features we had in the morning session and underlines that the depth of integration achieved under a given agreement is to be measured not only by looking into its foundation charters, but also by taking into account its reality. Of course, differences in scope between the EC Treaty and the EEA Agreement, as referred to by Professor Pescatore in the context of exhaustion of trademark rights, may gain a certain importance in individual cases. But overall, it seems fair to say that the structural differences between both models are of far less significance than is often alleged.

The third theme, which has been underlying the presentations of Professor Müller-Graff and of Professor Bronckers, concerned the question of whether non-legal factors and collective preferences may be relevant in the interpretation of EC/EEA law and WTO law or in the respective legislation. There seemed to be a certain mood in the room, in particular when Marco Bronckers spoke, that in the future, power could be shifted back to the Member States in these areas, not only in the WTO, but also in the European Union and the European Economic Area. This will probably happen whether we like it or not. I refer to the statement of former EFTA Court President Leif Sevón on that matter.

The fourth subject, which has been dealt with throughout the conference was, no wonder, judicial dialogue. Professors Graver and Stefánsson focused on the co-operation between the EFTA Court and the national Courts of the EFTA States. This could be referred to as a vertical dialogue. President Skouris spoke about the relationship between the European Court of Justice and the EFTA

Court, which is essentially horizontal in nature, and he has made it clear that although, like law on the books, this model of homogeneity appears to be a one way street, like law in practice, it is not. Judge Allan Rosas spoke on the difficult task of ensuring a homogeneous development of the case law of the Community Courts and the EFTA Court on the one side and the European Court of Human Rights on the other, which, as he has made very clear, is a very complex relationship.

But nevertheless, no major accidents have happened over the years; again, because there is dialogue on-going. President Wildhaber has rightly stressed its success in preventing conflicts. The notion of judicial dialogue is widely used in American contemporary literature. There are dozens of articles written on judicial dialogue right now, but in practice, there is not much dialogue in American Courts with regard to European sources. The dialogue takes place in Europe. In the United States, we have for instance read a famous dissenting opinion by Justice Scalia, who says that 'every reference to foreign material is dangerous and meaningless dicta'. That means that for once, Americans appear to be the talkers, while the Europeans are the doers.

I would like to thank our speakers for their outstanding contributions. I am personally looking very much forward to the publication of these speeches. Then I thank my colleagues Thorgeir Örlygsson and Per Tresselt for having presided over the morning and the afternoon sessions. I thank the participants in this symposium, not only for having accepted our invitation, but also for having taken part so actively in the discussions. With this, I declare the symposium closed.

III. Additional Speeches

The EFTA Court—Ten Years On

LEIF SEVÓN

Mr President, Ladies and Gentlemen,

SPEAKING AT THIS hour, of events that lie 15 years back in time, permits a precision and a clear picture of the events that only a retarding memory can provide. I shall start with the negotiations for the EEA Agreement, continue with the setting up of the EFTA Court and end with the first cases it heard.

As you know, the negotiations were carried out at three levels. The overall responsibility was bourn by a group of Ministers. They were assisted by group of senior civil servants. In addition, there were five groups dealing with specific issues. I had the privilege to participate in the group V on institutional questions. There the challenges were considerable. As a consequence, progress was slow. After one of the meetings the Swedish member of the group and I sat down in a lounge at the Brussels airport and made the reflection that if progress would be following the Swiss negotiations on insurance we would both be of the mature age of 152 years before we would reach the end of the negotiations. Finding that prospect a bit challenging, we started to list the open questions and to formulate possible answers to them. Having cleared that list in our respective countries, we approached the EC responsible for that group Jean-Louis Dewost with our proposals. The institutional questions were subsequently resolved on the basis of them.

At that stage, an EEA Court was envisaged with the participation of Judges from the EC Court of Justice and the EFTA countries. However, the thumb of Caesar, that is the ECJ, pointed downwards in its opinion 1/91. A new solution had thus to be found. The solution was the EFTA Court.

Then a number of questions submerged. The first one was how one, in such circumstances, could ensure that the EFTA Court would apply rules identical to those of the Community in the same was as the ECJ. That was the source of some crucial provisions in the EEA Agreement and in the EFTA rules. Secondly, the question arose how to organize the EFTA Court and the procedure before it. The answer was to use the model of the ECJ. That model was sufficiently strange and in part equally incomprehensible to all participants in the EFTA working group to convince them that none of them could smuggle in their own rules. But some serious problems presented themselves. For instance, in the ECJ there was a plenary, a small plenary, and chambers of five and three judges. The EFTA Court would be composed of six judges as it then was believed. A plenary of five was in order. A small plenary of three would presuppose a chamber of one. But as no one was enthusiastic about splitting himself or herself nothing would remain to correspond to a chamber of three judges. The shortcut was a court working always in plenary.

The second challenge was the Advocates General. That problem was resolved by the universal rule that if you do not have the money it may, at least occasionally, be advisable not to spend it. Thus, no Advocates General were envisaged.

Next, work started on the Rules of Procedure. The approach could be described as numismatic. There was hardly any rule in the context of which the question of the remuneration and pensions of the Judges would not be voiced.

Then came the inauguration and the first cases arrived. According to some, the crucial question was whether the case should not be inadmissible. Indeed, one may say that the EFTA Court was liberal in interpreting the expression 'court or tribunal'. However, two comments may be appropriate. Firstly, an international court that would go through great pain in finding cases inadmissible might be deemed an odd animal. Avoiding work, one might say. An international court following the example set by the ECJ might be expected to be somewhat bold. And that seems to have been the case with the EFTA Court both initially and later on. Never has it thought passed the line on appropriateness. Secondly, the subsequent case law of the ECJ seems to point in the direction that what the EFTA Court did was not all that extraordinary. Thirdly, not taking cases would also have meant a transfer of workload to the EFTA Surveillance Authority, which would then have been the only body for testing the compliance of the EFTA countries with the obligations arising out of the EEA Agreement.

The EFTA Court provided a pleasant environment. The cases were reasonably few and enabled the Judges to spend the time necessary on each of them, consistently learning their job. The role of the President was equally pleasant, and was exercised on the understanding that the Judges were equal and deserved every respect. I believe this is the case today, too. That was, and should always be, the case. The prerogatives of the President should never be exercised giving him advantages.

Life at the Court was not restricted to cases. The Members and the Court as a whole formed a family. In that family, wining and dining were not forgotten. In short, life was agreeable.

May I conclude by expressing the gratitude of all participants for a memorable seminar and for a splendid dinner. All former and present Judges of the EFTA Court are present, as well as many that I have not seen since the EEA negotiations. For all this and for much else, Carl Baudenbacher and the EFTA Court deserve our gratitude.

EFTA Court 10th Anniversary

BO VESTERDORF

Mr President, Your Excellences, Distinguished Guests,

I AM HONOURED TO have been invited to give a brief speech during this dinner in celebration of the EFTA Court's 10th Anniversary, with which we congratulate you.

Given the serious and interesting character of the discussions during today's symposium, I have chosen to strike a slightly lighter tone in my speech tonight.

At several occasions today, President Baudenbacher has referred to the ECJ and the CFI as its '*big sister courts*'. This, I find, loyally portrays the warm relationship that exists between our three Courts. I would, however, suggest adding one nuance. Indeed, the ECJ is 52 years old. The CFI is only 15 years old, not much older than the EFTA Court. I would therefore be tempted to view the ECJ more in the role as an older, more experienced, parent, with the CFI and the EFTA Court being her two daughters, still in their teens.

Life of 'younger sisters' is not always easy. Similarly, being the youngest sister in the 'European Court family' may not always have been easy. Had the EFTA Court been a normal child, the conditions surrounding her birth, infancy and early adolescence might have been considered less than ideal. Indeed, it is well known that, even before the EFTA Court's birth, in the famous opinion 1/91, her future 'mother', the ECJ—who had just given birth to the CFI—made it clear that she was not ready to have another sibling. Moreover, when the EFTA Court was finally born in January 1994, after a somewhat turbulent 'maternity' period, she was sent away to live in Geneva, far away from her family in Luxembourg.

Luckily, after a bit more than two and a half years, it was decided to unite the family in one country, on the Plateau Kirchberg, and that even within walking distance. Patterns of a European family life began to make themselves felt. I myself have noted this, in particular, during the bi-annual meetings arranged between the CFI and the EFTA Court, where the two 'sisters' meet. This has allowed a close exchange of ideas and views, not only about professional activities but also about every day life in Luxembourg.

I feel that I can say safely today that the EFTA Court has turned out to be a model sister. This was already clear in the EFTA Court's early rulings. Indeed, already in the first *Restamark* case, the EFTA Court made it clear that there was no need to 'invent the deep plate twice' and that the case law of the ECJ and the CFI would be relevant whenever the rules under the EEA Agreement were similar to those under the EC Treaty.

Moreover—and perhaps even more importantly—the 'little sister' has earned the respect of both its 'mother' and 'bigger sister'. Indeed, as was mentioned at several occasions during the symposium today, both the ECJ and the CFI have several times—in fact in 11 different cases—made direct reference to EFTA Court judgments in their rulings. Moreover, a number of Advocates General have made direct reference to EFTA Court rulings in their attempts to convince the ECJ.

The ruling of the EFTA Court in the *Kellogg's* case stands out particularly strongly. Indeed, in several rulings of both the CFI and the ECJ, direct reference was made to that case: it served as a clear inspiration to the CFI in the *Pfizer* and *Alpharma* cases and, in particular, to the ECJ in the *Monsanto* case and the *Danish Vitamins Cases*, as regards the *precautionary principle* and its application in the area of free movement.

Allow me also to mention the ruling in case *Erla María Sveinbjörnsdóttir* (followed up by the case *Karl K. Karlsson*), where the EFTA Court found the principle of State liability to exist within the framework of the EEA Agreement. The ruling is particularly forceful since the EEA Agreement explicitly excludes that legislative powers be conferred upon the institutions set up under the EEA Agreement, which in turn would seem to exclude that citizens of EFTA countries can invoke EEA rules directly against their Member States. As it has also been argued today, the Court by this ruling seems to have introduced a doctrine of 'indirect' direct effect, whereby citizens in EFTA countries have a remedy to compel their Member States to comply with the obligations that flow from the EEA Agreement (both primary and secondary legislation).

The EFTA Court in *Erla María Sveinbjörnsdóttir* case also clearly spells out that the EEA Agreement is more than a mere free trade agreement and is an international treaty *sui generis*, which contains a distinct legal order of its own.

I am also happy to say that your 'sister' (the CFI) took the first step in this respect. Indeed, in the *Opel Austria* judgment from 1997, the CFI stressed that the EEA Agreement 'involves a high degree of integration, with objectives that exceed those of a mere free-trade agreement'. This seems now also to have been—at least indirectly—recognized by the ECJ which, in the *Rechberger* case, refers to the possibility of obtaining reparation under the EFTA Court's case law, while making direct reference to the *Erla María Sveinbjörnsdóttir* ruling.

The fact that the three European Courts have inspired each other's case law does not mean, however, that the EFTA Court's rulings have always been followed by the CFI and the ECJ.

The first example, which was brought up during today's symposium and which deserves special attention, is the *Maglite* case, decided on 3 December 1997, in which the Court held that national rules of EC Member States providing for international exhaustion of trade mark rights are not incompatible with the Trade Mark Directive. As you are well aware, the ECJ later came to the opposite conclusion in the *Silhouette* case of 16 July 1998.

The second example is the ruling in the so-called *Husbanken II* case, concerning the application of Article 86(2) of the EC Treaty in the area of public service compensation, where the Court opted for what may be defined as a 'net' or 'State aid' approach, thereby showing deference to a number of rulings adopted by its older sister (in cases *FFSA* and *SIC*). It is well known, however, that the ECJ, first in the *Ferring* case and later in the important *Altmark* case chose to go in another direction.

As the above examples tend to show, the EFTA Court, like its teenage sister, is today firmly rooted in the 'European Court family' and has proven that she is both able to draw lessons from the case law of her older relatives while inspiring them. She has also shown that she is, when necessary, ready—and able—to stand on her own feet and step out of the shadow of her family.

Soon the European family of Courts will witness a further enlargement, as the '*Tribunal de la Fonction Publique*' sees the light, probably already next year. This will mean that the European Court family in Luxembourg is growing, and that the EFTA Court will have a little sister for the first time. Whether the family will grow further in the future remains to be seen.

Let me finish by once again congratulating the EFTA Court and wishing it all the best in the future.

Thank you.

List of Participants

President Heinz Aemisegger	Supreme Court of the Swiss Confederation
Joseph Jean Aghina	Managing Director Abalone SA
Knut Almestad	Former President of the EFTA Surveillance Authority Advokatfirmaet Schjødt
Nikolaos Apostolidis	Head of the President's Cabinet The Court of Justice of the EC
Judge George Arestis	The Court of Justice of the EC
Professor Dr Finn Arnesen	The University of Oslo
Karl Axelsson	Supreme Court Attorney Associate Professor of Law
Judge Josef Azizi	The Court of First Instance of the EC
Dr Inge Lorange Backer	Director General The Ministry of Justice and Police of Norway
Dr Marino Baldi	Legal Adviser EFTA Secretariat
Andreas Batliner	Chairman of the Supreme Administrative Court of Liechtenstein
President Carl Baudenbacher	EFTA Court
Dr Doris Baudenbacher-Tandler	Publisher
Dr Georges Baur	Deputy Head of Mission and First Secretary at the Embassy of the Principality of Liechtenstein
Judge Håkan Berglin	Kammarrätten
President Max Bizozzero	The Court of Appeal of Liechtenstein
His Excellency Monsieur Björn Bjarnason	Minister of Justice and Ecclesiastical Affairs of Iceland
Per Andreas Bjørgan	Senior Officer The EFTA Surveillance Authority

Judge Davíd Þór Björgvinsson	European Court of Human Rights
Fridgeir Björnsson	Former Chief Judge Editor Tímarit Lögfrædinga
Chief Judge Benedikt Bogason	The District Court of Vesturland
Judge Anthony Borg Barthet	President of the Sixth Chamber The Court of Justice of the EC
Professor Marco Bronckers	Wilmer, Cutler & Pickering, Hale and Dorr
Professor Dr Thomas Bruha	University of Hamburg
His Excellency Monsieur Hans Brunhart	Former Prime Minister of Liechtenstein President of the Board Verwaltungs- und Privat Bank
Einar Bull	College Member EFTA Surveillance Authority
Dr Henrik Bull	Ad hoc Judge of the EFTA Court Center for European Law
Dr Dirk Buschle	Legal Secretary EFTA Court
Justice Gustav Bygglin	The Supreme Court of Finland
Vice-President Gunnlaugur Claessen	The Supreme Court of Iceland
Evanthia Coffee	Lawyer-Linguist EFTA Court
Judge Ninon Colneric	The Court of Justice of the EC
Judge Ena Cremona	The Court of First Instance of the EC
Bjørn Daehlin	Head of Division Parliamentary Ombudsman of Norway
Þórsteinn Davíðsson	Political Advisor Ministry of Justice and Ecclasiastical Affairs of Iceland
Lucien Dedichen	Former Registrar of the EFTA Court
Linda Dragvoll	Translator EFTA Court
Peter Dyrberg	Member of the 2nd Board of Appeal Office for Harmonization in the Internal Market
Bjarnveig Eiríksdóttir	Solicitor
Bent Endresen	Solicitor
Niels Fenger	Director of Legal and Executive Affairs EFTA Surveillance Authority

Rolf Einar Fife	Director General Legal Department The Ministry of Foreign Affairs, Norway
Fabrice Filliez	Councellor Swiss Mission to the EU
John Forman	Legal Service of the Commission of the EC
Ian Forrester, QC	White & Case, Brussels
His Excellency Monsieur Mario Frick	Former Prime Minister of Liechtenstein Advocatur Seeger, Frick & Partner
Judge Rafael García-Valdecasas	The Court of First Instance of the EC
First Advocate-General Leendert Adrie Geelhoed	The Court of Justice of the EC
Þorsteinn Geirsson	Permanent Secretary Ministry of Justice and Ecclesiastical Affairs of Iceland
Dr Katja Gey	Office for Foreign Affairs, Liechtenstein
Roger Grass	Registrar The Court of Justice of the EC
Professor Dr Hans Petter Graver	University of Oslo
His Excellency Monsieur Bjørn T Grydeland	Ambassador of Norway to the EU
Dóra Guðmundsdóttir	Ad hoc Judge of the EFTA Court
Professor Fridtjof Frank Gundersen	Norwegian School of Management
Tryggvi Gunnarsson	The Althingi Ombudsman
President Hannes Hafstein	EFTA Surveillance Authority
Þórunn Hafstein	Head of Unit EFTA Secretariat
Professor Dr Waltraud Hakenberg	Legal Secretary Court of Justice of the EC
Chief Judge Hjördís Björk Hákonardóttir	Chairman of the Judges' Association The District Court of Sudurland, Iceland
Bernd Hammermann	College Member EFTA Surveillance Authority
Kristín Haraldsdóttir	Legal Secretary EFTA Court
Henning Harborg	Registrar EFTA Court

Bjørn Haug	Former President of the EFTA Court
Ragnhildur Helgadóttir	Former Minister of Education
His Excellency Monsieur Kurt Herndl	Ambassador Former Judge of the EFTA Court
Professor Dr Stephan Hobe	University of Cologne
Øystein Hovdkinn	Deputy Secretary-General EFTA Secretariat
Irvin Høyland	Department for Legal Affairs Ministry of Foreign Affairs
Judge Marko Ilešič	The Court of Justice of the EC
His Excellency Monsieur Thorbjørn Jagland	Former Prime Minister of Norway Member of Parliament (Stortinget)
Judge Peter Jann	President of the First Chamber The Court of Justice of the EC
Martin Johansson	Legal Secretary at the Court of Justice of the EC Former Legal Secretary of the EFTA Court
Erik Johnsrud	Ness & CO Advokatfirma
Chief Judge Helgi I Jónsson	Reykjavik District Court
Hans Jung	Registrar The Court of First Instance of the EC
Judge Küllike Jürimäe	The Court of First Instance of the EC
Professor Dr Christine Kaddous	University of Geneva
Justice Heikki Kanninen	The Supreme Administrative Court of Finland
Tom Kennedy	Head of Legal Service European Court of Auditors
Professor Dr Christian Kohler	Deputy Director The Court of Justice of the EC
Advocate- General Juliane Kokott	The Court of Justice of the EC
Högni S Kristjánsson	Minister Counsellor Embassy of Iceland to the EU
Vincent Kronenberger	Legal Secretary The Court of First Instance of the EC
Judge Pranas Kūris	The Court of Justice of the EC
Judge Ingrida Labucka	The Court of First Instance of the EC
Advocate-General Philippe Léger	The Court of Justice of the EC

Judge Egils Levits	The Court of Justice of the EC
First President Nils Erik Lie	Borgarting Court of Appeal
Judge Pernilla Lindh	The Court of First Instance of the EC
Vice-President Inge Lønning	Stortinget
Mads Magnussen	Legal Director at the Norwegian Competition Authority Former Legal Secretary of the EFTA Court
Sigurður T Magnússon	Chairman The Council of District Courts Administration, Iceland
Katinka Mahieu	Legal Secretary EFTA Court
Guiliano Marenco	Deputy Director General Legal Service The Commission of the EC
Judge Arjen WH Meij	The Court of First Instance of the EC
Judge Paolo Mengozzi	The Court of First Instance of the EC
Professor Ola Mestad	Centre for European Law The University of Oslo
Jean Mischo	Former Advocate General of the European Court of Justice
Professor Dr Peter Christian Müller-Graff	University of Heidelberg
Jonas W Myhre	Supreme Court Advocate Advokatfirmaet Wikborg, Rein & Co, Oslo
Dr Sven Norberg	Director at the Commission of the EC Former Judge of the EFTA Court
Thomas Nordby	Office of the Attorney General (Civil Affairs) of Norway Former Lawyer-Linguist of the EFTA Court
Professor em. Nils Nygaard	University of Bergen
First President Agnes Nygaard Haug	Borgarting Court of Appeal
Svala Ólafsdóttir	Lawyer
Judge Thorgeir Örlygsson	EFTA Court
Lic.iur. Martin Ospelt M.B.L.-HSG	Ad hoc Judge of the EFTA Court Advocatur Sprenger, Kolzoff, Ospelt & Partner

Bryndís Pálmarsdóttir	Administrative Officer EFTA Court
Professor Dr Pierre Pescatore	Former Judge of the Court of Justice of the EC
Judge Jörg Pirrung	The Court of First Instance of the EC
Fanny Platou Amble	Office of the Attorney General (Civil Affairs) of Norway
Advocate-General Miguel Poiares Maduro	The Court of Justice of the EC
Judge Jean-Pierre Puissochet	The Court of Justice of the EC
Kurt Riechenberg	Legal Secretary The Court of Justice of the EC
Judge Allan Rosas	President of the Third Chamber The Court of Justice of the EC
Dr Michael Sanchez Rydelski	Deputy Director Legal Service The EFTA Surveillance Authority
His Excellence Monsieur Georges Santer	Ambassador, Secretary General Ministry of Foreign Affairs of Luxembourg
Judge Sir Konrad Schiemann	The Court of Justice of the EC
Mr Marc Schlungs	Vice President of the Supreme Court of Luxembourg Adviser of the Constitutional Court
Professor Dr Helmuth Schröter	Former Director at the Commission of the EC
Dr Michael Schütte	Freshfields Bruckhaus Deringer
Professor Dr Erling Selvig	The University of Oslo
Gunnar Selvik	Head West Norway Office Former Registrar of the EFTA Court
President Leif Sevón	The Supreme Court of Finland Former President of the EFTA Court
President Markús Sigurbjörnsson	The Supreme Court of Iceland
Professor Johannes Sigurðsson	Reykjavik University
President Vassilios Skouris	The Court of Justice of the EC
Ragnheiður Snorradóttir	Head of Department Ministry of Finance
Róbert Spanó	Associate Professor

Eilert Stang Lund	Supreme Court of Norway
Hrafnhildur Stefánsdóttir	Chief legal adviser SA Confederation of Icelandic Employers
Professor Stefán Már Stefánsson	Ad hoc Judge of the EFTA Court University of Iceland
Ólafur Walter Stefánsson	Former Deputy Secretary General in the Icelandic Ministry of Justice
Titus Stiphout	EFTA Secretariat
Advocate-General Christine Stix-Hackl	The Court of Justice of the EC
Siri Teigum	Thommessen Krefting Greve Lund, Oslo
Professor John Temple Lang	Cleary Gottlieb Steen & Hamilton, Brussels
Professor Björg Thorarensen	University of Iceland
Professor Dr Daniel Thürer	University of Zurich
Stefán Geir Þórisson	Supreme Court Advocate Lögmenn Klapparstíg, Iceland
Skarphéðinn Þórisson	Attorney General of Iceland
Deputy Secretary-General Pétur G Thorsteinsson	EFTA Secretariat
Judge Virpi Tiili	The Court of First Instance of the EC
Judge Christiaan WA Timmermans	President of the Second Chamber The Court of Justice of the EC
Advocate-General Antonio Tizzano	The Court of Justice of the EC
Professor Dr Christa Tobler, LLM	University of Basel
Sabine Tömördy	Deputy Director EEA Coordination Unit, Liechtenstein
Diana Torrens	Lawyer-Linguist The Court of Justice of the EC Former Lawyer-Linguist at the EFTA Court
Judge Per Tresselt	EFTA Court
Karl Arne Utgård	Supreme Court of Norway
Amund Utne	Director Competition & State Aid EFTA Surveillance Authority
Judge Vilenas Vadapalas	The Court of First Instance of the EC

William Valasidis	Legal Secretary The Court of Justice of the EC
Professor Dr Christoph Vedder	University of Augsburg
Bjørg Ven	Ad hoc Judge of the EFTA Court Advokatfirmaet Haavind Vislie
President Bo Vesterdorf	The Court of First Instance of the EC
Judge Mihalis Vilaras	The Court of First Instance of the EC
Thór Vilhjálmsson	Former President of the EFTA Court Former Chief Justice of Iceland
Dr Hannu von Hertzen	Head of Unit, Juridical Service European Parliament
Henrik von Holstein	Deputy Registrar The Court of Justice of the EC
His Serene Highness Prince Nikolaus von und zu Liechtensteinr	Ambassador Head of the Mission of Liechtenstein to the EC
Ursula Wachter, MBL-HSG	President of the Liechtenstein Bar Association
Maria Westman-Clément	Former Legal Secretary of the EFTA Court
President Luzius Wildhaber	The European Court of Human Rights
Elisabethann Wright	Senior Officer The EFTA Surveillance Authority

Discussion Participants

Dr Inge Lorange Backer
Director General, The Ministry of Justice and Police

Dr Dirk Buschle
Legal Secretary, EFTA Court

Ian Forrester, QC
White & Case

Bjørn Haug
Former President of the EFTA Court

His Excellency Monsieur Thorbjørn Jagland
Former Prime Minister, Member of Parliament (Stortinget)

Dr Sven Norberg
Director at the Commission of the EC
Former Judge of the EFTA Court

Professor Dr Pierre Pescatore
Former Judge of the Court of Justice of the EC

President Leif Sevón
The Supreme Court of Finland
Former President of the EFTA Court

Professor Dr Christa Tobler, LLM
University of Basel

President Luzius Wildhaber
The European Court of Human Rights

Bibliography

K ALMESTAD, 'The Duties of Co-Operation of National Authorities and the Community Instutitions under Article 10 (ex Article 5) of the Treaty of Rome: The EEA Variant' (2000) *FIDE XIX Congress*, vol I, 427.

P ALSTON (ed), *The EU and Human Rights* (Oxford, OUP, 1999).

JE ALVAREZ, 'The New Dispute Settlers: (Half) Truths and Consequences' (2003) 38 *Texas Intl L J* 405.

C BAUDENBACHER, 'Homogenität–Parallelität–Going First–Betrachtungen zur Rechtsstellung des EFTA-Gerichtshofs am Beispiel der Rechtsprechung zur Betriebsübergangsrichtlinie', *Festschrift für Bernhard Grossfeld zum 65. Geburtstag* (Heidelberg, Verlag Recht und Wirtschaft GmbH, 1999) 55.

C BAUDENBACHER, 'Internationale Erschöpfung des Markenrechts und der Begriff der Zustimmung' (2001) *Eur L Reporter* 382.

C BAUDENBACHER,'Facets of an EEA Constitutional Order' in N Colneric, *et al* (eds), *Une communauté de Droit, Festschrift für Gil Carlos Rodríguez Iglesias* (Berlin, Berliner Wissenschafts Verlag, 2003) 343.

C BAUDENBACHER, 'Judicial Globalization: New Development or Old Wine in New Bottles?' (2003) 39 *Texas Intl L J: Special Symposium: Globalization and the Judiciary* 505.

C BAUDENBACHER, 'The EFTA Court—An Example of the Judicialization of International Economic Law' (2003) 28 *European L Rev* 880.

C BAUDENBACHER, 'Der EFTA-Gerichtshof, das EWR-Abkommen und die Fortentwicklungen des EG-Vertrages' [2004] *Festschrift zum 75. Geburtstag von Prof Dr Dr Herbert Batliner* (Vaduz, ex jure Verlagsanstalt, 2004) 59.

Sir C BELLAMY, 'Focusing on the European Perspective of Judicial Dialogue: Issues in the Area of Competition Law' (2003) 39 *Texas Intl L J: Special Symposium: Globalization and the Judiciary* 461.

U BERNITZ, 'The EEC-EFTA free Trade Agreements with special reference to the position of Sweden and the other Scandinavian EFTA countries' (1986) *CML Rev* 567.

J BORNKAMM, 'The German Supreme Court: An Actor in the Global Conversation of High Courts' (2003) 39 *Texas Intl L J: Special Symposium: Globalization and the Judiciary* 415.

T BRUHA, 'Is the EEA an Internal Market?' in P–C Müller-Graff and E Selvig (eds), *EEA-EU Relations* (Berlin, Berlin Verlag Arno Spitz GmbH, 1999) 97.

L BRITTAN, 'How to Make Trade Liberalisation Popular' (1995) 18 *World Economy* 761.

H BULL, 'The EEA Agreement and Norwegian Law' (1994) 5 *EBL Rev* 291.

R CAILLOIS, 'Tome 2 des Oeuvres Complètes de la Pléiade' in P Pescatore (ed), *La Séparation des Pouvoirs et l'Office du Juge, de Montesquieu à Portalis–Cahier Documentaire* (Luxemburg, Institut Grand-ducal, 2004) 4.

JI Charney, 'The Impact on the International Legal System of the Growth of International Courts and Tribunals' (1999) 31 *NYU J Intl L & Politics* 697.

T Christoforou, 'The Precautionary Principle and Democratizing Expertise: a European Legal Perspective' (2003) 30(3) *Science & Public Policy* 205.

RR Churchill and U Khaliq, 'The Collective Complaints System of the European Social Charter: An Effective Mechanism for Ensuring Compliance with Economic and Social Rights?' (2004) 15 *European J Intl L* 417.

A Clapham, 'The European Union before the European Court of Human Rights' in L Boisson de Chazournes, C Romano and R Mackenzie (eds), *International Organizations and International Dispute Settlement: Trends and Prospects* (New York, Transnational Publishers, 2002) 73.

PP Craig, 'Report on the United Kingdom' in Slaughter, *et al* (eds), *The European Court and National Courts–Doctrine and Jurisprudence* (Oxford, Hart Publishing, 1998) 198.

HM Enzensberger, *Ach Europa!* (Fankfurt, Suhrkamp, 1987).

J Forman, 'The EEA Agreement Five Years On: Dynamic Homogeneity in Practice and its Implantation by the Two EEA Courts' (1999) *CML Rev* 751.

IS Forrester, 'The Dangers of Too Much Precaution' in Hoskins and Robinson (eds), *A True European, Essays for Judge David Edward (*Oxford, Hart Publishing, 2003) 203.

G Gorton, 'Bestätigung der Staatshaftungsrechtsprechung des EFTA-Gerichtshofs' (2002) 7–8 *Eur L Reporter* 260.

E Gould and G Lesieur, T*he European Court of Justice on the European Convention on Human Rights: Who Said What, When?* (London, Kluwer Law International, 1998).

HP Graver, 'Mission Impossible: Supranationality and National Legal Autonomy in the EEA Agreement' (2002) 1 *Eur Foreign Affairs Rev* 73.

HP Graver, 'Die Ausdehnung des Europäischen Gemeinschaftsrechts auf Nichtmitglieder der Union–Das Beispiel Norwegens' in PC Müller-Graff (ed), *Europäisches Integrationsrecht im Querschnitt* (Baden-Baden, Nomos Verlagsgesellschaft, 2003) 45.

J Habermas, *Theory of Communicative Action* (Frankfurt, Suhrkamp, 1981) vol 2.

J Heliskoski, 'Fundamental Rights versus Economic Freedoms in the European Union: Which Paradigm?' in J Klabbers and J Petman (eds), *Nordic Cosmopolitanism: Essays in International Law for Martti Koskenniemi* (Leiden, Martinus Nijhoff, 2003) 417.

HH Herrnfeld, in J Schwarze (ed), *EU-Kommentar* (Baden-Baden, Nomos Verlagsgesellschaft, 2000).

F Jacobs, 'Judicial Dialogue and the Cross-Fertilization of Legal Systems: The European Court of Justice' (2003) 39 *Texas Intl L J: Special Symposium: Globalization and the Judiciary* 547.

HA Jakobsen, 'Offentligrettslig erstattningsansvar ved brudd på EF– og EØS-retten' 39 *IUSEF* (Senter for Europarett, Universitetet i Oslo) 91.

SS Jensen, *The European Convention on Human Rights in Scandinavian Law* (Copenhagen, Jurist- og økonomforbundets Forlagm, 1992).

G de Jonquieres, 'Europe Studies Radical Trade Veto Proposal' *Financial Times*, 5 February 2004.

C Kohler, 'Integration und Auslegung Zur Doppelfunktion des Europäischen Gerichtshofes' in E Jayme (ed), *Ein internationales Zivilverfahrensrecht für Gesamteuropa* (Heidelberg, CF Müller Juristischer Verlag, 1992) 11.

C L'HEUREUX-DUBÉ, 'The Importance of Dialogue: Globalization and the International Impact of the Rehnquist Court' (1998) 34 *Tulsa L J* 15.

LAMY, 'The Emergence of Collective Preferences in International Trade: Implications for Regulating Globalisation', paper presented at the conference *Collective Preferences and Global Governance: What future for the Multilateral Trading System*, organized by the European Commission (Brussels, 15 September 2004).

LEADER, 'Lamy's Big Idea', *Financial Times*, 10 February 2004.

K LENAERTS and P VAN NUFFEL, *Constitutional Law of the European Union* (London, Sweet & Maxwell, 1999).

PH LINDBLOM, *Progressive Process* (Uppsala, 2000) 465.

N LUHMANN, *Legitimation durch Verfahren* (Frankfurt, Suhrkamp, 1983).

W MATTLI and AM SLAUGHTER, 'Role of National Courts in European Integration' in Slaughter, *et al* (eds), *The European Court and National Courts–Doctrine and Jurisprudence* (Oxford, Hart Publishing, 1998).

JG MERRILLS and AH ROBERTSON, *Human Rights in Europe: A Study of the European Convention on Human Rights* (Manchester, MUP, 2001).

J MISCHO, 'Hoechst, Colas, Roquette: illustration d'une convergence' in N Colneric, *et al* (eds), *Une communauté de droit. Festschrift für Gil Carlos Rodríguez Iglesias* (Berlin, Berliner Wissenschafts-Verlag, 2003) 137.

PC MÜLLER-GRAFF, 'Die Rechtsangleichung zur Verwirklichung des Binnenmarktes' [1989] *Europarecht* 107.

PC MÜLLER-GRAFF, 'EEA Agreement and EC Law: A Comparison in Scope and Content' in PC Müller-Graff and E Selbig (eds), *The European Economic Area -Norway's Basic Status in the Legal Construction of Europe* (Berlin, Berlin Verlag Arno Spitz GmbH, 1997) 17.

PC MÜLLER-GRAFF, 'Supranationality and National Legal Autonomy: Community Law and EEA Compared' in HP Graver (ed), *National Judicial Reaction to Supranationality in the EC and the EEA* (Oslo, Universitetsforlaget, 2004) 35.

PC MÜLLER-GRAFF, in H von der Groeben (ed), *Vertrag über die Europäische Union und Vertrag zur Gründung der Europäischen Gemeinschaft* (Baden-Baden, Nomos Verlagsgesellschaft, 2004).

PC MÜLLER GRAFF and SELVIG (eds), *The European Economic Area–Norway's Basic Status in the Legal Construction of Europe* (Berlin, Berlin Verlag Arno Spitz GmbH, 1997).

N NEUWAHL and A ROSAS (eds), *The European Union and Human Rights* (The Hague, Martinus Nijhoff, 1995).

S NORBERG, 'Perspectives on the Future Development of the EEA Agreement' (Reykjavik, Bokautgafa Orators, 2000) *Afmælisrit Thór Vilhjálmsson* 367.

T OJANEN, *The European Way, The Structure of National Court Obligation under EC Law* (Helsinki, Gummerus Oy, 1998).

T ÖRLYGSSON, 'Hvernig hefur Ísland brugðist við ákvörðunum EFTA-dómstólsins?' (2004) 54 *Tímarit lögfræðinga* 375.

J PAUWELYN, *Conflict of Norms in Public International Law: How WTO Law Relates to Other Rules of International Law* (Cambridge, CUP, 2003).

M POIARES MADURO, 'Striking the Elusive Balance between Economic Freedom and Social Rights in the EU' in P Alston (ed), *The EU and Human Rights* (Oxford, OUP, 1999) 449–72.

Sir K POPPER, *Logik der Forschung*, 6th edn (Berlin, Akademie-Verlag, 1976).

D Prevost and P van den Bossche, 'The Agreement on the Application Sanitary and Phytosanitary Measures' in Appleton and Macrory (eds), *The World Trade Organization: Legal, Economic and Political Analysis* (New York, Springer, 2004).

C Romano, 'The Proliferation of International Judicial Bodies: The Pieces of the Puzzle' (1999) 31 *NYU J Intl L & Politics* 710.

A Rosas, 'The European Union and International Human Rights Instruments' in V Kronenberger (ed), *The European Union and the International Legal Order: Discord or Harmony?* (The Hague, TMC Asser Press, 2001) 53.

A Rosas, 'The Legal Sources of EU Fundamental Rights' in N Colneric, *et al* (eds), *Une communauté de droit. Festschrift für Gil Carlos Rodríguez Iglesias* (Berlin, Berliner Wissenschafts-Verlag-, 2003) 87.

A Rosas, 'International Dispute Settlement: EU Practices and Procedures' 46 *German Ybk Intl L 2003* (Berlin, Duncker & Humblot, 2004) 284.

Rosett, 'Unification, Harmonization, Codification and Reform' (1992) *American J Comparative* L 683 *et seq.*

A Sapir, 'Trade Liberalization and the Harmonization of Social Policies: Lessons from European Integration' in JN Bhagwati and RE Hudec (eds), I *Fair Trade and Harmonization: Prerequisites for Free Trade?* (Cambridge, MA, MIT Press, 1996) 543.

Schilling, 'The Autonomy of the Community Legal Order—An Analysis of Possible Foundations' (1996) 37 *Harvard Intl L J* 389.

L Sevon, 'Primacy and Direct Effect in the EEA—Some Reflections' in *Festskrift til Ole Due, Liber Amicoru*m (Copenhagen, Forlaget Thomson, 1994) 34.

L Sevon and M Johansson, 'The Protection of the Rights of Individuals under the EEA Agreement' (1999) 24 *European L Rev* 373.

F Sejersted, 'Between Sovereignty and Supranationalism in the EEA Context: On the Legal Dynamics of the EEA Agreement' in PC Müller Graff and E Selvig (eds), *The European Economic Area: Norway's Basic Status in the Legal Construction of Europe* (Berlin, Berlin Verlag Arno Spitz GmbH, 1997) 43.

F Sejersted, in F Sejersted, *et al* (eds), *EØS-rett*, 2nd edn (Oslo, Universitetsforlaget, 2004) 108.

V Skouris, 'Introducing a Binding Bill of Rights for the European Union: Can Three Parallel Systems of Protection of Fundamental Rights Coexist Harmoniously?' in *Verfassung im Diskurs der Welt, Liber Amicorum für Peter Häberle* (Mohr Siebeck 2004) 261–73.

AM Slaughter, 'Judicial Globalization' (2000) 40 *Virginia J Intl L* 1003.

AM Slaughter, 'A Global Community of Courts' (2003) 44 *Harvard Intl L J* 201.

M Slotboom, 'Do Public Health Measures Receive Similar Treatment in European Community and World Trade Organization Law?' (2003) 37(3) *Journal of World Trade* 553.

O Spiermann, 'The Other Side of the Story: An Unpopular Essay on the Making of the European Community Legal Order' (1999) 10 *Eur J Intl L* 763.

J Steiner and L Woods, *Textbook on EC Law*, 8th edn (Oxford, OUP, 2003) 115.

Stokes, 'New Trade Barriers: National Preferences', *National Journal*, 24 April 2004, 1276–77.

U Sverdrup, 'Compliance and Conflict Management in the European Union: Nordic Exceptionalism' (2004) 1 *Scandinavian Political Studies* 23.

AS Sweet, 'Integration and the Europeanisation of the Law' (2002) *Queen's Papers on Europeanisation,* No 2/2002, 15.

AS SWEET and TL BRUNELL, 'The European Court and the National Courts: A Statistical Analysis of Preliminary References, 1961–95' (1997) *Jean Monnet Working Paper* No 14/97.

J TEMPLE LANG, 'The Duties of National Courts under Community Constitutional Law' (1997) 22 *ELR* 3.

G TESAURO, 'The Role of the Court of Justice in the Protection of Fundamental Rights' in N Colneric, *et al* (eds), *Une communauté de droit. Festschrift für Gil Carlos Rodríguez Iglesias* (Berlin, Berliner Wissenschafts-Verlag, 2003) 103.

P TRESSELT and K MAHIEU, 'Hugtakið Skaðabótaábyrgð Ríkisins Innan EES-Réttar' (2004) 54 *Tímarit Lögfræðinga* 335.

T TRIDIMAS, *The General Principles of EC Law* (Oxford, OUP, 1999).

C TURNER, 'Human Rights Protection in the European Community: Resolving Conflict and Overlap between the European Court of Justice and the European Court of Human Rights' (1999) 5 *European Public L* 453.

W VAN GERVEN, 'The Genesis of EEA Law and the Principles of Primacy and Direct Effect' [1992/93] 16 *Fordham Intl L J* 955.

JHH WEILER and U HALTERN, 'Constitutional or International? The Foundations of the Community Legal Order and the Question of Judicial *Kompetenz-Kompetenz*' in Slaughter, *et al* (eds), *The European Court and National Courts—Doctrine and Jurisprudence* (Oxford, Hart Publishing, 1998).

L WILDHABER, 'Foreward' in R Blackburn and J Polakiewicz (eds), *Fundamental Rights in Europe: The European Convention on Human Rights and its Member States, 1950–2000* (Oxford, OUP, 2001) xiv.

Index